Ratio et Fides

RATIO ET FIDES

A Preliminary Intro-duction to
Philosophy for Theology

Robert E. Wood

FOREWORD BY
Jude P. Dougherty

PICKWICK *Publications* • Eugene, Oregon

RATIO ET FIDES
A Preliminary Intro-duction to Philosophy for Theology

Pickwick Publications
An Imprint of Wipf and Stock Publishers
199 W. 8th Ave., Suite 3
Eugene, OR 97401

www.wipfandstock.com

PAPERBACK ISBN: 978-1-5326-1957-1
HARDCOVER ISBN: 978-1-4982-4593-7
EBOOK ISBN: 978-1-4982-4592-0

Cataloguing-in-Publication data:

Names: Wood, Robert E., 1934–, author. | Dougherty, Jude P., 1930–, foreword.

Title: Ratio et fides : a preliminary intro-duction to philosophy for theology / Robert E. Wood ; foreword by Jude P. Dougherty.

Description: Eugene, OR : Pickwick Publications, 2018 | Includes bibliographical references and index(es).

Identifiers: ISBN 978-1-5326-1957-1 (paperback) | ISBN 978-1-4982-4593-7 (hardcover) | ISBN 978-1-4982-4592-0 (ebook)

Subjects: LCSH: Philosophy—History. | Philosophy, European. | Philosophy and religion. | Religion.

Classification: B72 .W66 2018 (print) | B72 .W66 (ebook)

The chapter on Hegel is reprinted with permission from the Ohio State University Press.

Manufactured in the U.S.A.   10/08/18

To my seminary students, past, present, and to come

CONTENTS

FOREWORD

John Henry Newman, in a letter to his friend John Delgarins (dated October 1846), recounts a conversation he had with a Jesuit priest (whose name is not disclosed) at the Collegio di Propaganda. Newman asked the Jesuit about the status of Greek studies at the college, specifically whether the students read Aristotle. The Jesuit tells Newman that neither Aristotle nor St. Thomas is in favor in Rome, or for that matter in Italy. "I asked him," writes Newman, "what Philosophy they did adopt?" The Jesuit said. "None, odds and ends, whatever seems best, like St. Clement's *Stromata*. They have no Philosophy, facts are the great things, and nothing else, exegesis but not doctrine." He went on to say that many Jesuits privately were very sorry for this, but no one dared oppose the fashion.

That conversation took place one year after Newman had been received into the Catholic Church. In the same year we find Archbishop Gioacchino Pecci in Rome, and that may account for Newman's remark, "There is a latent power in Rome which would put a stop to the evil." The Jesuit may have misunderstood the remark for he shrugged his shoulders and said, "The Pope can do nothing if the people do not obey him." Decades latter, Pecci would become Leo XIII. Within a year after being elected in 1878, Leo had named Newman a cardinal and the same year published his encyclical *Aeterni Patris*, promoting the study of St. Thomas. The encyclical endorsed a fledgling Thomistic movement and was to exercise considerable influence on Catholic higher education through most of the twentieth century. Both Newman and Leo recognized that the effectiveness of the Church, supernatural aids apart, depended on an enlightened and superior clergy, and both devoted considerable effort to the education of future priests.

Newman, for his part, was steeped in the Fathers of the Church, both Greek and Latin, and he knew the role that classical philosophy had played in their understanding of the Gospels. He wanted as much for the clergy of his day, even before he entered the Church. Leo, no less than Newman, venerated the Fathers whose assimilation of pagan philosophy he found "prepared and smoothed the way to the faith." But Leo was confronted with the agnosticism and materialism that followed the Enlightenment repudiation of classical philosophy. Recognizing that philosophy can only be fought by philosophy, he turned to the doctors of the Middle Ages for assistance, and in the encyclical *Aeterni Patris,* wrote, "The Faith can expect no more reliable assistance than it has already received from St. Thomas." *Aeterni Patris,* subsequently endorsed by Pius X in his motu proprio *Doctoris Angelici,* and by Pius XI in his encyclical *Studiorum Ducem,* stimulated an interest in classical and medieval philosophy and, in fact, produced a scholastic revival that enlisted scholars of the rank of Gilson, Mercier, Noel, Maritain, Pegis, Fabro, Garrigou-Lagrange, DeKoninck, Van Steenberghen, and Yves Simon, to name only a few. Thomas became the *Doctor Communis* of North American seminaries and colleges alike. "Midwestern Thomism" became a euphemism for programs of study that could be found in Toronto, Milwaukee, South Bend, St. Louis, Cincinnati, and points south. Not only Thomas but Bonaventure and Scotus were given a place in the curriculum of most Catholic institutions of higher learning. For many, to study Thomas also entailed some acquaintance with the Arab philosophers Avicenna and Averroes.

Benedict XVI, following the lead of his predecessors, has similarly stressed the importance of classical learning for an understanding of the Apostolic Fathers, who represent the faith as received in the first and second generation after the death of the apostles. The Fathers, as he presents them in his book, simply entitled *The Fathers,* are a lively bunch of intellectuals as they grapple with the truths presented in the "Memories of the Apostles," as the Gospels were first called. To Benedict, it is clear that Athens prepared the way for the intellectual reception of the teachings of Christ. As the story unfolds in Benedict's telling, the names flow by: Ignatius of Antioch, Justin, Philosopher and Martyr, Irenaeus, Clement, Origen, Tertullian, Cyprian, Eusebius, Athanasius, Cyril, Basil, the two Gregories, Ambrose, Jerome, and Augustine. Their extant writings are of major importance not only for the history of the Church but for an understanding of Western culture. Many of those writings have been amazingly preserved. The "Fathers of the Church" series, published in English translation by the Catholic University of America Press, numbers 117 volumes. Apart from the two great works of Augustine that have entered the Western literary canon, *The Confessions* and *The City of God,* we have more than three hundred letters of Augustine and almost six hundred of his homilies that through the centuries have served as models for other bishops and priests.

It is easy to detect in Benedict a great love for the Bishop of Hippo. The Holy Father speaks of his personal devotion and gratitude for "the role he has played in my life as a theologian, priest and pastor." One can surmise that Benedict himself is following the example of Augustine. At one point in his career, Augustine informed his colleague, Bishop Evadius, of his decision to suspend his dictation of his books on *De Trinitate* "because they are too demanding and I think few can understand them; it is therefore urgent to have more texts which I hope will be useful to the many." Since the beginning of his pontificate, Benedict has published, one may say, delightful books accessible to the layman, on the Fathers, on Jesus of Nazareth, and on the Doctors of the Church, with more to come.

That brings me to the merits of the present volume by Robert E. Wood. Although prepared for a specific audience, namely, candidates for the diaconate in two Texas dioceses, it can be used as an introductory course in philosophy in any program of priestly formation. Clearly it partakes of the effort of Leo XIII and his successors to elucidate the rational nature of the Faith. The Catholic Faith is not a Kierkegaardian leap into the dark. As many of the Fathers believed it to be, it is both a continuation and fulfillment of the classical learning inherited from the Greeks and the Stoics. Wood speaks of the "Wisdom of the Church" and the need to explore the sources of that wisdom. He recognizes that it is the task of every generation to appropriate that wisdom while acknowledging its source. Wood, like John Paul II, believes that there can be multiple approaches at the philosophical level as the Church attempts to engage the modern mind. He finds in the work of Husserl and the phenomenological movement that he launched elements that enable the Catholic mind fruitfully to engage the contemporary intellectual. He is attracted to Bernard Lonergan and to Hans Urs von Balthasar because he finds them so engaged. It is to Wood's credit that, like Gilson, he sees a unity to philosophical experience, but he never forgets that the Greeks and their medieval commentators over the centuries remain a constant source for modernity.

Jude P. Dougherty

Dean Emeritus, School of Philosophy
The Catholic University of America

AN INTRODUCTION

This is the Introduction to the book. The book itself is an introduction to philosophy for theology—i.e., it is not preliminary but
structured to bring the reader into [Latin *intro-ducere*] the heart
of the matter.

1.

Though this book had its origin in and for a Catholic context, I have approached it in a nonsectarian manner such that anyone can gain an introduction to philosophy from it, for or not for theology. Indeed, it begins
with Pope John Paul II's letter *Fides et Ratio*, which is not sectarian but is
addressed to all people. The message is: In the face of widespread skepticism and relativism, Believe in Reason! His most memorable idea is that
the human spirit soars on two wings, faith and reason. Either one without
the other never gets off the ground but flutters around itself.

The current text was a response on the side of Reason. It was developed
in a one-year long, two-credit course for the Deacon Candidates' Program
in the Diocese of Tyler, Texas, and also for the Diocese of Dallas. My intent
was to construct a background text for reading classic sources with a view
toward the students' being able to read papal encyclicals, the documents of
Vatican II, the Fathers and Doctors of the Church, and the most formative
theologians of the twentieth century: Hans Urs von Balthasar, Karl Rahner,
Bernard Lonergan, and, as a kind of devil's advocate, Hans Küng. Though
the people in the pews do not need to know theology beyond some preliminary level, those who lead the people, deacon's as well as priests, need
to be able to read the tradition of theology with profit, for they will be the
preachers and guides to those in the pews. To that end, it is not enough to
be able to repeat what the Church teaches, but, more important, to know
why it teaches what it does.

Von Balthasar took the history of biblical understanding and Western philosophy, literature, and theology together as the field out of which he addressed current theological issues. Central to his work is a theological aesthetics and crucial for this work is Hegel's aesthetics which he finds summarizing the whole tradition. Crucial also is Heidegger, whose project, von Balthasar claims, we (Catholic thinkers) must make our own. For Rahner, both Hegel and Heidegger are crucial to an understanding of Aquinas, and through that, to reawakening issues in contemporary theology. Lonergan's thought is grounded in a kind of phenomenology of the field of experience and a careful reading of Aquinas, though he has also learned from Hegel and Kant in significant ways. The readings we select have these thinkers especially in view.

2.

I call this text an "intro-duction," a "leading into," with the hyphen indicating that it leads one into the heart of philosophy. I call it such because, unlike many introductory texts, it is not watered-down philosophy, often presented as a history of opinions. It is not *about* philosophy, but is an *example* of philosophy, and philosophy in a specific mode. The approach is through certain select highlights in the history of philosophy presented in the words of the thinkers themselves. But the approach is taken through the phenomenological method. That method describes various types of evidences and the modes of awareness having the evidence. It shows how to see for oneself is the only adequate basis for seeing the cogency of what the philosophers claim.

Because we are studying philosophy as preliminary to the study of theology for deacon candidates, the first text we chose is Pope John Paul II's encyclical *Fides et Ratio*, on faith and reason. Here the pope exhorts contemporary culture to trust in the power of reason—in effect, to cultivate *fides in ratio* or *ratio in fides* and not fall into scepticism and relativism or biblicism and fideism. He exhorts thinkers not to abandon the attempt to develop a comprehensive view of things. And he lays stress again and again upon the autonomy of reason. The understanding of the faith depends upon the developed capacity of reason and gives to reason the further task of developing our understanding of revelation in theology. He points to the continual use of the independently developed philosophies of Plato and Aristotle by the Church Fathers and medieval Scholastic theologians. In general, he makes the case for mandating the study of philosophy for those preparing for ministry.

John Paul II developed his own thought through a study of phenomenology. Our second text is thus a short work in phenomenology entitled "Phenomenology of the Mailbox: Much Ado about Nothing." It shows the various types of evidences involved in our everyday activities: the various features of differing modes of sensation, the different levels of awareness involved in attending to these modes, the functioning of systems of production and exchange involved in the postal system, speech and writing, the nature of language, as well as personal presence and absence, matters presupposed in all our dealings, everyday and scientific. The piece especially aims at recovering a reflective sense of the differentness of awareness from any externally given evidence. It is reflection upon awareness which drives the wedge into contemporary attempts to reduce the human being to externally combined bits of matter and human awareness to brain functions.

3.

Armed with the battery of evidences attended to phenomenologically, we then set about our reading of the tradition. Since the course meets only once a month, candidates are invited to read the whole of each text, although they will be expected to focus only upon particular parts of each. We begin with parts of Plato's *Republic*, the most basic text in Western philosophy. The themes we focus upon are the moral virtues, the structure of the soul, the levels of knowing involved in the pursuit of the Good as Principle of the Whole, death, immortality and the judgment of the dead.

A chapter on Aristotle shows how he developed in relation to Plato, his teacher, and prepared the way for the incarnational view of Christian existence developed by Thomas Aquinas and brought forward in our own day by John Paul II in *Theology of the Body*. We focus upon the nature of the soul and its various functions, upon the virtues required for self-mastery and human coexistence, upon the fundamentally sociopolitical character of the human being whose rationality develops in and through language, and upon the way to the Unmoved Mover as Self-Thinking Thought.

We then go on to examine the way in which the two greatest Catholic theologians, Augustine and Aquinas, developed their theologies by employing Greek philosophy. Our next reading is thus from Augustine's *Confessions*. Here the philosophic themes we focus upon are his assimilation of Neoplatonism which helped him in thinking of God and the soul in other than material terms, as well as the key notions of the restless heart, time, and memory.

Readings from Thomas Aquinas's *Summa theologiae* show how Aquinas shifted the grounds for developing theology from basically Platonic thought to basically Aristotelian thought. The shift involved a view of embodiment as essential to the character of being human. The human being is not a spirit trapped in a body for a period, as Neoplatonists thought, but an essentially incarnate spirit destined by nature and grace for the resurrection. Embodiment is such a good thing that God himself became incarnate and prefigured our own resurrection. In this life God's grace is mediated through the sacraments as material signs, most especially by the transformed bread and wine in the Eucharist. Aquinas's approach entailed the principle that grace presupposes and perfects a rational nature.

René Descartes's *Discourse on Method* is a short work that inaugurated distinctively modern philosophy. Like Plato he attempted to back off from the tradition in order to show the fundamental evidences available to reason. He developed a mode of thinking that involved a notion of body exhaustively treatable by scientific method and culminated in what became the view of the Clockwork Universe in modern physics. It entailed a dualism in human existence between a mechanized body and a separate substance mind/soul. Descartes set the conceptual framework for the way modern science has developed and the way body is considered today in natural science. He inaugurated the modern project by developing science for its practical application in medicine and technology.

G. W. F. Hegel presented a mode of thought that attempted to gather the various philosophic positions into a single System. He taught us to think in philosophy both historically and systematically. His System laid out the conditions—ontological, cosmic, historical, and personal—for the rationally free society. But he also taught us to think with constant attention to revelation. His own thought was rooted in his self-avowed Lutheranism. We have chosen selections from the introductions to his *Lectures on the Philosophy of Religion* and *Lectures on the History of Philosophy*.

Finally, we have selected a small text from Martin Heidegger presented as a "Memorial Address" to peasant villagers of his hometown in Messkirch in Bavaria. Heidegger attempted to get back to what he called "the ground of metaphysics" as first philosophy and to rethink the tradition from there. The ground of metaphysics lies in a sense of the encompassing

Mystery that is brought to awareness through the kind of thinking awakened by the arts and that emerges from meditation on ultimate things, such as one's own mortality. The tradition of philosophy is fueled by that but has not considered it as such. Heidegger saw each great philosophy as a way of revealing fundamental truths about our position in the whole scheme of things, but also simultaneously as a way of concealing what is revealed in other philosophies; and he especially focused upon the rootage of thought in the life-world, in everyday life. As we noted previously, von Balthasar claimed that today theology must make Heidegger's project its own. In effect, this involves the rootage of theology, not only in philosophy, but also and especially in the life of prayer. The current work provides an introduction to each of the works selected as well as lists of questions for focus and discussion and suggestions for further reading.

4.

There is no such thing as philosophical reading; there is only philosophical rereading and rereading and rereading. The idea is to consider each claim within the context of the philosopher's view of the Whole, but also to think of that in terms of reflection upon one's own experience. So when reading one has to anticipate and recall, correcting one's preliminary understanding in the light of what comes later. By this tacking between part and whole of the text and between text and experience, one gradually builds up a view of the Whole to which each philosopher directs us. It is upon the habits developed in this manner that theology essentially draws in thinking through revelation.

One way to read well is to respond regularly and reflectively to what is read. Students would do well to keep a reflective journal in which they develop reasoned reactions to what might especially strike them, positively or negatively, in the texts. In this way they will learn to think for themselves, following the paths laid out in the readings.

Finally, the texts and the introductory remarks are meant to be supplemented by a seasoned teacher who, through lecture and discussion, can help bring to life what might otherwise remain only the dead letter.

* * * *

Two of the chapters have already appeared in print: "Phenomenology of the Mailbox" in *Philosophy Today*, "Hegel and Religion" in my *Placing Aesthetics: Reflections on the Philosophic Tradition*. They are reprinted with permission and with some modification.

FIDES ET RATIO

The human spirit soars on two wings, reason and faith.

—*Fides et Ratio*, John Paul II

READING

John Paul II, *Fides et Ratio: On the Relationship of Faith and Reason* (Boston: Pauline, 1998). You are invited to read the entire work, but you are expected to have read the following sections:

Introduction: 1, 3–5

I. Revelation: 12, 15

II. Credo ut Intelligam: 16–19

III. Intelligo ut Credam: 26, 30–33

IV. Faith and Reason: 36, 38–40, 43, 45–46, 48

IV. Magisterium: 49, 51–52, 55–56, 62

V. Philosophy and Theology: 64–68, 71–73, 75–77, 79

VI. Current Requirements and Tasks: 81, 83, 85, 86–90, 97, 106

1.

The epigram to *Fides et Ratio* presents an image that governs Pope John Paul II's thought: "Faith and reason are like two wings upon which the human spirit rises to the contemplation of truth." The image is suggestive: with one wing a bird cannot take off but only flutters around in a circle, pivoting around itself. One wing—faith alone or reason alone—gets one nowhere in the greater scheme of things. Fideism or rationalism are the extremes to be avoided. But there is also a third option to be avoided: rejection of both faith and reason.

In this encyclical John Paul II addresses the contemporary intellectual situation. He finds currents of materialism, scientism, positivism, phenomenalism, historicism, subjectivism, relativism, skepticism, agnosticism, atheism, evolutionism, pantheism, nihilism, and fideism, as well as, linked to fideism, biblicism and radical traditionalism.

Materialism is a position that claims to be the upshot of scientific development: everything is reducible to elementary particles that combine and separate according to invariant laws. Human awareness is wholly governed by brain-functioning (*Faith and Reason*, #80, p. 101; henceforth 80/101). It is also called *reductionism*. It appears as *evolutionism* insofar as it sees no link between matter and spirit but reduces the latter to the former. Materialism is linked to *positivism*. The pope also calls it *scientism* (88/109), which claims that our only knowledge is sensory (46/62). It is also linked to *instrumentalism*, which the pope sees as in turn linked to *pragmatism* (89/110–11), which holds that through science we can know how to develop the means to our ends without any ability to assess ends (47/63). *Phenomenalism* is broader than positivism because what appears is more than sensory, for example, our own awareness; but phenomenalism denies knowledge of ultimates beyond phenomena (54/71; 83/105).

Relativism is the generic position that denies all absolutes (5/14; 80/101). Its two variants are subjectivism and historicism. *Subjectivism* claims that all opinions and especially all values are merely relative to individual preference. Certain brands of *existentialism* make that claim with regard to values. *Historicism* broadens the claim to cover cultures and epochs: truth and goodness are determined by culture or the historical time frame within a culture and there is no way to judge better or worse with regard to differing cultures or different historical time frames (54/72; 87/109). *Skepticism* withholds judgment on everything. *Nihilism* (from the Latin *nihil*, which means "nothing") goes further than skepticism to claim that there is nothing at all to value or even to ultimate intelligibility (46/62; 90/111). *Agnosticism* withholds judgment on the existence of God (5/14), while *atheistic humanism* denies the existence of God as a block to the maturity of humankind (46/62), and *pantheism* claims that everything together is God (80/101). On the other side of the ledger are fideism, biblicism, and radical traditionalism (52/69; 55/73–74). *Fideism* refers to the position of those who accept absolutes by reason of their religious belief system and reject the work of reason. *Biblicism* narrows the belief system to what the Hebrew-Christian Bible is thought to teach, *radical traditionalism* to what has been taught in the past. All these forms either distrust or place unwarranted limits on reason. With a distrust of full-fledged reason goes reliance upon individual feeling regarding the most fundamental things.

The pope discerns in all of these movements a denial of the competency of reason, except as merely instrumental reason, as a tool to get what we want. But there are also positions which affirm that competency. He singles out three that he finds inadequate: rationalism, ontologism (52/69), and eclecticism (86/108). The term *eclecticism* is derived from the Greek for "selection." It refers to a position that accepts truths wherever they might be found, but without a comprehensive view of the compatibility of the frameworks within which they have been formulated. *Rationalism* claims the omni-competence of reason and its superiority to faith, though (for example, in Hegel) it is not necessarily opposed to the truths of faith. *Ontologism* involves the claim that in the notion of Being (Greek *on*, genitive *ontos*) we intuit God himself. John Paul also points to "some forms of idealism" that attempt to transform faith into reason (45/62), though he recommends the idealism of Rosmini, who had been condemned for ontologism (59/77). *Idealism* holds that there is nothing outside of mind, at least outside the mind of God.

2.

One problem involved in most of these movements is the problem of the fragmentation of human experience. A vision of the Whole is lacking and, in most cases, denied. Metaphysics, as the discipline, based upon the all-inclusive notion of Being, which aims to ponder the most fundamental and comprehensive principles, is ignored or denied (83/104). The pope calls for a rehabilitation of reason as critical and constructive, aiming at a metaphysical view of the Whole that is coherent, systematic, and organic (4/12). Against the general cultural denial of the competence of reason aimed at the Whole, the pope exhorts contemporary thinkers to have confidence in reason (6/16) and to develop a philosophy rooted in the notion of Being (97/119). Against fideism, biblicism, and radical traditionalism, he speaks for the *autonomy* of reason, its being a law (*nomos*) unto itself (*autos*), governed by its own intrinsic principles which cannot be dictated to from the outside. This is a theme that appears throughout the encyclical as one of its central claims (13/23; 14/24; 75/94; 77/97; 45/61).

John Paul sees metaphysics or the philosophy of being as involving the basic principles of noncontradiction, causality, and finality (4/12). What first occurs in intellectual awareness is the notion of Being as a notion of unrestricted scope: outside of being there is nothing, and the notion of Being concerns everything about everything. The principle of *noncontradiction* follows from the notion of Being: whatever is is such that it cannot both have and not have the same property at the same time and in the same respect. This is the basis for all rationality. What is claimed in one area of experience, e.g., in physics, cannot contradict what is claimed in another area, e.g., in moral experience or in the Bible. If there appears to be a contradiction, we have to learn to wait and work—for centuries if necessary—for a more comprehensive way of understanding. The principle of *causality* follows from experience: that nothing finite is the cause of its own being. The principle of *finality* (a.k.a., *teleology* from the Greek *telos*, as end) also follows from experience: that every agent acts for an end or purpose (Latin *finis*). The three principles together form the bases for a comprehensive metaphysical view.

3.

Though he sees the deficiencies of the modern philosophies listed above, nonetheless the pope cautions that they also contain "precious insights" which we neglect at our peril (48/64). In particular, he underscores the historical character of thought by distinguishing between enduring truths and historically conditioned formulations, and he sees a growth in the adequacy of formulations through time (95/117). That is linked to a legitimate pluralism of philosophies as differing angles on the Whole which calls for dialogue and not simply condemnation. He exhorts us to an extension of the dialogue from an exclusively intra-Western focus to one that includes Eastern thought as well (7072/88–92). And because human beings are by nature explorers, the quest for understanding never ceases (64/83).

What does that mean for the faith tradition? The pope reaches back to the Bible to point out the role of reason in the wisdom literature (16/29) and St. Paul's dialogue with the Greek philosophers. The latter involved both an acceptance of the quest for God and a caution not to be misled by inadequate views (24/47). The pope goes on to show the assimilation of Platonic philosophy in thinking through revelation on the part of the Church Fathers and medieval Doctors. The latter transformed theology through the assimilation of Aristotle as well, reaching a high point in St. Thomas Aquinas. (In succeeding chapters we will examine the assimilation of Platonism in Augustine and of Aristotelianism and Platonism in Aquinas.) One of Aquinas's basic principles was that grace presupposes and perfects nature (43/58). His appreciation of the integrity of nature bypassed what the pope views as an unnatural tendency to negate the world and its values which persists as a noxious strain in Christianity (43/59). (Readers of Dostoevsky's *The Brothers Karamazov* can see this in the monk Fr. Ferapont as an archetypal world-negating figure. Such negation is the main target for Friedrich Nietzsche's atheistic critique of Christianity.) As regards theology, for Aquinas revelation presupposes reason in that God speaks to humans who are defined as *rational animals*.

The God who reveals himself in history is the same God who gave us reason (34/47). Faith demands that the rational being seek to understand its belief: the truths of revelation are to be understood in the light of reason (35/48). The pope cites St. Anselm: *fides quaerens intellectum*, faith seeking understanding. He also cites St. Augustine: *credo ut intelligam*, I believe that I might understand. And he refers to the unusually strong words of St. Augustine that a thoughtless faith is *nothing* (79/99)—rather strong words, indeed!

When we take up the Bible as the record of revelation, we understand it in terms of our own experience. The problem with biblical fundamentalism is the poverty of reflective self-understanding exhibited by its practitioners as well as a failure to understand the peculiar literary form and role of each of the books of the Bible. As Aristotle said, human beings cannot avoid philosophizing; their only options are to do it well or poorly—that is, attend carefully and reflectively to experience or attend casually and unreflectively. Belief does not excuse one from careful and comprehensive reflection on experience. And that is just what philosophy at its best is. Both the Church Fathers and the Doctors of the Church understood that. They spoke of certain rationally discernible *prolegomena fidei*, certain prerequisites to faith such as the existence of God as source of revelation and the credibility of the Bible itself as putative divine revelation (67/85–86). And they saw that revelation, far from being antithetical to reason, is an invitation for reason to extend its scope (14/24). That extension is theology as a logically consistent body of knowledge (66/84). It presupposes "reason formed and educated to concept and argument" (77/97).

4.

The encyclical hearkens back to a recovery of tradition initiated in modern times by Leo XIII's 1879 encyclical, *Aeterni Patris*, which called for a renewed study of Scholastic thought, especially though not exclusively that of Thomas Aquinas (57/76). In subsequent papal teaching, this had the unfortunate consequence of adopting Thomistic philosophy as official Catholic philosophy and requiring the defense of the 24 Thomistic Theses by all Catholic teachers of philosophy and theology. That requirement denied the autonomy of philosophy and turned Catholic professors into rationalizers of Thomistic teaching rather than responsible and independent thinkers. John Paul II expressly repudiates that (though prudently avoiding the claim that he is overturning previous papal authority): there is *no longer* any official Catholic philosophy (49/66; 78/98). When the defense of Thomistic Theses view dominated, there was a lack of dialogue with modern philosophy (62/81) and a consequent failure to appreciate modern philosophy's "precious and seminal insights" (48/64). The pope claims a legitimate pluralism in philosophy since no philosophy can embrace everything adequately (51/68).

He goes on to recommend, in addition to twentieth-century Thomistic philosophers like Jacques Maritain and Etienne Gilson, late nineteenth-century Catholic thinkers who were not Thomists, thinkers like John Henry Newman and Antonio Rosmini, the latter of whom, remember, had been condemned by the Vatican for "ontologism." He also recommends twentieth-century Catholic thinkers like phenomenologist Edith Stein (now *Saint Theresa Benedicta of the Cross*) and Maurice Blondel, as well as Russian thinkers lesser known in the West like Soloviev, Florensky, Chaadev, and Lossky (59/77; 74/93), to initiate dialogue with the Orthodox tradition. And with regard to earlier thinkers, in addition to Thomas Aquinas, he recommends non-Thomists like Gregory of Nyssa, Augustine, Anselm, and Bonaventure, who were philosophers of some stature and whose philosophic development served as the basis for their theologies. (Pope Benedict wrote his doctoral dissertation upon Bonaventure.)

The motto of Leo XIII's encyclical was: *Vetera novis augere et perficere*, "To extend and perfect the old with the new." That involves not only a recovery but also a renewal, exactly the twin movement behind Vatican II: *aggiornamento* and *resourcement*, an (Italian) updating of Catholic thought and a (French) return to the sources. However, the updating following from Vatican II involved a dialogue with modern thought which had been largely condemned from without by the papal tradition, and the return to the sources involved going back behind the Middle Ages for a recovery of the early Church Fathers and a methodically enriched study of the Bible. The latter was rooted in Pius XII's 1943 encyclical, *Divino afflante spiritu*, which permitted the use of historical-critical method forbidden by previous Vatican pronouncements. So while John Paul explicitly underscores the continuity of Vatican II with the modern papal tradition, he also, subtly and without calling attention to it, reverses elements of that papal tradition in the light of the study and development of tradition as a whole launched by Vatican II.

The overall aim of the encyclical is to restore trust in reason and to recover philosophy's dignity (6/16; 56/75) in order to "develop for the future an original, new, and constructive mode of thinking" (85/107), a philosophy not restricted to repeating antique formulae (97/119), but open to all that human inquiry uncovers. The understanding of the faith itself grows through that inquiry. That is why the pope underscores the importance—indeed, the indispensability—of the study of philosophy for the priesthood (62/81).

QUESTIONS

1. What is the main thesis of the book? What is its basic claim? What reasons are offered to support the claim?

2. What do you understand by "faith"? By "reason"? Identify the various passages in which the pope explains what he means by these terms.

3. Consider the basic outline of the text. Is it like a shopping list or is there some basis for the order?

4. What do you understand by "philosophy"? Do you have a philosophy? What is the basis for it?

5. President Bush said that his favorite philosopher was Jesus. Would the pope say that? What does the pope understand by "philosophy"? How is it related to "theology"? How are both related to "faith"?

6. List the thinkers favored by the pope. List the philosophical and theological positions he does not favor. What are his reasons for favoring or not?

7. What are we to do with the plurality of philosophies, theologies, and faiths? Why is there this plurality?

8. What are the "current requirements and tasks"?

FURTHER READINGS

1. Kenneth Schmitz, *At the Centre of the Human Drama: The Philosophical Anthropology of Karol Wojtyla / Pope John Paul II.*

2. George Weigel, *Witness to Hope: The Biography of John Paul II.*

3. D. Foster and J. Koterski, eds., *Two Wings of Catholic Thought: Essays on Fides et Ratio.* An expository collection.

4. L. Hemming and S. Parsons, eds., *Restoring Faith in Reason.* A Latin-English text, a commentary, and a reaction by people from different traditions.

* * * *

PHENOMENOLOGY
OF THE MAILBOX

Grant unto us men the skill, O God, in a little thing to descry
those notions as be common to things both great and small.

—AUGUSTINE, *CONFESSIONS*, XI, 23

INTRODUCTION

Fides et Ratio spoke of several levels of truth: first of everyday experience,
second of the sciences, third of philosophy, and fourth of religion (*FR*
§30 / p. 42). They are all both distinguished and linked. The first three have
their origins in common human experience independent of revelation; the
fourth depends upon revelation, i.e., upon special human experience. That
might be said of any religion. In this exercise we will focus attention upon
common human experience—at least in our culture which is literate and
has a mail system: we will explore the structures of experience found in
doing a phenomenological description of a mailbox. Though not all cultures are literate and have mail systems, many of the features of experience
involved in knowing and using the mailbox are found in cultures generally.
And *Fides et Ratio* from the very beginning (*FR* 1/9) sets our sights upon
Eastern as well as Western cultures.

Everyday experience is presupposed by the other levels. Even revelation is addressed to everyday experience. *Fides et Ratio* claims that God
comes to us in the things we know best and can verify most easily, the things
of our everyday life, apart from which we cannot understand ourselves (*FR*
12/21). Science itself takes root in and presupposes ordinary experience.
The evidence that science appeals to is based upon looking and manipulating as well as upon linguistic communication. The latter is not only that
which appears in scientific literature but that which is used by scientists

15

when they talk to one another: Can you fix this spectroscope? How about a cigarette? (Horrors!) What are you doing for lunch? A scientist might even say, Lord, help me to see things aright and make a contribution to my field! None of this is communicated in scientific language.

We already know how to operate in the sensory environment and in the world of everyday linguistic communication before, during, and after we set about engaging in science. Being involved in the everyday world, doing science, and living religiously present the data that philosophers reflect upon. So, before we set about these other tasks, it is important to reflect upon what we always already know as fully formed adults. Such knowledge is purely functional and is usually not made explicit. Often what we might think about experience—our "theories" about it—do not match what we know in the mode of "how to," but not in the mode of explicit description. We might, for example, think that knowing is a matter of sense experience alone and that it takes place inside our head, as a matter of brain processes—though the deliverances of ordinary experience speak against those views.

The article employs the method singled out by the John Paul as the phenomenological method (*FR* 59/78). (He wrote his own doctoral dissertation on the German phenomenologist Max Scheler.) The term "phenomenology" is derived from the Greek terms *phainomenon* or "appearance" and *logos* or the attempt to get at essential, universal, and necessary features (the same as in bio-logy, psycho-logy, theo-logy). The fancy term for the universal and necessary is "the eidetic" from the Greek word *eidos* which translates as "type" or "kind" or "form." Phenomenology is based upon careful description of the essential types of features of things appearing and of modes of attending to that appearing. Using the phenomenological method of isolating essential features involved in such appearance, the piece that follows distinguishes several aspects involved in recognizing and utilizing a mailbox.

The first is the level of so-called *empirical objectivity*. What that technical philosophic expression indicates is the environment of things presenting themselves through our senses "objectively," that is over-against us (from the Latin *ob-jectum*, that which is cast—*jectum*, from *iacere*, to throw—over against—*ob*, as in "obstacle"). The term "empirical" is from the Greek *empeiria* or experience. We see, handle, hear, smell, and taste things: that is the realm of empirical objectivity. The senses are the ways in which we come to know things; they are the immediate phase of how things appear to us; they present the original phenomena. John Paul says that it is a great challenge at the end of the millennium to move from *phenomenon* to *foundation* (*FR* 83/105). Our descriptions will prepare the way for that.

The second aspect is most important: it is that of our own consciousness. It is the crucial feature in following the command "Know thyself" with which *Fides et Ratio* begins and which originates in the ancient Greek oracle at Delphi followed by Socrates (*FR* 1/9). How do you think about your own consciousness? It is surely that which is most intimate to you. But it is not like the things that appear to consciousness. It has no color, shape, smell, etc. No one can touch it. And it is not locked into what the senses deliver: through our reflective awareness we can come to know something about the senses that the senses do not immediately deliver. Human awareness not only senses, it reflects. Most significant, it can know the universal, necessary features of each of the sensory fields, not simply the individual things that happen to appear within them. Awareness is not an object, but the central feature of the subject who knows objects; it is the sphere of *subjectivity*. Its most crucial feature is the employment of the notion of Being, an odd notion that includes absolutely everything, and everything about everything; but it includes it all initially in an *empty* manner. That is, we do not know everything, but we are by nature *referred* to everything in the mode of a set of questions peculiar to humans: What's it *all* about? How do we fit into the whole scheme of things? What is this "whole scheme"? Religions and philosophies are attempted answers to those questions. That is closely linked to the John Paul's calling for a recovery and renewal of the philosophy of being (97/119).

Third, the mailbox is not given by nature but by human artifice: it is an arti-fact. In order to make a living, someone made it to function within the mail system. So it fits into a system of production and exchange as well as into the mail system. Such systems function in independence of my own individual awareness and mediate my relations to those connected indirectly to me by these systems. Humans live with one another mediated by regular, habitual practices developed over significantly longer time periods than the time of those who now operate within them. Institutional mediation is an essential aspect of my relation to the mailbox. It involves our essentially belonging to a community (*FR* 31/43).

Further, the foundation of this mediation is the primal institution: language. It is the clearest indication that we are not self-made humans but are essentially embedded in tradition. Language has two central modes:

spoken and written. It can also be signed by hand signals or semaphore or embossed in braille.

Human are believed to have existed on the earth for some one and three-quarters million years. Writing emerged very recently, around 3000 BC. It changed essentially our relations to time and space and to one another. The mailbox functions in terms of written communication.

Finally, the mailbox functions in the absence of the person or persons addressed. There are essential differences between the ways in which persons, animals, plants, and nonliving things present themselves and the ways they are absent.

The general features uncovered reflectively from what we already know functionally furnish the bases for the "big questions" and the test for the adequacy of the answers offered in terms of how such answers do justice to the whole field of experience. The inventory of such features is presupposed but not made explicit in the attempt to interpret scripture and tradition in theology.

* * * *

PHENOMENOLOGY OF THE MAILBOX

Earlier in the century Adolph Reinach, one of the pupils of Edmund Husserl, founder of phenomenology, devoted an entire semester to a course on the phenomenology of the mailbox. Given the great questions of human origins and destiny, human freedom and responsibility, and the meaning of the cosmos, such inquiry seems trivial. However, these larger questions arise on the basis of certain features of the field of human experience in their different relations. And it is features that appear in the field of such experience in their peculiar modes of togetherness that furnish the evidence for testing the larger claims. People are free to make whatever ultimate claims they wish, but it is only appropriate evidence that tests the validity of those claims, so that the prior quest should be a making explicit of the initial forms of evidence that found our theoretical claims. Such is the role of phenomenology or the discipline that attends to the essential features of what is given within the field of experience. Such givenness entails both features of objects of attention and the always, but usually only implicitly present, features of the conscious subject in the togetherness of his or her different acts of attending.

The mailbox has a certain advantage in that recognizing and using it involves several different strata in its appearance. It is first of all an object within our sensory fields: we see it and take hold of it. When we open it, it emits a certain sound. We might also smell and, less likely, taste it. Second, it is an artifact which exhibits features over and beyond its being like sensory objects of nature. Third, it functions within the mediations of institutions like the production and exchange systems which manufacture and sell mailboxes. But we buy it in order to function within the postal system. Fourth, it presents the written word, which is to be set in contrast with and in relation to the spoken word. Fifth, it involves the absence of the communicator, which is to be set in contrast with and in relation to his or her presence. We could go on to consider other features, but let us limit ourselves to the five we have listed—at least for the time being: empirical objectivity in general, artifaction, institutional mediation, writing and speech, intersubjective presence and absence. In and through all these considerations we have to attend to the differing intentional acts or modes of attending involved in such layers of recognition.

What we are after in philosophy are the basic concepts that determine a given field, not the particulars that may occur or be discovered in that field. Thus we are not as such interested in seeing this or that but in what is *essential* to seeing and what is *essential* to being seen. In the form of first philosophy or ontology or metaphysics (it has been given different names historically), philosophy is after the basic concepts that are found in *all* things. In fact, it takes one of its names, *ontology*, from the most basic of notions, the notion of being (Greek *to on*, genitive *tou ontos*). We will make a great deal out of that in studying the thinkers and the matters about which they speak.

For purposes of better illustrating some points, let us consider a rural mailbox set on a post by a roadside at some distance from the house and encompassed by the rolling fields of farmland.

1.

Consider first the mailbox as a visual object. It has a kind of silver-gray surface set upon a light brown post. On one side it has a moveable little red flag attached to a pivot. To appear as a visual object it must exhibit a certain color or set of colors. Even the so-called color-blind see shades of black, white, and gray. What appears as colored must be extended, ultimately linked to three-dimensional solids which have an inside and an outside. In the case of the mailbox proper, it has a hollow inside. In the case of the post upon which it is mounted, it has a full inside. Further, it can only appear in a space separated from the viewer and filled with light. The filled space does not extend indefinitely: it appears within a horizon as the limit to the field of vision. We look out beyond the mailbox to the surrounding hills, beyond which perhaps we see the sky and the clouds. Such horizoned space moves ahead of us as we move forward. We carry it with us as a kind of psychic hoopskirt, though it is not merely psychological. It is the condition for the visual appearance of things to a bodily situated observer. Though the perceived space is limited by the horizon, it nonetheless always presents itself as linked to an indeterminately surrounding space spread out in all directions from our bodies. And by reason of the relation between the bodily location of our viewing and that horizon, three-dimensional objects appearing within the horizon are perspectivally shortened, shrinking as they recede from our viewing position. Again, any extended thing only exists in measurable relation to other extended things in its environment. Within the visual field the objects upon which we focus are set off from the others that then appear only marginally or obliquely until we attend to each of them successively. When we do so, the others we attended to earlier become marginal in their turn.

We have spoken as if the viewing subject were immobilized. As a matter of fact we are always changing our visual viewpoint, moving our heads from side to side and moving ourselves bodily to differing positions vis-à-vis the objects present visually. As we do so, the perspectives alter. And yet, they perspectively present themselves as coherently relating to previous perspectives and as linked, immediately and spontaneously, to those that will follow. As conscious subjects we retain the immediately past and expect the immediately following presentation. In fact, what we have previously experienced mediates our expectations as to what will follow the perspectives we have just experienced, not simply in terms of the peculiarities of a given situation, but in terms of empirical objects generally. We expect, for example, that every front will have a back, even though we might have never seen the back of a particular body. We walk around to the other side of the mailbox and see that it has a dent in the back.

2.

Even though our current interest is theoretical, our basic lived relation to the mailbox is not theoretical but practical: we check it to see if we have mail. Seeing is for the sake of apprehending. We go up to it, reach out, and open it. When we do so, its metal sides feel hard and smooth. If in the winter, they would feel cold and usually dry. In the summer they might feel hot and sometimes damp. When I might have first set it on its post, it would have felt rather light. Hardness, smoothness, coldness, dampness, lightness: all are not absolute but relative terms. The sides of the mailbox are harder than the muscle on my arms, slightly tensed when I first carried the box to its current location and installed it; but not as hard as, let's say, the gaudy diamond ring on my finger. Furthermore, properties such as coldness are relative to the thermal state of the one who takes hold of the object. For one who is hot, it might feel cooler; for one who is cold, it might feel warmer. But though doubly relative—to their opposites and to the bodily state of the one who feels them—that is their objective nature; that is what such properties actually are: relations of a manifest object to an embodied conscious subject.

I open the box and take out the mail. I notice that there is a lingering fragrance left from a perfumed letter I received yesterday. As I close it, it emits a peculiar clank, louder or softer, depending upon how hard I push it closed. I knock on it and it produces a different sound. Both fragrance and sound diffuse themselves into the space surrounding the smelling and sounding object, diminishing in intensity as they recede from their irradiating object, with the fragrance lingering longer, but in a more reduced area, than the sound. I open one of the letters: it is a valentine with some little red candy hearts. I pop one in my mouth: it is smooth and hard with the sharp but sweet flavor of cinnamon. Taste is a variation on touch: the object exhibits the tactual qualities and adds its own specialization: flavor with variations between sweet/sour, sharp/flat, and the like. Flavors interplay with smells; hold your nose and you can't taste anything.

Now all these features—visual, tactual, olfactory, audile and also gustatory—are spontaneously linked together as features of the object I have come to call my mailbox. But it is not these features to which we ordinarily attend. Regularly we attend *through* each feature *to the thing*, the aspects appearing only subsidiary in our attention focused on the thing. And each presentation points beyond itself to the sum total of possible perspectives within each of the senses in their togetherness. I intend the mailbox itself in and through the subject-dependent perspectives on it that sensation affords me. The mailbox presents itself as exceeding each of the perspectives but containing all of them.

3.

Now we have been attending primarily to the mailbox itself. The thing presented through the continual variations of its sensory features stands present to me outside my body. Attend now more carefully to that awareness. Though my awareness is grounded in my body which furnishes me my mobile point of view on the thing and the organs for sensation, awareness itself is not in the body the way my eyeballs and brain are. I attend *from* my body *to* the thing outside. My awareness is literally *with* the mailbox, not as one body alongside and perhaps in contact with another, but in the distinctive mode of *manifestation*, of *appearance*. The mailbox is shown as existing outside me, its viewer and user. It is present as other than me. The condition for that happening is my self-presence as a conscious being, other than which the other is present. Embedded within the darkness of material processes with their blind action and interaction, a clearing, "a lighting" occurs, an open space in which things not only *are* but are *shown*, they *appear*, they become *manifest*, they become *phenomena*.

The first condition that makes this possible is involved in every sensing being, namely touch. Some animals, like worms, seem to have only touch. Animals who have other senses must also have touch. The reason for this is that the point of sensing is to present opportunities and threats to organic development and sustenance. The latter is served by apprehending the appropriate objects, eating them, mating with them, struggling with them, caring for them.

One of the peculiarities of touch is that, though the hands are the typical locus of its operation, the organ for touch is the whole surface of the body. That contrasts with the other senses that have specifically localized organs: eyes, eardrums, mouth, nose. There is another feature linked to that: touch involves the suffused self-presence of the animal that is functionally, pre-focally aware of its entire body. As aware, it lives in and from its body, not as something that it simply has, as it has any other instrument, but as something that it *is*, with which it is identified. The body is mine as consciously self-directive and is me myself in one of my phases. Awareness is related to body, not as one thing to another, but as a pervading, overarching presence to the whole functioning organism, a kind of concrete universal in relation to the particulars of its organic parts. Of course, that presence does not involve even implicit awareness of *all* of the body's parts. There is no lived awareness of one's own cell-structure nor of one's brain. Most of the body remains beneath the threshold of awareness: an animal is present to it as a *functioning whole*, implicitly aware of what it needs to do to move itself in reacting to its environment. The field of awareness in its pervading the lived body is an expression of the fundamental pervading of the whole organism in all its parts by the unifying principle of its kind of life, by what Aristotelians call the "soul" (*psyche*). The soul is the principle of holistic functioning involving conscious, and in the human case reflectively self-conscious capacities.

The lived body is both other than and the same as the body observed in physiology. Analogous to the same body seen and touched, each human body is both exteriorly apprehensible and lived from within. But in the latter mode of access, it is not entirely other than the awareness that lives it. Its otherness is more like the otherness of the liver in relation to the brain: two features of the single functional whole we call an organism. But unlike the relation between the liver and the brain, the relation of feeling to its organic base is not a relation of two separable parts but of a self-presence to its own dark basis.

The diffuse self-presence of the animal organism in the mode of feeling is the basis for the manifestation of what is other than the conscious organism. Manifest otherness presupposes self-presence, other than which the other is manifest. Tactual sensitivity spread over the whole surface of the organism is the result of primordial self-presence in the mode of feeling. It is the basis for the differentiation of sensibility found in relation to localized organs.

Linked to this are the kinesthetic feelings whereby I operate through the organism, moving from position to position, sensing in various ways and taking hold of things. As I take hold I feel myself feeling things, feeling the effect things have upon me. There is, in addition, the sense of balance as there might be a sense of dizziness as I stand and move from place to place. Pervading my awareness of identity with my body there might also be a sense of vigor or weariness or perhaps nausea.

Again, there is the frequent recurrence of hunger, thirst, and sexual desire experienced in relation to certain organs of the body. Whereas the various sensory capacities are oriented toward *aspects* of things in the environment, the natural appetites are oriented toward the *things* presented through these aspects, namely those kinds of things that can nourish or can fulfill sexual desire. Feelings expressive of such appetites are linked to the appearance of certain sensorily present objects in the environment or even to the inner recollection of such objects. When such desires become intense, they seem to pervade our whole organism and magnetize our attention. When they become very intense, they rise to the level of pain. But when they are being satisfied, there is the feeling of pleasure.

Awareness is thus rafted upon an underlying organism whose needs dictate the way in which I am engaged in the environment outside my organism. I find myself always thrust "outside," always engaged in the things that are opportunities or threats to my organic well-being. I am always "tuned," anticipating feeling pleasure and pain in relation to the things given outside.

The organically based desires are latent as I approach the mailbox, but other desires are operative. Perhaps I am a bit anxious about a letter I am expecting. Will I get the grant for which I applied? Did my friend accept my apology for having offended him or did the offense produce a final breach to our long friendship? So I am engaged in another way: in expectations linked to my relation to other persons mediated by practices that are not themselves directly organic.

As I go to open the mailbox, I cut my finger on a sharp edge. There is a feeling of pain. Pain arises both from bodily injury and from the frustration of intense desire as pleasure does from the satisfaction of that desire and in proportion to the intensity of the pain of desire. If I receive the grant and secure forgiveness from my friend, I am pleased; if I do not, I am saddened. Both being pleased and being saddened are in proportion to the value I attach to the objects of that happiness or sadness.

4.

There is another feature involved in our attention thus far. In order that the thing may be manifest as enduring through the variations of its various presentations to me, I myself must be self-present as likewise enduring, as the same one who first saw the mailbox at a distance, approached it, opened it, smelled its slight aroma, and heard the clank of its closing. I must—or rather my psycho-neural system must—retain the first moment of encounter through the whole experience. Indeed, I must further retain the integrated experience as the ground for my re-visiting the mailbox in my mind while in its absence as the condition for my intending tomorrow to revisit it as the same mailbox I approached yesterday.

Attend to still another factor involved in the analysis thus far. As I look, apprehend, smell, and hear the object, my attention is focused upon it as an individual in the field of my own individual awareness and as having its own peculiar individual sensory features. The features are all actual and the individual thing is immediately present in them. However, our interest now is not in those individual features but in the eidetic constants they exhibit. Our aim is to disregard the contingent variations in order to attend to the universal and necessary constants that constitute the framework of each of the sensory fields. To that end, the real presence of a mailbox is irrelevant: an imaginative construct, such as the reader is now employing, is sufficient. What we apprehend as eidetic is characterized as universal, and that means as possibly instantiated in an indefinite number of particular instances, wherever and whenever we might encounter it. The senses give us the individual and actual; what we then come to call "the intellect" gives us the universal and possible.

The recognition of the redness of the flag on the mailbox is not given in the single experience of the flag. *This* red is given now in sensation, but *redness* is not. It is the result of past experience and the extraction of an ideal object which given sensory instances approach or from which they deviate in various degrees. The red on the flag is not the identical red of the cardinal fluttering through the tree above the mailbox nor the red on the pickup truck coming down the road. Other ideal types of visual objects are isolated: blue and yellow together with red being primary, pleonastically called "chromatic colors" (or *colored* colors) in contrast with black, white, and gray as oxymoronically termed "achromatic colors" (or non-colored colors) which "color-blind" people see. Particular shades and borderline cases are produced by combination of these "elements." But, we recognize, overarching these color variations, color as the genus correlative to the power of seeing. Whenever I see, I see color. But it is only in individual colored things, things of a particular shade, that I come to know the genus color. Indeed, I only come to recognize the genus when I recognize the species in the individual instances. But whereas redness has visible instances, there is no instance that exhibits just color the way the cardinal exhibits redness. Color is free of both species and instances of it as capable of being applicable to both.

When we come to recognize the generic object of seeing in color we at the same time come to recognize the nature of the capacity to see. The actuality of both the act of seeing and the seen color are always individual occurrences in a given Here-and-Now. But the capacity of seeing is a universal orientation toward the kind of object we call color, whenever and wherever its individual instances can be seen. Kinds are naturally correlative to powers. Furthermore, the seen individual has the natural capacity of being seen; and that, too, involves a universal orientation toward the kinds of organisms that can see. So individuality is manifest on both sides of the subject-object relation in sensing generically, but universality is involved on both sides in the reflectively discernible active and passive capacities and their objects. Kinds or types are correlative to the natural powers, active and passive, of individual things. Though it takes the work of sorting and thus abstracting from the welter of concrete visual experiences, such work is a matter of focusing what is already operative in things, namely, their natural powers. Universality in these cases is thus no relatively arbitrary construction of the human mind but a revelation of the inner nature of natural things as such, with the intellect as one of the functions of nature, nature as manifest *in its capacities and kinds* and not simply in its individuals.

From the proceeding, we can see that the recognition of the eidetic is not fixation upon an isolated universal. Each such universal presents itself as embedded within a hierarchical structure of samenesses and differences. The silver-gray of the mailbox, the red of its flag, the light brown of the post upon which it is mounted fall under the general notion of color as the sameness running through all of the kinds and individual instances of color, each of which is at the same time different from all the rest. Color, in turn, is a sensory feature set off from other such features by being perceptible through sight. And each sensory feature is a dependent feature of things, set off from other dependent features such as weight, height, and functionality. Specific clusters of types of features identify things of various sorts that are themselves linked in hierarchies of sameness and difference.

Such features as universality and particularity, sameness (generic and specific), and difference (universal and individual), along with other features like affirmation and negation, possibility, contingency, necessity, and existence, thing and properties are categories that operate through the other more directly present features like silver-gray, red, light brown, or heavy and light, smooth and rough, and the like. The level of the categorical, of both the sensorily restricted and the non-sensorily restricted universals, stands fixed atemporally over against the flux of sensations (both external and internal), sensorily given things, and our awareness. Categorial awareness invades our immediate sensory awareness since we always attend to the individual given features and their clusters *as* something, as instances of types. But categorial awareness is subsidiary to my focus upon the individual: in our example, upon the mailbox and its perceptible features. The universal structures function like glasses: I look *through* them, not *at* them—except in the present case where I am making them the object of my reflective attention. By reason of this reflective capacity I am able to take apart my experience by isolating some of these features and then relating them back to the objects in the judgments I make about what is focally given in perceptual experience.

But just that attention involves another structural level of my awareness. Not only am I, as conscious, outside the body that grounds and situates my awareness; I, as eidetic inquirer, am outside the Here-and-Now of the embodied sensory situation by being referred to the whole field of space and time where instances of the eidetic are found. That is, I come to apprehend the eidetic constants as holding *anytime* and *anyplace* the conditions for their instantiation are met. Reflection puts me at a distance from my immersion in the Here-and-Now because it is based upon my reference to the whole of space and time. It involves a shift in my disposition: from one engaged in the world of hopes and fears gathered in the mailbox to the simple desire to attend to the eidetic features apart from any other motivation.

There is a final consideration along these lines. The overarching notion within which all the sorting of samenesses and differences goes on is the notion of *Being*. Whatever I recognize, I recognize *as being*. And everything I recognize about anything I recognize as being. Everything, and everything about everything, is included indeterminately in the notion of Being. Consequently, the horizon of all our wakeful life is the totality of things. We live out of an anticipation of the character of the Whole within which we find ourselves—not only the cultural whole or cultural world, but the Cosmos itself. As the Stoics saw, we are, by nature, *cosmo-politan*, our home is the Cosmos as a whole.

The notion of Being pries one loose from all determinants, organically produced, culturally shaped, and personally chosen. It sets one at a reflective distance, making possible both the simple desire to grasp the eidetic as such and making possible and necessary our each choosing our way among the possibilities afforded by our situation and our understanding thereof.

5.

Providing various handles in and through my various sensory capacities, the mailbox is in general the same as any other empirical object. But it stands over against the general class of things provided by nature and stands in the class of things provided by art. As we already noted, the mailbox is also embedded in a general system of production and exchange.

The relatively perfect geometrical shape of the box itself indicates not only a refashioning of what is given by nature but a developed process of machine technology that allows for great exactitude in shaping things according to geometric idealization. Mass production supersedes hand-work. Over time various techniques develop of extracting raw materials from nature and of transforming such materials into forms that serve the ends for which we produce them. The early techniques were rather crude. The people who developed them have died long ago; but the techniques are passed on to others, some of whom refine them and, in turn, pass them on to still others.

Monetary exchange supersedes simple barter as things are subjected to quantitative evaluations that establish equivalencies. Again, the system of monetary exchange is developed and passed on as the institutional framework of operation in which we now live. So I was able to go to the store and purchase the mailbox instead of building one for myself.

In addition to functioning within the production and exchange system, the mailbox functions as the end intended by those systems within another system, the postal system. Its final end is the exchange of written statements.

6.

Such systems within which I function involve the mediation of my relations by anonymous others through those I directly encounter: the salesperson or the postman. The postal system aims at a mediated presence, a presence-in-absence, of others whom I intend directly as the recipients of my own letters or the authors of those directed to me. Such presence-in-absence develops out of an original situation of immediate encounter.

I see the postman bringing the mail. He is an empirical object, in that respect like other such objects: the trees, the hills, the dog running around the yard, the mailbox, the birds fluttering above, the clouds. He is set off from the hills and the mailbox which are *inanimate* objects. He has something in common with the trees in that he is an organically living process. The latter is set off from the inanimate by exhibiting developmental phases of a single, functional whole. An organism is a self-formative process, self-sustaining, self-repairing as well as self-reproducing. It thus necessarily appears as an individual of the kind belonging to its reproductive line. The notion of "self" here refers to a kind of centeredness, operating "from inside outward" and resisting that which would dissolve it. Its self-formation depends upon specific kinds of mineral elements, oxygen, and light in its environment. Its native powers, active and passive, are oriented toward the kinds of individuals in the environment correlative with those powers.

The postman is an organism, but he is different from the trees in that he is, like the birds, sensorily aware. Such awareness adds a dimension of self-manifestation as correlative to the manifestation of what stands outside it as sustaining, threatening, or indifferent to its own existence. Its sensory life is focused upon individuals and is immediately linked to its organic needs experienced in terms of desire and the pleasure and pain of possession or its lack regarding beneficial and harmful goods.

The postman is different from the birds, not only in physiological structure, but in his whole style of behavior. For one thing, he is clothed—usually in a uniform that identifies his functioning in an official capacity within the postal system. Being clothed places him within a set of cultural practices with its different styles of dress, but also, as with the mailbox he opens, in the systems of production and exchange. He functions by reason of knowing his way about within these systems.

But he is not simply a different sort of object sharing identical traits with other sorts of objects appearing in the environment. He is another self whom I experience as "you." He looks; he smiles; he speaks to me. The look and the smile are expressive of the inwardness of his disposition. His state of mind is directly available in his comportment. But the fuller content of his mind is available through his speech. Here he rests, like I whom he addresses, within the same linguistic conventions as I do.

7.

The postal service is itself made possible because of the invention of writing. Writing is a kind of surrogate presence of other subjects as it is a kind of surrogate for living speech.

Speech itself is a temporal flow. Sentences are generated in such a way that the sound of the beginning of each has passed away before the sound of its end is generated. And each sentence flows into the next. Indeed, we do not ordinarily think in terms of sentences but in terms of the objects about which we speak in continuous discourse. Sentences are analytically isolatable from the flow of discourse. We can carry out the analysis further when we isolate the words: the nouns, verbs, adjectives, adverbs, articles, prepositions, conjunctives. Some are subjectable to inflections of various sorts: declensions in terms of gender, number, and case with regards to nouns and (in some languages) adjectives; conjugations, for example, in terms of time-relations (variations on past, present, and future) and relations to the intent of the speaker (declarative, interrogative, optative, and imperative) as well as the abstract infinitive in the case of verbs.

Speech is embedded in sound. When we carry on a phonological analysis, we find that the unit proximate to words is the syllable, but the ultimate units are vowels and consonants. The vowels are basic: a, e, i, o, u; the consonants "sound with" (*sonare con*) the vowels by clipping them in various ways termed dentals (d and t), labials (b, f), gutturals (c, g, k), sibilants (s, z), and the like. Vowels and consonants are based upon the sound possibilities of the human oral cavity on the one hand and an idealized selection of certain ranges of sound that carry absolute identities. In the case of "a," for example, there are many concrete individual modulations for individuals or groups when sounding out the same identical "a" sound. And to determine how a given sound counts for "a" one has to hear it in relation to the way in which the other vowels are sounded by that individual or in that group. In other words, the vowels and consonants form part of an eidetic system of humanly selected ideal units. They are subservient to communicating identical meanings abstracted from and applied to things originally given in the environment, for example, features like colors, tactual qualities and the like. Linguistic sounds arise by historical selection out of the sound-generating capacities of the organism that situates human awareness in the environment. They are themselves the incarnation of distinctively human awareness. We come to ourselves as thinkers as we incarnate our thought in speech or writing.

The spoken sentence persists in memory, until it is forgotten. Of course, much depends upon the quality of one's memory. It is memory—good or poor—that allows one to return to the same singular historical event long after it has flowed down the stream of time. But writing rescues memory from its tendency to weaken over time. Memory also implies that the past event, long since flown away, still retains the sameness of objective immortality to which our memory refers and which we attempt to revisit through deliberately employed techniques of recovery.

Writing is an exterior supplement to the native, interior memory which is inclined over time to forget what was said. The Romans noted: *Verba fluunt, scripta manent*: Spoken words flow, written words remain—a warning by the pragmatists to be careful what you commit to writing, but also a significant observation about the relation of speech to writing.

Writing also changes the scope of the audience. Speech is restricted to the immediate situation of the interlocutors—or eavesdroppers: to the space within which the voices can be heard and the time within which the conversation occurs. But writing opens up to all those capable of reading the language, wherever they might be spatially located and whenever they might read the text for the duration of the time when the material medium supports the text. The same words can be read again and again. But the flux will inevitably overtake the medium. However, these same words can be written again and again by copyists and later reproduced by mechanical means. Indeed, today the living voice itself can be transcribed electronically—thus significantly disambiguating by tonal dynamics what, as written, could remain ambiguous.

Not only the written message sent and received through the postal service, but the very account we are giving is made possible both because of the various levels of structure involved in my awareness and because of the antecedent development of the English language. Language places me from the start into a peculiar space together with others. Those who taught me language brought me out of my bodily point of view as a needy sensing being and into a common set of eidetic structures. Language holds in place the eidetic recognitions and creations of those long dead. It is the system within which all the other systems function, the basic openness of the Whole for a tradition. Each of us lives in it in such a way that we are brought out of our own privacies and into a public space. It is within this space that we carry on all the operations we have been examining. It is within this space that we are able to carry out the sciences that have inter-subjective validity.

8.

Return now to the character of the subject who is carrying on this inquiry. It is a single, embodied subject. As such it is in the midst of a career as an organism that began as a fertilized ovum replete with the unobservable potentialities directed toward the adult stage of a human being. It will inevitably end with the dissolution of the organism. The most detailed inventory of all the empirically available features of the fertilized ovum will yield absolutely nothing of its potentialities. Only reflective intellect can uncover them by working backward from the actual course of development to the powers. But reflective intellect, operating out of the horizon of orientation toward the whole of Being, also lives out of the horizon of anticipating its own demise. The human being exists as one of the mortals. Running ahead in thought to that term, one can bring one's own life as a whole into focus.

The mailbox appears as such because we are able to recognize the eidetic, because we situate it within a shared horizon of institutions governed by collective ends and personally appropriated by placing our individual ends within those institutional frames. But the eidetic appears because the immediately present things like mailboxes are finally horizoned by our anticipation of the Whole and the whole of our own life as sealed by our own demise. How we view the Whole (our philosophy or theology) and how we anticipate the final shape of our own individual lives governs how we approach even the simplest things in life—things like the humble mailbox.

With all this attention to the eidetic, to the system of essences as the glasses through which we look at things in the environment, have we not lost existence, have we not lost this actual mailbox? There are certain privileged moments when the individuality of its existence might come to the fore. Consider the mailbox alongside the road just after sunrise. The clouds are tinged with an orange-gold glow reflected on the surface of the mailbox. The morning dew is still on its surface. A spider has woven its web between the edge of the box and the post on which it sits. The dew on the web and on the box glistens in the sunlight. A sense of freshness and promise pervades the cool air. We are gripped by the display, held by its beauty. In the functional world within which we operate, the pre-understanding in virtue of which we take up things in certain ways involves our focus upon the goals under which we subsume what presents itself. Being halted by the beauty of a particular display pulls us up short, sets us in the Now in a transformed way—even opening out to a possible theophany. As Martin Buber said, "Sunlight on a maple twig and a glimpse through to the Eternal Thou is worth more than all the [mystical] experiences on the edge of life."

But no matter what our focus, the lure of the Whole constitutes the implicit background within which we come to understand anything and to grasp and pursue our goals. It is that lure which generates the questions that set in motion the history of philosophy. What is the nature of the Whole? How can we come into proper relation to that Whole? How does that relate to our everyday focal concerns? How is our awareness related to the dark biological ground that underpins it? How is it related to the community that antecedes it as the source of the institutions whereby I define and realize my own individual possibilities? What does it portend with respect to my own inevitable demise? The descriptively available evidences we have explored both lead to such questions and relate the putative answers back to the togetherness of such evidences in order to test the adequacy of our larger claims.

9.

These observations lead us to a view of human nature as culture-creating nature and thus as essentially historical. Human nature is the constant; culture and history are the variables. Based upon what we have seen, human nature presents itself as bipolar, as organically based reference to the Whole.

We are obviously organisms, some of whose organs are the basis for sensory experience. The organs serve the powers of perception but also the desires for food, drink, and sex served in turn by perception of what is beneficial or harmful to our flourishing as organic beings. The objects of perception and biological desire are ever present in wakeful life as individual and actual. They are the most obvious inhabitants of "reality." This establishes one pole to our experience.

The less obvious feature of experience is an empty reference to the whole of what-is that founds the questions, What's it all about? What is our place in the whole scheme of things? And, What is the whole scheme of things? That reference is a function of the notion of Being which makes the mind to be a mind. Everything is included in its scope, for outside being is nothing. But by itself it yields no knowledge of anything in particular. We begin to fill in that empty reference by experience and inference governed by the principle of noncontradiction that holds for the whole of experience and what we might infer from it.

It is that reference to the Whole via the notion of Being that is the basis for both what we call *intellect* and what we call *will*. Being directed to the Whole of what is, we are also directed to the whole of space and time which allows us to abstract eidetic features that refer to *anytime* and *anyplace* such features might be met in the individuals given in sensory experience. Abstraction leads to judgment which puts the abstractions together with the experienced objects. And judgment allows for inference when we put judgments together in reasoning processes following the principle of noncontradiction.

That same reference to the Whole is what makes will possible as the freedom to choose. Referred by our nature to the Whole, we are free in the face of anything less than the Whole and are thus able to determine ourselves. But that can only happen insofar as we understand the possibilities for our choice given by intellectual operations. Thus intellect and will are like two sides of the same coin: each presupposes the other. We cannot understand unless we choose, and we cannot choose unless we understand the options.

The building up of our view of the Whole is linked to the limitation of our experience and the inadequacy of the frameworks for understanding that experience. That is why science has a history of uncovering nature. And our choices are limited by our understanding of possibilities. At first they were extremely limited. Over time each of us attains to habitual ways of understanding and choosing. Passed on to others, these ways sediment into institutions, that is, loci of practices that focus and hone our possibilities for acting. Because of the differing ways of understanding and the differing character of institutions, cultures are necessarily plural. And because understanding and choice develop over time, cultures have a history—much of it brought about by interaction between cultures.

Each of us is born and raised in a determinate culture as mediated by the more or less limited understanding possessed by those who raised us. That process focuses the possibilities given by each of our individual genetic makeups. So when reflective awareness begins to emerge in each of us, we are already determined by two structures we did not choose: our genetic makeup and our cultural shaping. These give us the initial motivational structure for choosing. When we begin to make our own choices, we further determine our own habit-structure within the frameworks of the genetic and cultural stamps given to us. At any given moment then we have three already determined levels that constitute any given Me: a genetic level, a cultural level, and a personal-historical level. We cannot erase the fact that Here-and-Now we are each determined by these three levels, in the peculiar forms they have taken in each of us. But any given person has the bipolar structure sketched above. Reference to the Whole grounds the I as the ability to understand and choose from among the possibilities afforded by the I's own Me. The Me is the artist's material for the I, the already determinate stuff for the I's choosing. What am I going to do with Me? is the question each one of us always faces. And what we do depends upon how we understand the possibilities afforded by that tri-level structure.

The interplay of these levels sediments into a dynamic center that a long tradition has called "the heart." It is the ground of our spontaneous tendency to move in certain directions, to be attracted by certain possibilities and repelled by others. It is our more or less automatic pilot, the default position for everyday action. But being directed toward the Whole, I am always placed in conscious life at a reflective distance from Me, on account of which I have to ask myself: Where is my heart? Is it where it ought to be? Where ought it to be?

Reflective distance makes the individual responsible for its own actions. It becomes the cutting edge of the culture which it can sustain, develop, or subvert. Its full development lies in the cultivation of its spontaneous proclivities for action when thought reaches the heart. Religiously, that means when God moves from object of thought to a living Presence.

Now the function of philosophy is to make the invariable structures explicit, those that are present phenomenologically and those that underlie foundationally. That is why John Paul points to a move from phenomenon to foundation. We will follow that move in the treatment of the various philosophers we have selected.

The practice of philosophy stands at a distance from our own hearts in order to arrive at an understanding of what and why our hearts desire what they do and in order to arrive at criteria for judging the movements of our hearts within a responsibly developed view of the Whole. Philosophy holds open the space for the fullest development of the heart and clarifies the heart to itself. But philosophy itself is not directly a matter of the heart; it is a matter of the intellect and its pure, unrestricted desire to understand, apart from how we might feel about things.

* * * *

Armed with the basic concepts we have highlighted in our dealing with everyday things, we turn to focus upon select highlights in the history of thought, beginning with Plato, passing through Aristotle, on to Augustine and Aquinas, who took up Plato and Aristotle respectively, and then to Descartes, Hegel, and Heidegger. The aim is not to present how they *used* to think and thus satisfy historical curiosity, but to learn *how* to think by attending to the things with which the classic texts deal. The lives of the thinkers are to that extent irrelevant. It is the things themselves that we learn to focus in various ways by studying the great philosophers.[1]

QUESTIONS

1. What are the essential features of each of the sensory fields?

2. What is the difference between the "lived body" and body object? You know of bodies by sensing them in various ways as objects appearing within your sensory fields. But you know your own body in a different way. Describe that difference as exactly as you can.

3. What is different about touch than is the case with the other senses?

4. How is intellection different from sensation?

5. How is a natural capacity different than a sensory object? How is it like the intellect? How is it different?

6. Heraclitus once said: All things flow and nothing remains the same. You can't step into the same river twice. Is that true of *all* of experience and its objects?

7. Red thing, redness, color, sensory feature, quality, property: these terms are arranged from more concrete to more abstract. Each more abstract term covers more items in experience than the more concrete terms that precede it. This is an instance of a logical hierarchy—parallel to the Church hierarchy in which you find broader and broader spheres of authority. How do the notions of sameness and difference function in this logical hierarchy?

8. Universal notions function like glasses. How so?

1. This essay is the result of a collaborative effort in a phenomenology workshop at the University of Dallas. I wish to thank Glenn Chicoine, Michael Jordan, Landon Lester, Lynn Purcell, Michael Tocci, and Matthew van House for their contributions to the development of the work.

9. How are humans related to space and time?

10. The pope says that what we need is a renewal of the philosophy of being (*FR* 97/119). How does the notion of Being enter into the discussion of the mailbox? What features of human experience does it make possible?

11. What are the essential features of the way in which different kinds of things present themselves: the nonliving, the living, the animal, the human?

12. What are the essential features involved in speech? How does writing modify those features?

13. How does aesthetic experience move us from essence to existence?

14. How are the big questions made possible by the structure of human awareness?

15. Describe the bipolar structure of human existence. How does that make the human being the culture-creating animal?

16. Describe the distinction between I and Me. How does the heart fit into the picture?

FURTHER READINGS

1. Edmund Husserl, *The Crisis of European Sciences and Transcendental Phenomenology*. This is one of the founder of phenomenology's most readable works, set against the background of modern thought from Galileo and Descartes through the British Empiricists and Kant in relation to the development of Western thought generally.

2. Robert Sokolowski, *An Introduction to Phenomenology*. Short and readable, it gives a good sense of phenomenological method by practicing it.

3. Dermot Moran, *Introduction to Phenomenology*. A substantial history of the phenomenological movement.

4. Dermot Moran, *The Phenomenology Reader*. Readings from the thinkers covered in Moran's history (3, above).

* * * *

PLATO'S *REPUBLIC*

The philosopher keeps his eyes always fixed on the Whole
. . . and the universal nature of every thing that is, each in
its wholeness.

—PLATO, *THEAETETUS*, 173C

. . . always devoting himself through reasoning to the idea
of Being.

—PLATO, *SOPHIST*, 254A

READINGS

The Republic of Plato:

1. The opening and the discussion with Cephalus: death, justice, and philosophical reflection (327a–329e)[1]

---

1. The sections to be read are indicated by Roman numbers and by section numbers, not by page numbers. The reason is that there are many different translations with different page numbers. The Roman numerals refer to the traditional division by "books" (or what we today would call "chapters"). The section numbers refer to the first critical edition of Plato's work by Stephanus in 1578. Critical editions of Hebrew, Greek, and Roman antiquity were first produced in the Renaissance. They arose because of problems involved in copying and dissemination throughout geographically separated regions. A copyist may misread some words, skip others, or add his own bright remarks. His copy, being, in turn, copied and disseminated widely, produced variant manuscript traditions. Those who produced the critical editions studied the variant traditions and the time of their reproduction in order to arrive as close as possible to the original text. The Bible did not escape the problems of copying and disseminating: it too was subjected to the same dissemination process that required a critical edition. Referring to the critical edition gives us a common way of referring that cuts across the multiplicity of translations.

1.

Twentieth-century mathematician and philosopher Alfred North White-head said that the history of philosophy is a series of footnotes on Plato.[2] American essayist Ralph Waldo Emerson said that "Philosophy is Plato, and Plato, Philosophy."[3] The best introduction to Western philosophy is a careful study of Plato's works. Plato is particularly important for understanding the way reflection upon revelation occurred among the Church Fathers, for early theology was dominated by Platonic ways of thinking. And that influence continued unabated—for better *and* for worse—throughout the centuries.

Plato (429–348 BC) was originally a tragedian—until he met Socrates who subjected him to a philosophic grueling. After that he burned his plays (alas!) but turned his literary talents to writing philosophic dialogues where he combines the use of imagery, the description of character, dramatic action, allegorizing, and myth-making with philosophic questioning and construction. His early work was a retelling of the trial and death of Socrates who was killed for unsettling Athenian authorities by his relentless questioning of their understanding of ultimate things.[4] Thereafter Socrates becomes the main character in the dialogues; but later he becomes secondary, finally disappearing in favor of other major speakers. So it becomes difficult to say what is Socrates's and what is Plato's

---

2. Whitehead, *Process and Reality*, 63.

3. Emerson, "Plato or the Philosopher," in *Representative Men*.

4. The story of Socrates's trial, imprisonment, and death is told by Plato in *Apology*, *Crito*, and *Phaedo*. These and the rest of Plato's dialogues are found in *Plato: Complete Works*.

in the dialogues. But that is only of historical interest and irrelevant to understanding their philosophic content.

2.

In the center of Plato's works stands the *Republic*: all the chronologically previous dialogues lead up to it; all those subsequent follow from it. The work is structured around an ascent and a descent, beginning with the first line where Socrates said "I went down" and was about to "go up."[5] "Down" is allied with darkness, "up" with light. These are the central metaphors that structure the work: up/down, darkness/light. Plato chose them because they are metaphors used in everyday life for our own thinking in terms of meaning. When we are "down" our life is dark and gloomy, when we are "up" it is bright and sunny, etc.

"Down" at the beginning is literally the Piraeus, the sea port *down* by the sea from Athens that stands *up* on a hill. The occasion is the celebration of the feast of the goddess Bendis, a goddess of the dark underworld. Socrates and his companion Glaucon are playfully threatened with the use of force to keep them down in the "underworld" in order to watch a torchlight procession at night. They consent to stay, though Socrates says there is always the option of his persuading them to let him and his companion go *up* to the city. At the conclusion to the main argument in Book IX Socrates speaks of "the city laid up in heaven," looking to which one can become the philosopher-king of one's own life (IX, 592B). The actual city of power is "down" in relation to the city "constructed in words" that is the true measure of what is "up" in life. The dialogue is about persuading the city of power that the philosophy Socrates practices will not harm it but could bring it the greatest benefit.

They come to the home of old Cephalus who is concerned about death and the darkness of the Underworld, and this prompts him to think about how he had lived his life (I, 328B–331d). First he thought a meaningful life was one of bodily pleasure; then he thought it was money (he made a bundle with a shield-manufacturing company); but now he thinks it might be what the "old foggies" had said all along: it was a life of *justice*.

---

5. Henceforth, references to Plato's *Republic* will be indicated in parentheses within the body of the text. We will refer to the book (or chapter) by a capital Roman numeral followed by the Stephanus numbers. Subdivisions in the pages are indicated by an alphabetical character.

The dialogue consists in probing what justice really is, beginning with common opinions that Socrates proceeds to take apart. The opening argument moves *up* in complexity as Socrates refutes one character after another, but the characters seem to move *down* in motivational structure. Cephalus presents a commercial understanding of justice: paying what is owed. His son Polemarchus presents a civic view where justice is helping the citizens and allies and harming enemies. Thrasymachus presents a "realist" view: he claims it is the benefit of the stronger who make the laws in their own self-interest; but for the average person it is obeying those laws.

In the main argument that follows in the first book, Socrates claims a parallel between the city and the soul (that is, the conscious life of human beings): it is the city that shapes the soul and the soul that reinforces the city (II, 368d). He constructs three levels of a city, moving *up* from a level of biological necessity (providing food, clothing, and shelter by a division of labor) to a city of luxury that becomes "bloated and feverish," and on further *up* to a "purged" city that orders the chaos of the luxurious city.[6]

Setting up his argument about the nature of justice as right order of the soul, Glaucon introduces the legend of the Ring of Gyges (I, 359d). Gyges was a shepherd who fell in a hole that led to an underground cave in which a corpse was laid out with a ring on its finger. Gyges took the ring and discovered that when, at the fireside with his fellows, he turned the ring around, he disappeared. He then used the ring to seduce the queen and to kill the king.

Through this story, Glaucon is asking us to perform a mental experiment. Suppose you had such a ring, what would you do? Most people would probably say they would continue to do what they usually do. But if it was discovered that the ring made one disappear *from the gods* as well, *then* what would they do? Fyodor Dostoevsky in *Brothers Karamazov* has one of his characters, Ivan, say, If there is no God, all is permitted.[7] God's watching is what keeps naturally disorderly people in place, for he is ready to punish and reward. Plato has Socrates argue from the premise of disappearance from men *and gods*, and argue that there is an intrinsic order and disorder to the soul, with consequences of satisfaction and dissatisfaction for how we think and act, whether seen or not, whether rewarded or punished externally or not. In effect, the right order of the soul lies in its being

---

6. The first city is treated in II, 369b to 372c; the second, the luxurious city, in 372c–374d; and the third, the purged city, in 374d–427E.

7. Dostoevsky, *Brothers Karamazov*, 244 and 599.

oriented by love of the Good as the principle of the Whole. This directly parallels being moved by the love of God rather than by the stick and carrot of punishments and rewards in an afterlife.

3.

The classes in the purged city parallel the levels of the soul: the biologically desirous level (pleasure- and money-loving artisans), the competitive level (victory- and honor-loving military), and the rational level (learning- and wisdom-loving guardians) (IV, 427d–445e). The development of the higher levels of the soul entails restriction of the lower. The three levels are the basis for the introduction of what the Catholic Catechism calls "the four cardinal virtues." (They are called "cardinal"—from the Latin *cardo*, meaning "hinge"—because human flourishing hinges upon them.) Prudence (practical wisdom) belongs to the rational level, fortitude to the competitive level, and temperance to the submission of the lower levels to the higher. Justice consists in each level "doing its own thing," with the lower not attempting to take over the role of the higher and the higher fulfilling its proper functions. The major question that remains is whether the work of the rational level consists solely in "looking down" to ordering the appetites or whether its major task is rather "to look up" to contemplate the order of the cosmos (VII, 529a).

The argument continues *up* to the level of the famous "philosopher-king" (V, 473d) and on to the study of that which he seeks, "the Good" as "principle of the Whole" (VI, 505a–509c).[8] The Good is presented at first metaphorically as "the sun of the intelligible world," the Top of the cosmos, the ultimate Up. Just as seeing can view the seen only in the light provided ordinarily by the sun, so also intellect can grasp the intelligible only "in the light" of the Good. In the famous Cave Allegory human beings in general are presented as chained from birth *down* in a *dark* cave looking at shadows (VII, 514a–517a). Someone frees them from the chains and forces them to "turn their heads around" (reflect) to see what produces the shadows. Someone then drags them *up* outside where they are at first dazzled by the *light* of the sun. Then they are put back *down* in the cave.

The allegory needs "cashing in": what does it really mean? That is the task of the Line of Knowledge which begins to "remove the chains" that tie us to thinking only in terms of sensory images (VI, 509e–511e). The

---

8. We ask you to read about the Sun, the Line, and the Cave in Books 6 and 7.

ascent from the sensory to the intelligible is presented through the Line, the real center of the work, and indeed, the spindle around which philosophy has developed ever since. We have developed aspects of the Line in our Phenomenology of the Mailbox. So it is crucially important to understand what is going on there.

3.

In attempting to explain his notion of philosopher-king, Socrates draws a line between the lovers of beautiful things, the highpoint of education in the purged city, and the lovers of the vision of Beauty itself. Socrates further says that what makes a philosopher a philosopher is the study of the Good, for which he gives the image of the sun. So he has drawn a line, so to speak, twice: one distinguishing the lovers of beautiful things from the lovers of the vision of Beauty itself, the other distinguishing the realm of the visible from that of the intelligible, though we are not told what that means. That is the job of the Line of Knowledge.

Socrates's treatment begins with a line drawn according to any proportion and subdivided by the same proportion. We are invited to move from looking in the light of its visual presence to "turning our heads around," that is, reflecting. If we do so, we may come to see "intellectually" that, no matter what proportion we take, the central segments will always be equal. What we discover is a *geometric theorem*. Socrates then asks us to reflect metaphorically, something we have been accustomed to doing from the very beginning by thinking in terms of the metaphorical pairs up/down, light/dark. Such reflection is one of the basic features of poetry, which is thus a kind of intellectual activity, but one tied to imagery. The philosophic task is to get beyond images to the intelligible.

The Line is taken to stand for the different relations between states of mind and manifest objects, arranged from lowest to highest. On the side of the objects we have images, then things that produce the images (both manifest through sensation), then mathematical objects (the theorem we grasped when reflecting upon the visible line), and then the level of what Socrates calls "Forms" (the Greek term is *eidos*, from which we got the expression "eidetic features" in "Phenomenology of the Mailbox"). The level of Forms is the level of philosophic reflection. We are invited to think about the eidetic differences between a visible object (the drawn line) and an intelligible object (the theorem), between the objects of *sight* and the objects of *insight* or intellection. Socrates places the level of the sensory (of which the visible is an instance) under the general heading of "Becoming" (Greek *genesis*), noting that everything sensible and indeed our own life is subject to change: it exists in time. The upper levels (mathematics and philosophy) are placed under the general heading of "Being" or "Beingness" (Greek *ousia*). The drawn line that I see with my eyes was generated and will be destroyed. It appeared in a stretch of space within a span of time. But the theorem, and the Forms involved in theorems and things that are their instances, are not limited to a given span of time or stretch of space and thus confined to an individual instance: they apply *whenever* and *wherever* their instances are found. They exist as in some way eternal: they do not come into being and pass out of being, they just *are*.[9]

This might seem rather juiceless, but what it helps us to see better are the levels of our own soul revealed in our conscious life. At the sensory level we are immersed in segments of space and time; at the intellectual level we transcend such immersion and grasp intelligible constants that hold *anytime and anyplace* their instances are found. At the sensory level we are immersed in the biological desires evoked by sensory objects; at the intellectual level we are moved by deeper desires. This determines what is truly "up" in life: our relation to the eternal, to what is beyond time. When we begin to uncover the eternal relations, we stand more and more "in the light."

The cave condition is not only one of being chained by nature to sensations, it is being chained by culture to opinions (the realm of *doxa* or "how it seems" or opinion) that may or may not be correct. Traditional *doxa* provides the basic measures of truth and value without itself being subjected to measure. Plato's work attempts to find a measure beyond cultural opinion.

4.

But the deeper point is to get us to reflect further, because the aim is to get us to see something of what Socrates calls "the Good," the "Sun" of the intelligible world and the ultimate aim of philosophy, the final "Up," the "Top of the Cosmos." He asks us to think of geometric procedure as an aid. Geometry proceeds, not only by piecemeal insights—such as we might have gained by our initial reflection upon the proportionately drawn line. If

9. See the appendix to this chapter for a diagram of the Line of Knowledge.

you can think back to geometry classes, you will note that geometry has already moved "up" from geometric theorems to a few axioms and postulates, and then "down" by logical deduction to prove the theorems, linking them together in a single coherent whole in the system of geometry first developed by Euclid. Socrates suggests that we could move "up" further from the few axioms and postulates. What could that mean? It means moving from the few principles of each science toward "the One," the single principle of all intellectual development. Socrates called the Good "the principle of the Whole." It is what generates intellectual "light."

To see what that might be, think of what intellectual understanding is—as distinct from sensory experience. Consider geometry again. It began as *geo-metria*, that is, "earth measurement." Metric regularities were discovered by builders through trial-and-error methods. Just as they carry an assortment of tools lying randomly in their tool bags, so they carry an assortment of metric regularities "lying randomly" in their minds. But what geometric science did was demonstrate the underlying intelligible unity of the whole metric region of experience. What is most surprising is that by pure deduction one could not only unify already discovered regularities, one could deduce not yet observed regularities *without even looking or needing to look!* But what is most startling—and remains so—is that the demonstration takes place solely in the mind through an act of reflective withdrawal from looking at and manipulating the "outer world." One moves "inward" and "upward" from the "outside" spatiotemporal world *up* to the "eternal" world of underlying intelligible coherence. There is a movement from scattered multiplicity to unified wholeness.

Consider also an everyday example. Suppose someone who knew no English got a hold of this paper. What they would see is a scattered multiplicity of visual marks that offer no clue as to how they fit together. Suppose someone who knows English gets a hold of it: they understand that there is a scattered multiplicity of English sentences. Now suppose you begin to understand what's going on: you begin to "see" that there is unity (I hope) in that multiplicity. In both the simpler case of understanding what is written in an introductory philosophic paper and the more complex case of understanding a whole geometric system, understanding takes place "in the light of" seeking unity in what would otherwise appear as a scattered multiplicity. When you grasp unity, you "see the light"; if you remain stuck in multiplicity, you are "in the dark." Einstein said that the task of physics is to find the single equation from which all known and future metric regularities could be deduced; but that applies only to the measurable. If you could see "the One" you would attain to the highest intelligible principle whose scope would extend to everything—not only the whole of the metric realm, but the Whole of what-is. And that would include the whole of the mind that negotiates between the sensible and the intelligible.

The human intellect is linked to the sensory field provided by the bodily organs. The organic body is the way a mind is rooted in the world of space and time. But it is a *mind* that is so rooted, and what the mind seeks is named "the Good" (the nature of any good is to be what is sought). The Good is "the principle of the Whole," the One. The deepest native desire of the human soul is to see the One and to see everything it experiences in the light of the One. "Doing justice" to the soul is turning it upward toward that One. He who does that will not be unjust to others, but will aid them in that turning. Part of the problem of human existence is that we are so buried in our desires and so turned outward that we are often oblivious of what, underlying everything, our nature seeks. Unaware of that, we are unable to do full justice to others, or even to ourselves.

The discovery, both of the intelligible unity of the measurable world underlying sensory experience, *and* of the fact that one discovered this "inside" the mind, led to the establishment of the first monastic order in the West, the Pythagorean brotherhood, with its strict ascetic practices: no sex, limited diet, strict silence for long periods. Why? To shift the pattern of experience from our usual focus "outside" in service of our appetites to a concentrated focus "inside" where we are able to move "up" to the eternal. However, this had the unfortunate consequence of leading to the consideration of the body as the tomb of the soul: rational reflection was "buried" in its bodily-based appetites and fixed on the sensory surface of things. Having discovered rational inwardness, the Pythagoreans in effect asked: "What's a nice inwardness like you doing in a place like this?"—a spirit linked to eternity living in the darkness of bodily desires caught in and tumbling through time? There must have been some sort of Fall, and our task is to turn inward and upward from time to eternity, freeing ourselves from "this world."

There is another aspect to the ascent. Remember the distinction between the lovers of beautiful things and the lovers of the vision of Beauty Itself. One of the aspects of the Good is its being "an incomparable Beauty." The aspect of human existence that is drawn by such Beauty is *eros*, described in Plato's *Symposium* as being in all living things—plants, animals, and humans—and as the love of the mortal for the immortal, of what has to die for the continuance of its type. Sexual desire is the next generation saying to us, "You have to die. Let us live in your place." Philosophic eros is the desire of the whole soul for the Good as Beauty Itself as the Source of the deathless order of the intelligible governance of the cosmos.

Part of the philosophic task is to fill in the level of the Forms by thinking through the eidetic features of the field of experience. We have attempted to do that in a preliminary way in "Phenomenology of the Mailbox." The reading of the *Republic* shows how to use that eidetic inventory to think about the soul and its relations to the Whole and how that spells itself out throughout the whole of our lives as human beings.

After directing us toward the Highest, Socrates uses the structures uncovered to rank-order types of character and the regimes that produce them and that they sustain (VIII, 544C–592b). The best is rule by the one ("mon-archy" from *monas* and *arche*) or by the many who are "the best" ("aristo-cracy" from *aristos* and *cratia*)—best, not by birth, but by the criteria developed in the work as the highest form of human existence. Next is rule by adhering to the noble tradition without understanding its bases ("tim-ocracy" or the rule of honor—*timey*), then rule by the few who are rich ("olig-archy" from *oligoi*, the few, or "pluto-cracy," from *plutos*, the rich), then the rule of the many ("demo-cracy" or rule of the *demos*, the city as a whole) who generally follow their appetites, and finally "tyranny" or the rule of one in his own base self-interest. (This is treated in Books 8 and 9, perhaps the most readable sections of the *Republic*.)

The last book (X) contains a contrast between philosophy and poetry to the detriment of the latter (remember Socrates converted Plato from poetry to philosophy), then a consideration of the rewards and punishments for justice and injustice in this life and in the next. The latter contains several attempts to show that the soul is immortal. Finally, Plato turns poet at the end by concocting the Myth of Er as a fantasy about the judgment of the dead based upon their justice or injustice in life. It is the last "descent into darkness" of the work, returning us to the beginning where Cephalus's reflection upon the afterlife set in motion the discussion of justice.

THE SUN, THE LINE, AND THE CAVE

THE GOOD

Source of *Aletheia*

Incomparable Beauty, Principle of the Whole, Beyond Forms

[Seeing the Sun]

| *NOESIS* | FORMS |

EPISTEME --*OUSIA*--BEING

[Intellect..Intelligible]

| *DIANOIA* | MATHEMATICALS |

[Outside the Cave]

_____

[Conversion of Attention]

| *PISTIS* | THINGS |

DOXA--*GENESIS*/BECOMING

| *EIKASIA* | IMAGES/SHADOWS |

[Chained in the Cave]

[vision..visible]

[Inside the Cave]

Source of Light

SUN

* * * *

QUESTIONS

Beginning of Book 1

1. How are the metaphors "up" and "down" and "light" and "darkness" used in everyday speech? What role does thinking about death play in human life?

End of Book 4:

2. What does Socrates mean by "soul"? (Check both the end of Book and Book 10).

3. What is the relation between the individual ("the soul") and the city (society and its tradition)?

4. What are the levels of the soul? What makes one level of the soul "higher" than another? Why does the development of the higher involve restriction of the lower?

5. What is the basis for the cardinal virtues?

6. Discuss the two roles that rationality plays: its downward and upward looks.

7. (Compare the end of Book 4 with the readings from Books 6–7.)

Books 6–7:

8. Discuss the levels of awareness laid out in the Line of Knowledge. Show how the lower levels lead to the higher. Show especially how geometry is an aid in the "upward" movement. How does all of this lead to some understanding of "the Good"?

9. How was Pythagorean monasticism tied to the discovery of demonstrative geometry? Based on this discovery, what did the Pythagoreans think of the soul?

10. How does all of the above (6–8) cash in on the image of the sun and the Cave Allegory? Consider how "up and down" and "light and darkness" function here.

11. Relate the Line of Knowledge to "Phenomenology of the Mailbox."

Book 10:

12. What evidence does Socrates offer for the immortality of the soul? What is there about the soul that supports belief in an afterlife?

13. How do you understand the Myth of Er? Is it an allegory of this life as well as the suggestion of a next?

FURTHER READINGS

1. Alan Bloom, "Interpretive Essay," in *The Republic of Plato*, 307–436.

2. Paul Friedländer, *Plato: An Introduction* (3 vols.).

3. Eric Voegelin, *Order and History*, vol. 3, *Plato and Aristotle*.

4. Catherine Zuckert, *Postmodern Platos*.

5. Plato, The Ladder of Ascent to Beauty Itself, 201d–212c, *Symposium*.

* * * *

ARISTOTLE: SOUL, ETHICS, AND THEOLOGY

The soul is the place of the forms. . . . Intellect sees the forms in the phantasms.

—*On the Soul*, 429A 28, 431B 2

READINGS[1]

1. Four causes: *Physics* II, iii, 194b 16—195a 26.

2. The nature of the soul: *On the Soul* (henceforth *OS*), II, i, 412a 1—413a 10.

3. Sensation: *OS* III, ii, 425b 12—426a 26.

4. Intellect: *OS* III, iii—iv, 428b 18—429b 10. *OS* III, v, 430a 10—25.

5. Mind and appetite: *OS* III, x, 433a 10—433b 10.

6. Political animal: *Nicomachean Ethics* (henceforth *NE*) I, iv, 1095a 14—1096a11.

7. Virtues: *NE* II, vi, 1107a 1—1107b 23. *NE* VI, iii–v, 1139b 14—1140b 21.

8. Justice: *NE* V.

9. Friendship: *NE* VIII–IX.

10. Contemplation: *NE* X, vii, 1177a 12—1178a 9.

---

1. As with Plato, given many different translations and editions, we refer to the Stephanus numbers of the first critical edition of Plato's works, so with Aristotle, we refer to the Bekker numbers after the critical edition by August Immanuel Bekker in the middle of the nineteenth century. For generous and judicious selections, we recommend Hippocrates Apostle, *Aristotle: Selected Writings*.

11. God as Self-Thinking Thought: *Metaphysics* XII, vi–vii, 1071b 4—1072b 34.

1.

Up to the thirteenth century, Christian theology operated under the aegis of Plato and Neoplatonism. We will see that in the case of Augustine. The philosophy of Aristotle, Plato's pupil, was unavailable to the West until the middle of the twelfth century. During the Crusades, the West contacted a rich Islamic tradition that had assimilated the thought of Aristotle. Translations began to pour into the West in two waves, first from the Arabic, then from the original Greek. The process was completed in the middle of the thirteenth century where Aquinas became one of the leading commentators as a theologian interpreting Christian tradition in the light of an Aristotelian understanding of nature, and especially of human nature.

Aristotle (384–322 BC), a Macedonian, spent some twenty years in Plato's Academy in Athens which is said to have had a sign over its door: Do not enter here if you do not know mathematics. Plato is also said to have paid a goodly sum for Pythagorean books. Pythagoras is the grandfather of deductive geometry, best known for the Pythagorean Theorem. Legend has it that it was in Plato's Academy that Euclid wrote his widely read *Elements*, the first systematic treatment of geometry that hooked up known metric regularities into a consistent whole. It involved basic axioms and postulates from which all known and future metric relations could be deduced. It provided the model of rational proof and the basis for Aristotle's making explicit the logic it presupposed.

Remember that, in our treatment of Plato, reflection upon the psychological conditions of geometrical concentration involved a turn "inward and upward" from the sensory world in relation to our bodily needs to the intelligible realm that is thought to govern the material world, part of which is displayed in sensation. This led to the notion that the rational soul was somehow trapped in the body through sensations and appetites and needed to gain as much distance from it as possible so as to be able to see the intelligible order more clearly. This provided grounds for the consideration of the immortality of the human soul, since the death of the body would seem like the removal of an impediment.

Although many lines of text in Plato look askance at bodiliness, there are other texts that view the body as the *house* rather than the *prison* of the soul. The resolution of this conflict lies in the distinction between a *psychological* consideration where the senses and bodily passions get in the way of concentrated intellection[2] and an *ontological* consideration where the body is, by the character of its being, the house of the soul, the place where the soul dwells as in its proper place.[3] The *Republic* also presents a fine analogy of the unity of the soul in the image of a spinning top. When it attains the upright position, the outer movements (bodily desires) support the upright position; whereas, when it strays from the upright, it wobbles; and if it leans too far away so that it hits the ground, it is carried erratically by the outer movements. The soul dwells properly in its house when it is upright; it loses its uprightness when it allows the outer movements rooted in biological desires, to rule its decisions.[4]

In contrast to the mathematicians who were Plato's paradigms of rationality, Aristotle's father, Nichomachos, was a physician and the son named a book on ethics after him: the *Nichomachean Ethics*. His relation to his father's work may explain his own central preoccupation with empirical, especially biological, investigation. In such inquiry, we do not, as we do in mathematics, *construct* and deduce facts but find them available only by patient sensory examination. Aristotle was tutor to Alexander the Great as a young man; and Alexander, like Napoleon imitating him, was accompanied by scientific field workers who collected samples of all the flora and fauna found in the regions of Alexander's wide-ranging conquests, from Egypt to the Ganges. They sent them back to Aristotle for analysis and classification. Aristotle wrote the *History of Animals*, *Parts of Animals*, and other empirical works on animal behavior, for which he provided the theoretical framework in his *Peri Psyches* or *On the Soul*. And here we rejoin our brief consideration of Plato's views on the soul. But we also move along the lines of *Fides et Ratio* which called for a move from phenomena to foundation, from a description of the field of experience and its object-types to its non-appearing ground in the notion of the soul.

Aristotle followed the direction of Plato's late claim that the body is the house of the soul, with the basic addition that the soul *constructs* its

2. E.g., *Republic*, X, 611c–612a; *Phaedo* 80e.

3. To describe the way the body is related to the soul, in his *Timaeus*, Plato uses various terms linked to *oikazw*, to house (69d, 70e, 72d, 89e).

4 *Republic*, 436c.

own house. To understand how he might have arrived at that notion, consider the overall immediate, empirically available context in which humans perennially find themselves. In our exposition we will recall several of the considerations involved in the Phenomenology of the Mailbox.

2.

The clouds arise, billow, drop their liquid load, and dissipate. The wind blows as one front yields to another. Stirred by the wind, wave after wave crashes onto the beach. Lightning flashes and kindles a fire in the forest. The earth lies beneath, supporting all, but also occasionally sending shock waves throughout a given region. Air, water, fire, earth: the elements, each in its own way amorphous, move, each in their own way, and intermingle.

On the earth, in the midst of the elements, drawing *back* from the intermingling of the elements as they draw *from* them, living forms circle back upon themselves, setting themselves off from the causal networks within which they remain embedded and which they require for their nourishment. Even the simplest forms are of remarkable complexity. Like fire and unlike computers, they are continually in process; but each always retains the constancy of a single process contained within the overall circle which ramifies itself into different mutually supporting aspects. Once fully developed, each life-form always repeats the same components, always repairing and reproducing itself. Beyond the one-celled forms, as developed instrumentation will later show, adult organisms reproduce cellular substructures which, like the whole processive entity, circle back upon themselves. They remain within the overall encircling of the whole entity and enter into the articulation of a system of biological instruments, the organs that develop serially, heading toward a state of maximum articulation called the adult state of the organism. At this point each organism is enabled, through a sexual or asexual process, to reproduce replicas of itself outside itself that go through the same developmental and reproductive process that founds a species.

An organism is a kind of self, a *proto*-self, a distinct entity set off from others. It is self-formative, self-repairing, self-sustaining, and self-reproducing. Beneath the level of the living there are no such selves. (There are, of course, regularly recurring forms like crystals, but they do not constantly metabolize and ramify into complex functional systems. And at a level Aristotle couldn't reach, there are also the atoms and molecules for which most of the same distinctions apply as apply to crystals.) But the selfhood of living form, in turn, is a function within a larger whole that we call an ecosystem. Without such a system the organic self cannot be. As a process, it draws the materials for its own self-sustenance from its environment: light, heat, air, water, and earthly nutrients. The energy constituting the living being, in its turn, is employed through destruction and assimilation by other living forms to develop and sustain themselves— and so on up the food chain.

In the case of the animal organism, a much more complicated articulation occurs. In addition to the organs for extracting and processing energy from the environment and reproducing itself, new instruments for a completely different function emerge: organs of perception. Embedded also within the causal networks of pre-living processes, a new kind of process occurs: awareness. Animals *experience*, they *feel* the causal impact of various forms of energy upon the organs of perception. Correlated with that feeling, things not only are and operate, they *appear*. That appearance involves the selective manifestation of things outside the organism as colored, sounding, smelling and the like. The manifestation of things outside involved in awareness is correlated with the self-experience of the upsurge of desire and serves such desire that eventuates in pursuit or avoidance. Emergent out of the self-enclosing character of organic process, animal selfhood is tied to the manifestation of what is outside itself in function of its organic needs. With the emergence of the manifestation of the environment goes the emergence of hunger and, in the case of the fully adult organism, of sexual desire and aggression as well. Another appears as a necessary complement of itself, and from relation to that other, still others emerge as offspring. Central to sensory manifestation is the display and instinctive recognition of appropriate instances of its own kind essential for the work of reproduction and nurturing. The point of awareness is to afford flexible adaptation to the environment through learning. Animal awareness presupposes a non-reflective self-presence as the other to any manifest other. And, as in the case of plant forms, one organism is in essential continuity with its line, an instance of a type.

But emergent out of the field of animal consciousness, as animal consciousness is emergent out of organic processes, is the distinctive field of human consciousness. It is tied even more closely to the appearance of the significant human Other, especially through the mediation of language. Language binds the human community across generations. But it is itself a kind of self-enclosing process that separates one linguistic community from another as it forms that community from out of the differences of multiple human individuals. Nonetheless, human selfhood is such that it is able to move beyond the self-sealing, binding, and isolating character of the ethnic community in order to translate one language into another. The ultimate ground of such translatability is the notion of Being, an initially empty notion that refers the human individual not only to significant Others but to the All and to everything about each thing within the Whole. Such reference simultaneously sets the individual human away from the self-enclosing character of organic, animal, and ethnic specificity and condemns that individual to be an I, a unique center of choice and responsibility, responsible finally only to the truth of the Whole. As Aristotle said, Plato is a friend, but truth is a greater friend.

Such are the basic eidetic features of experience that will furnish the grounds for Aristotle's reflections in his *On the Soul* (*Peri Psyches*) which we proceed to examine.

3.

For Aristotle, the human soul (*psyche*) is the basis for a single three-level process, the lowest level of which—growth and sustenance—it shares with plants; the next—sensation, desire, and self-initiated locomotion—with the animals; while the third is distinctively its own: rational understanding and choice. The rational power is embodied because it is the kind of rational power that requires sensory input upon which it works for understanding and for directing itself in the environment and in relation to its desires. In order to have sensory input, it needs a set of organic instruments. To the implicit question raised by Pythagoras, What's a nice inwardness like my intellectual soul doing in a place like this, the body with its multiple needs, sicknesses, and distractions? Aristotle replied, in effect, that this is the only place it can develop as the kind of soul it is.

It may seem odd to speak of the souls of plants since, in our more recent tradition, "soul" has meant the spiritual principle of a human being. But if one understands the continuity between the three levels of human development, one can see why the notion is extended to plants which exhibit the characteristics of the first level of human development. "Soul" names the principle of unitary functioning that sets a living thing off from its environment and makes it to be a self-enclosed and self-sustaining self. Evolutionary theory would only serve to strengthen this view where ontogeny recapitulates phylogeny, that is, the stages in the genesis of the individual being (ontogeny) recapitulates the stages of development of the phylum or generic type to which the individual belongs. So the three levels in us would have come into existence sequentially over millennia, as they come to function serially over several years in the case of the individual human being.

Aristotle described the soul as the formal, efficient, and final cause of an organized body (II, 312a, 1—413a 10). To see what this means, we have to look at Aristotle's notion of the four explanatory factors involved in any process. Consider an artist who has an idea and a block of granite. The granite is what Aristotle called the *material cause*: the ensuing statue is as it is because of what it is made of. The idea is called the (extrinsic) *formal cause*; and when it has shaped the matter, it is the *intrinsic formal cause*. The artist herself is the *efficient cause*, not as one who works in the most economic way possible, but as the factor that effects or brings about the result. If she is making the statue for money, this is referred to as the *final cause*, in the sense that it is the cause of the causality of the other causes, that which sets them in motion (*Physics*, II, 2 and 3, 194a, 22—195b, 30).

Both the artist and her medium are the products of nature. The artist is the result of a series of stages of growth. Her soul is the principle of the process: the soul draws materials from the outer world and organizes them into an organ-system or interrelated set of instruments for the realization of the ends immanent in its form. Once having achieved its adult stage, the organism is the continuing work of the soul's nutritive power. The soul then is the formal, efficient, and final cause of the way the body is organized and the ground of the way the higher powers use the organs. Introduced into a tradition of art, the artist learns to tap her native talents. Without the tradition, the talents would lay largely fallow or develop only in a rudimentary manner.

Technically expressed, Aristotle defined the soul (whether human, animal, or vegetative) as the *form* or *first act* of an organized body having life potentially within it (II, 412b 5). In the definition, *form* is not simply shape: it is what determines the type of process a given living thing is. Aristotle often uses two terms together to express this: *morphe kai eidos*, form and intelligible principle (II, 414a 9). This heads off an equation of form with shape. The observable shape (form) is an external expression of the inward principle. Soul is first act or fundamental determinant that, through its active powers, develops through second acts or the actualization of the basic powers.

Soul's being first act leads to the basic level of functioning that is the construction and maintenance of the organism—what Aristotle calls the *nutritive* function (II, 416a 20—416b 32). The organism is a system, an -ism, consisting of organs or instruments coordinated for the fulfillment of its basic functions. The physical organism, considered purely from the viewpoint of the stuff that composes it, is only the potentiality for such organization. Its being actually organized is the continuing work of the soul. When the soul dies, the body soon returns to the elements out of which it was composed. The sign of the full maturity of the organism is its ability to reproduce, which Aristotle considers its basic goal: to imitate the eternal divine life by keeping the species going forever, at least as he saw it (II, 415b 1).

In the animal case, the nutritive function is involved in constructing organs for the emergence of sensory functions: the manifestation of things in the environment as beneficial or harmful for its own individual and species needs. Eyeballs, eardrums, nose, tongue—each a localized organ for a distinctive kind of manifestation: colors, sounds, smells, tastes. But not all animals have the full panoply of senses; some have only the sense of touch. What is peculiar about touch is that it has no localized organ: the whole bodily surface is the organ of touch. And what that involves is the animal's being in touch with its body as a functional whole. It is aware of itself as integrally engaged with the things with which it is in touch. Touch reveals the hard and the soft, the smooth and the rough, the heavy and the light—all factors of resistance. In addition there is the hot and the cold as well as the dry and the moist that follow special conditions of the resistant body.

All this is grounded in the central function of sensation which Aristotle calls "the common sense," that is, the sense common to all senses (III, 425a 15—425b 15). It involves, in the first place, awareness that we are seeing and hearing and the like because it can't be by seeing that we know we are hearing, etc. Further, in order for the common sense to operate, there must also be a retention and a reproduction of the various aspects appearing contemporaneously and spread out through time. He calls this capacity *phantasia*, often translated as "imagination," but it is linked to *phainomenon* or appearance (III, 427a 1—429a 9). As capacity for retention and reproduction of experiences, it is what makes appearance fundamentally possible on the part of the perceiving animal. The information coming in through the different senses has to be retained and reproduced in order to be subjected to the automatic synthesis of what appears from each of the senses into what Aristotle calls a "*phantasma*" or appearance (III, 428a 1). Here the appearance is not simply the display of differing *aspects* of things through the differing senses; it the total way in which *things* of differing sorts present themselves. To have experience is to have an inventory of standard ways in which differing kinds of things present themselves and consequently standard ways of responding to them. A phantasm is a unification of experiences of types of appearing things.

The perceiving organism is a functioning synthetic whole to which functioning synthetic wholes appear. As that synthesis occurs, what becomes apparent are aspects distinct from each of the sensory aspects, but found in them all: what Aristotle calls the "common sensibles" which are basically aspects of quantity: shape, size, weight, motion, rest (425a 15). We can see shape as well as feel it. So, the "common sense" has three aspects: awareness of being aware of all sensory presentations, synthesis of these presentations, and recognition of the common sensibles.

In all these and other distinctions, Aristotle resists the tendency to separate aspects. He claims that the sense power and the sensible thing in act are the same, but their "to-be" is different (II, 425b 27); similarly with intellect and the intelligible object in act (III, 430a 1–25). Here he sits between two other basic ways of viewing the relation of mind to things. At the sensory level, there is naïve realism: colors are on things independent of perceivers. There is also the distinctively modern position that colors, sounds, and the like are internal effects of external objects. It is the contemporary default modes for scientists who know the way light or sound relates to bodies and affects the nervous system, terminating in the respective areas of the cortex that steer the particular processes involved in each sense. Seeing and hearing are subjective acts inside the perceiver. This raises the huge problem that naïve realism does not have: how do you get outside to know things and encounter persons? Aristotle's notion that the sensible thing in act is the sense power in act holds the intermediary position of *cognitive identity*. The sense quality is a new emergent beyond physical interaction from the meeting of things and perceivers. It is a distinctively new mode of relation beyond physical causation: the relation of *manifestation* or *appearance*. Just as the horizon is the limit of the field of vision and the perspectival distortion involved in the point of view of the perceiver are not simply subjective but distinctive features of the subject-object relation called the *appearing of* things, so also with the color. Things shrink in appearance as they recede from the seer within the manifest limit of the seer's field of vision. But the phantasms produced by experience automatically discount these factors and anticipate the real size and shape of given objects. This discounting is a function of previous perspectives gained by moving in relation to the objects. Horizon, perspective, and color are not absolute features of things nor merely inner subjective experiences, but *relational* properties of the appearance of things to a biologically situated observer.

Aristotle makes the same claim of identity-in-difference in the relation between sense power and organ, and between sensation and desire (III, 424a 26, 425b 27, 426a 24, 431a 13). Though there are distinguishable aspects involved in perception—organ, power, act, desire, outside things perceived and desired—there is an underlying oneness.

To further illuminate the character of the soul, Aristotle says that if the eyeball were an organism and not an organ in an organ-system, its soul would be the power of seeing and its fulfillment would be in the act of seeing (42012b). In both cases of power and act of seeing, we have a non-seeable higher function, with nutritive power sustaining the seeable eyeball, visual power informing the eyeball, and seeing itself as term of the visual process.

Aristotle claims that the senses give us only the individual and actual, while the intellect yields the universal. Sensation itself does not give us the *powers* of things and the *types* to which the things and their powers and acts belong; it always yields the individual and actual. Intellect is the power to apprehend individual things as instances of types—this black lettering as instance of black and of lettering—and the powers of things to act and be acted upon. Words refer to concepts which are universal in scope and which refer to the kinds of things about which we speak. But underlying the appearance of individual things are their powers that are not simply individual, but are also *universal* orientations toward the *kinds* of things in the environment corresponding to the powers. It is intellectual power which enables us to recognize the universality involved in the individuals presented by sensation.

But what makes an intellect an intellect is the notion of Being which refers us to absolutely everything, though only in an initially empty way. We are *referred* to the Whole, but initially in the mode of questioning, not in the mode of possession. We have to fill in that emptiness by beginning with sensory experience and inferring from that all that it and our distinctively human awareness of it implies. Such filling is supplied by the tradition in which we were raised.

It is important to underscore that the sensory and intellectual showings of the things around us belong to the things as their expression relative to sensing and understanding beings. We are not locked up inside our brains but are really with the things outside, in cognitive identity with them; and we are simultaneously beyond the Here-and-Now of our bodily existence, inhabiting a common linguistically mediated world; and we are with being as a whole by way of basic reference.

4.

Given human structure as analyzed above, Aristotle defines the human being in operation as the *political animal*.[5] He also defines it as the *animal that has the logos*. The latter term can be understood in two related ways: as the medievals understood it, *logos* is reason, and the human being is the rational animal; or, as is actually necessary for the development of rationality, taking *logos* as language, the human being is the linguistic animal. The latter relates back to the political animal in as much as it is through language that one is inducted into, and continues to participate in, the institutions of a given society. Only in this way can individual rational animals develop. This also follows out Aristotle's claim that we live our subjective lives "out there," with things and other people.

Aristotle's ethics is the first part of his work on politics.[6] His ethics consists in uncovering the kinds of permanent dispositions required for life with others. He devotes one chapter of his ethics to justice and two to friendship.[7] But both are underpinned by a set of moral virtues. He carries on Plato's treatment of the four cardinal virtues: practical wisdom, justice, courage, and temperance, but Aristotle expands the list to include generosity, nobility, gentleness, honesty, wit, friendliness, and modesty (II, vii 1107b 1—1108b 8). He sees these virtues as lying in a mean between two extremes: courage is between cowardice and foolhardiness; temperance between over-indulgence and complete abstinence; generosity between

---

5. *Nicomachean Ethics*, IX, ix, 1169b 20; *Politics* I, 125a 2.

6. Quotations will be from *Nicomachean Ethics*, the Ross and Urmson translation. I, ii, 1094b 12. Since the Bekker numbers 1094a–1131b indicate this work, we will refer to it the same way we did to *On the Soul*, in parentheses within the body of the text. According to convention, we will indicate the book and the section numbers in capital and lower case Roman numerals respectively.

7. Book V on justice and Books VIII and IX on friendship.

stinginess and prodigality (II, vi, 1107a 1ff.). In each case, the exercise of the virtue depends upon a particular *intellectual* virtue: *phronesis* or practical wisdom, the ability to size up contexts and find the mean in the context (VI, vii, 1141b 12—1142a 30). Thus, when is conduct in a war cowardice or foolhardiness or true courage? When it is linked to doing the right thing as the situation requires. Thus retreat in battle may be a strategic withdrawal, with attack or holding one's place foolhardy, while in other situations it might be the opposite. A wise person always or for the most part finds the mean. Of course, that requires a clear mind and control of appetites. So what we translate as temperance, Aristotle calls *sophrosune*, which he claims is rooted in *sozein phronesin*, preserving your *phronesis*, keeping a clear mind so you can assess your situation and act wisely (VI, v, 1140b 12). So one learns what overindulgence in food or drink is by learning for yourself how far you can go without losing control or getting out of shape. That's why temperance is relative to the individual. Some, like Socrates in Plato's *Symposium*, have greater capacities for alcohol and are not fazed by consuming what, for another, would be totally intemperate. For some, no alcohol at all would be required for temperance. Practical wisdom, temperance, and courage are conditions for the possibility of justice and friendship, the most basic virtues of community life. One needs control of oneself in order to do justice to others. In one way of speaking, justice refers to complete virtue with respect to others, as in the biblical tradition, when one speaks of the just man. Aristotle speaks further of political justice, that is, justice between free and (actually or proportionately) equal persons, living a common life for the purpose of satisfying their needs. Hence between people not free and equal, political justice cannot exist, but only a sort of justice in a metaphorical sense. For justice can only exist between those whose mutual relations are regulated by law (V, v, 1134a 30). Within a political community, Aristotle distinguishes distributive and corrective justice. In each it is a matter of what is due. The first concerns the sharing of the goods of the community wherein Aristotle speaks of proportionate equality or proportionate reciprocity—that is, goods are justly distributed in terms of merit. Corrective justice concerns punishment proportionate to public offense in order to restore political order.

We said that he devotes two whole books to friendship as a fulfilled relation to others which presupposes but stands above justice itself. At the widest level, good will (*eunoia*) should be extended to all humans, like-mindedness (*homonoia*) pertains to citizens, while friendship (*philia*) involves some form of intimacy (IX, iv, 1166b 30—1167b 8). Intimate friends recognize their mutual liking, wish to do good to each other, each for the sake of the other, share goods in common, and live together. Young people tend to form friendships for pleasure or fun, older people for utility (like business partners), while the noble pursue excellence together. Although the most intimate friendships are between equals, there are also friendships between unequals: elder and younger people, father and son, husband and wife, teacher and pupil, and finally, ruler and subject. If the distance is too far, friendship is not possible—e.g., friendship between men and gods. A life without friendship is not a complete life, for the human being is a political animal (*zoion politikon*), living in a community bound together by language (*zoion logon echeon*), and able to develop only on the basis of an extended articulation of institutions.

But besides life with others, there is a private virtue that Aristotle thinks is the highest of all: *theoria* or the life of contemplation, precisely the life led by Aristotle, his teacher Plato, and his teacher's teacher, Socrates (X, vi, 1177a 13—vii, 1178 8). It is the life of doing what we are doing here: laying out the features of experience and what they entail. It is ultimately solitary, like the solitariness of God, but it is aided by friends engaged in the same pursuit.

5.

Finally, Aristotle moved from his careful phenomenological descriptions to the ultima foundation: he developed a notion of God as the Unmoved Mover and as Self-Thinking Thought.[8] For Aristotle, all things move in virtue of trying to imitate the divinity. His starting point, interestingly enough, is what he took to be the necessary *eternality* of the world. People are inclined to think that it is just the inability of time to be eternal that leads to the necessity of a God. Aristotle arrived at his counter-position through considering the nature of time as involving past, present, and future, so that the meaning of each of the three lies in their relation to the other two. "Now" has no meaning apart from past and future: it is the end of the past and the beginning of the future. Consequently, there can be neither a first Now nor a last Now, neither a beginning nor an end of time. Paradoxically from our usual point of view, time is itself eternal.

---

8. *Metaphysics*, XII, vii, 1072a 25—1072b 28.

With that as a premise, Aristotle argued that each thing in the world is able not to be and would eventually have actualized that ability. What accounts for the continuing existence of an eternal world of such things is something that is not subjected to change. Change for Aristotle is rooted in the principle of materiality, a kind of negativity in things that makes it such that they were not at one time, are not at any given time what they were or are to be, and eventually are not at all (*Metaphysics* IX, i, 1046a 10ff.). Their actuality is found in their natural form that determines the type of process a given thing is. As principle of change which is linked to a material thing's having parts outside of parts and thus being able to come together and come apart, materiality is the ground of spatiotemporal existence. Material beings come in types that apply to an indeterminately many instances. The ground of the individuation of a given type lies in spatiotemporal location that is grounded, in turn, in materiality. Intellect is the ability to abstract from spatiotemporally located, sensed individuality and to apprehend the types and underlying powers of what is sensorily present. That implies that intellect stands above the Here-and-Now in relation to space and time as encompassing wholes.

Things that are purely material, like the elements, are, so to speak, sunk in darkness; so are plants. In animals and in humans, cognition happens because their forms are above immersion in the opaque principle of materiality and can function as the place where they are at least implicitly self-present and thus can be aware of other things. In the case of animals, that self-awareness cannot become reflective and the appearance of things is restricted to the conditions of matter, that is, individuality and its spatiotemporal location (*On the Soul*, II, v, 417b24). In the human case, we recognize sensorily appearing entities as individual instances of *types*, that is, we recognize the universality of the type as such.

Words are conventional expressions of the apprehension of types. At the level of intellect, we ourselves are free from materiality and the conditions of materiality, transcending space and time. With our roots in matter through our bodies, and our attention to the environment in sensation, we rise above both to apprehend the universal and to think in terms of the Whole. It is this capacity that has been the basis for claims to the immortality of the soul—which Aristotle himself did not hold.

This is a long way about—though it gives us a fuller picture of Aristotle's cosmology—to understand how God has to be Self-Thinking Thought. A being not subject to change is thus immaterial and fully self-present as a consequence. However, being changeless, God cannot be specified by things either cognitively or practically. He cannot change by coming to know the changing things, and so he is oblivious of all; nor can he act upon things because that would involve being specified by them and thus changing. He is the self-presence of the fullness of being to which we are emptily directed as his imitators.

How then can he be the Unmoved Mover? Only by being an exemplar for others: things strive to be as much like him as their type admits. The elements strive to be in their natural places as he is beyond the fixed stars. The plants strive to become as fully actual as they can be by maturing, and as immortal as they can be by reproducing their kinds. Animals add awareness and the pleasure that comes from fulfilling their natural ends. Humans alone are able to be aware of being as a whole and to become as mature and self-possessed as any natural being can be. The being of all things is their striving to be like God.

The upshot of this view is that it does no good to petition or thank him or express sorrow for failing to be as like him as one can be, for he cannot hear what is outside nor act directly upon it. One can only contemplate him from afar and praise his eternal, changeless glory.

QUESTIONS

1. How does Aristotle understand the soul? How is that related to Plato's understanding of the soul? Why does he think it is also found in plants and animals? Is that foolish or wise?

2. What are the powers of the human soul? What is the function of the nutritive power? What are the sensory functions? How do they work together? What are the distinctive intellectual functions? How are they related to the will?

3. Why does Aristotle think that we are basically political and linguistic animals? How is that linked to our being rational animals?

4. What are the ethical virtues? Name and discuss them. What is the meaning of their consisting of the mean between extremes? How are they related to the intellectual virtue of practical wisdom?

5. What is the nature of justice and what are its differing forms?

6. What is the nature of friendship and what are its differing forms?

7. How does Aristotle understand *theoria*?

8. What is Aristotle's proof for the existence of God as Self-Thinking Thought and as the Unmoved Mover?

FURTHER READINGS

1. Marjorie Grene, *A Portrait of Aristotle.*

2. Henry Veatch, *Aristotle: A Contemporary Appreciation.*

3. Mortimer Adler, *Aristotle for Everybody.*

4. W. D. Ross, *Aristotle: A Complete Exposition of His Works and Thought.*

* * * *

AUGUSTINE'S *CONFESSIONS*

You have made us for yourself, O Lord. Our hearts are restless and will not rest until they rest in You.

—*CONFESSIONS*, I, 1

READINGS

AUGUSTINE'S *CONFESSIONS*. MANY EDITIONS are available, but the common way of referring makes any reputable translation acceptable for our purposes. However, our quotations will be from the William Watt translation in two volumes. As in Plato, the Roman numerals refer to the "book" while the Arabic refer to a subsection. We will make references to the *Confessions* by brackets within the text.

1. The restless heart: I, 1.

2. Beyond images: VII, 1.

3. The Neo-Platonists: VII, 9.

4. The vision at Ostia: IX, 10.

5. Memory: X, 7–30;

6. Time: XI, 12–31.

1.

Aurelius Augustinus lived from AD 354 to 430. He wrote his *Confessions* in the period from 397–403. Literarily they are a peculiar form:

autobiographical, theological, and philosophical reflections, but set within the form of a prayer. The title "Confessions" is not simply, given the story of his own dissoluteness, a confession of sin. It is much rather a *confessio fidei*, a profession of faith. But though the focus is theological, theology is philosophy reflecting upon what the thinker takes to be revelation. Theology is the application to revelation of human experience, its explication, analysis, and interpretation as it is an application of revelation to human experience. Aristotle noted that one cannot avoid doing philosophy, that is, developing a set of principles for action based upon a general view of the place of human-ness in the scheme of things. One cannot avoid that; one can only do it more or less explicitly, hence more or less carefully, more or less thoroughly. We chose this text for a course in philosophy not only because it exhibits the employment of Neoplatonic philosophy in thinking about revelation, but also because it shows independent philosophical investigation, especially in its treatment of time and memory. But once again, keep in mind that this work theologizes and thus also philosophizes in the presence of God, in the form of prayer. We have here a fruitful dialectic or interchange between philosophy and belief and between life and thought.

The whole exposition is couched in prayer. It is addressed to God, and we are invited to listen in on that address. It is divided into three parts. The first and longest (books 1–9) is autobiography. The second part (book 10) reflects upon memory as the condition for carrying on the narrative. The third part (books 11–13) is a commentary on the first part of *Genesis* in which, among other things, Augustine presents an intriguing philosophic reflection upon the notion of time. The first book begins with the desire to praise the God who made and guided him through his time on earth; the last part of the work reflects upon this God as the Creator of heaven and earth, of all time and being.

In the autobiographical section, Augustine describes how he underwent four basic conversions. First of all, he was converted to philosophy by reading Cicero's Hortensius (a work that is, unfortunately, no longer extant). Trying to understand his inability to control his own sexuality led him to his second conversion, to Manichaeism in which he remained for nine years (ages 20–29).[1]

1. The founder of Manichaeism was Mani or Manes who stood in the line of Zoro-aster, founder of Persian Religion, and was linked to the Judaizing Christian Elkhasaites. He was influenced by Marcion and Bardesanes. Born in 216, he claimed to be the in-carnation of the Holy Spirit, and was "crucified" between AD 264 and 277. The religion he taught spread widely in the East and West into the fifteenth century, reaching Rome

Eventually he came to know the works of the Platonists, Plotinus in particular, which led to his third conversion. Plotinus (AD 204–270) had developed a systematic way of reading Plato. The phenomenological basis is the same: a two-leveled cosmology, the flowing realm of time revealed in sensation over against the eternally fixed realm of the eidetic, grounded in the Good as principle of the Whole, with the human soul occupying both regions. The Good is understood as the single principle, source of "intelligible light." As we have seen, intellectual understanding is a function of finding unity in what would otherwise be a scattered multiplicity. "In the light of" our search for unity, we come to understand. The more unity apprehended, the more understanding. The source we seek as the Good is therefore the One.

But the One shines forth with the radiance of Beauty Itself, the experienced term of the ascent of the ladder of Beauty described by Plato near the end of his *Symposium*. Plotinus knew that experience. But also, according to the testimony of Porphyry, his disciple and biographer, he knew the experience of transcending the duality of seer and seen, even when what is seen is Beauty Itself: he knew the experience of identity with the One, being "alone with the Alone."[2] He was, indeed, a mystic. But that mysticism was closely linked to a severe Platonic intellectual ascent.

The experience of unity with the One was related to a deepening of Plato's understanding of the eidetic. In effect, Plotinus asked where he was when he ascended from the Cave of his own private subjectivity—his sensations, desires, preferences and opinions—and was able to apprehend the eternal Forms. His answer was repeated by Schopenhauer centuries later: he had become "the one eye of the world";[3] he was identified with the cosmic Nous, the World Mind, the Logos as it looks to the Forms within Itself.

Plotinus went further. He took Plato's analogy of light applied metaphorically to the Good. Just as the light automatically diffuses itself into the surrounding darkness, so the One spontaneously overflows into the

---

ca. 311, China in 675, and becoming the official religion of the Uighur kingdom in 745. It was linked to the Paulicians (7th-c. Armenia), who led to the Bogomils (10th-c. Bulgaria), who, in turn, were linked to the Cathari (founded 1149 in France). The latter were centered in the town of Albi; hence they were called Albigensians. The Dominican Order was founded to battle that as a heresy. One of the Manichaeans' key teachings was that the body was evil. The Church instituted the feast of the Body of Christ, Corpus Christi, to counteract that view. Thomas Aquinas wrote the office for that feast.

2. *Enneads*, V.1.6; VI.7.34; VI.9.11.

3. Schopenhauer, *World as Will and Representation*, vol. I, 3, §38, 198.

multiplicity contained within the subject-object correlation, that is, the relation between the mind and the Forms. That correlation constitutes the Logos as the locus of the possibilities of instantiation of different forms of unity within the world, i.e., of there being things outside God. The diffusion process continues on toward the temporal and material world through the World Soul. The togetherness of the One, the World Mind, and the World Soul constitutes the eternal Trinity which radiates further into the darkness of time and space.[4] That darkness represents the principle that multiplies Form. It accounts, for example, for there being many instances of a given species at different times and places and with differing degrees of perfection. The "dark principle" is materiality, ground of extension or having parts outside of parts and hence the ability to come apart or to come together through change. Mutable extension involves space and time. Being a material instance of a Form involves spatiotemporal location. Schopenhauer will later refer to space and time together as the *principium individuationis*, the principle in things that allows for their being multiple instances, at different places and times, of the same Form.[5] Following Parmenides who preceded Plato, both change and multiplicity involve the introduction of nonbeing into being, for change involves being no longer what one is and not yet what one will become, while multiplicity involves one thing not being another and within any given thing, each aspect not being any other. The principle of materiality is hence a principle of nonbeing within being. It is existent nonbeing as the ultimate limit of the diffusion of the light of the One into the darkness of multiplicity. A being that is immersed in matter is thus in the dark, without any self-presence, and thus without any awareness of what is other than itself.

As in Aristotle, intellectual knowing is apprehending the Form "without matter and without the conditions of matter," that is, without change and the multiplicity that involves spatiotemporal location. This is possible insofar as, at the higher levels of our awareness, *we* are without matter and its conditions. But to be without matter is to be self-present as the condition for the manifestation of otherness that all knowing involves. We are born in utter darkness and awaken slowly as animal beings, gradually coming to self-awareness as free and responsible beings. As we live more at the biological pole of our being, in "animal extroversion," we become dis-tracted, torn in various ways, unintegrated and clueless, "in the dark." "Returning to

4. *Enneads*, V, 2; V, 1, 4; I, 4, 12, 16.
5. *World as Will and Representation*, vol. I, 3, §45, 222.

ourselves" in reflection as rational selves, we are able to move "inward and upward" toward the unity of the eidetic and toward the One as principle of the Whole. However, for the most part we are stuck "in the Cave" of personal and collective *doxa* and are not even dimly aware of what we are at our deepest levels. We are even inclined to think of our awareness on the pattern of sensorily given things, as a body among bodies, like all too many neurophysiologists and the plethora of their popularizers.

Plotinus's reading of this situation is that we are really pure spirits who, before our Fall into the body, were within the Logos. Turning away from the One, we were thrust into the body as our prison.[6] There has to be some intervention into the situation of biological-cultural reflex, taking off our chains and forcing us to a complete 180 degree turn, an *epistrophe*, a conversion, so we can understand our Cave as, indeed, a cave, a place of darkness with our backs toward the light. Further, we have to be dragged out of the Cave into the world of the Forms where the sunlight of intelligibility always shines. The way up, back to the One, requires purgation, discipline, asceticism, forcing oneself into the reflective, inward pattern of experience and out of animal extroversion and cultural reflex. The point of the asceticism is instrumental to making the turn inward and upward so that we can put ourselves in the position to understand more fully the context of our existence, that is, to become "illumined." But the final point of illumination is to attain to union with the One which grounds the cosmic process.

Now Augustine claims that he read in the Platonists very much of Christianity. In fact, he found a great deal of the prologue to St. John's Gospel.[7] In the beginning was the Logos who was from all eternity with the Father as the One, the Source. Through the Logos as the locus of the Forms, of all the ways the One could be imitated outside the divine—through Him all things were made. In the Logos was the Life that was the light of men, the ground of intelligibility in the Forms. And the light shone in the darkness, but the darkness grasped it not. People remained chained in the Cave, forgetful of their heavenly origin. The return to the One required the threefold way—purgation, illumination, and union—which became a staple in the Christian ascetical and mystical tradition. Neoplatonism showed Augustine how to think beyond the imagination that pictures all

---

6. *Enneads*, IV, 8, 4.

7. *Confessions*, translated by William Watt, vol. 1, VII, 9. We will cite this work in parentheses by Roman numerals, the first for the book, the second for the section.

things, including God, as bodies.[8] (Think of the pictures of the Father as an old man seated on a throne and the Spirit as a dove. Of course, in Jesus God becomes really and not simply imaginatively picturable.) Neoplatonism introduced Augustine to the verifiability of the spiritual realm we have been at pains to show throughout this text. But it also led him to turn from the outer world and follow the Plotinian desire to be "alone with the Alone." Hence his famous declaration: "*Noli foras ire; in te intrare. In interiore hominis habitat veritas*" ("Do not go outside; enter into yourself. In the interior of man dwells the truth").[9] And again, "I would know God and the soul and nothing else."[10]

Further and along the same lines, based on a Neoplatonic demeaning of the body, Augustine misread St. Paul's proclamation that "the flesh wars against the spirit"—or rather saw it in only one of its obvious modes. His own sexual problems led Augustine to understand this relation as bodily desire warring against the mind. "Flesh" becomes body, whereas scripturally "flesh" means the whole of humanness and "spirit" here means the Holy Spirit. The dimension of humanness most inclined to rebelliousness is the proud self-sufficiency of the pagan "saint" who practices asceticism, has his passions under control, and sees very clearly the human condition within the cosmic order. He is most inclined to look upon the claims to revelation as myths concocted for the childish who can neither control themselves nor think deeply, clearly, and consistently. This is especially the case in the possible closure to revelation of the developed philosopher.

What Augustine did not find in the Platonists was what was peculiar to Christianity: that the Word was made flesh, that the Logos humbled himself to take on the form of a servant. The Platonists only saw the way but did not know the Mediator who alone allows us to walk the way. That was hidden from the proud pagan saints and was revealed to the humble. In fact, Augustine said that the virtues of the pagans were splendid vices.[11] It was Ambrose, bishop of Milan, who turned Augustine's attention back to the Christianity of his early youth and led to his fourth and final conversion (V, 14).

---

8. *Enneads*, VII, 1.

9. *On True Religion*, 39n72.

10. *Soliloquies*, I, 2, 7.

11. *City of God*, XIX, 25. John Henry Newman paints an admirable portrait of the pagan emperor Julian the Apostate only to undercut it by a claim similar to that of Augustine. Newman, *Idea of a University*, 147–49.

Laced through his conversion accounts is his attempt to come to terms with his sexuality. He had a child out of wedlock whom he named Adeodatus, "gift of God." After he met Ambrose, he prayed to God to grant him chastity, but added "not yet!" (VIII. 7). He still enjoyed his sex life too much. But then came the experience in the garden where he heard a child, probably playing some game, saying, *"Tolle, lege! Tolle, lege!"* ("Take and read!") (VIII, 12). Viewing this as a sign, he picked up the New Testament and opened it randomly. He happened upon St. Paul's Letter to the Romans (xiii): "Not in chamberings and drunkenness . . . , but put on the Lord Jesus Christ." Then it was that he gained the strength to overcome his overweening desires. This conversion finally helped him to unify his life in practice.

The life-narrative culminates in the "Vision at Ostia" during a conversation between Augustine and his mother Monica near her death (IX, 10). The two of them were then taken up in a strange interpersonal mystical vision. I say "strange" because mystical experience is almost always described as taking place in solitude. What he described was a mutual and progressive experience of silence: first of the tumult of the soul, then of the mind itself, after which the things outside point in the direction of the eternal wisdom that fashions them and they themselves fall silent.

2.

One of the dominant strands running through the book—indeed, one might argue it constitutes the very heart of the book—is the notion of the *cor inquietum*, the restless heart found in the opening paragraphs. "You have made us for Yourself, O Lord, and our hearts are restless and will not rest until they rest in You" (I, 1).

The *cor inquietum* indicates an underlying dynamism having by nature a final goal. Augustine sees it linked with the teleological (that is, goal-seeking, from the Greek *telos*, goal) dynamism of the inward-upward turning of the soul toward the Good as principle of the Whole. In our ordinary life, we are unaware of this teleology. Plato drew a parallel between Eros or sexual desire and the deep desire of the rational soul, which desires he saw as in some sense continuous.[12] But, for the most part, the conscious I (*animus*) is unaware of its deepest desire. Sexual desire arises from the principle which animates the body, from the *anima* in Augustine's way of speaking. It comes into the field of experience as a feeling of unrest linked

12. Plato, *Symposium*, 210a–212a.

to a promise of delight brought about by the perception of the beautiful form of another member of the species. It is not necessarily experienced as a desire to produce offspring. As desire, it is rooted—once again speaking Augustinian language—in that aspect of the *anima* which juts into the field of experience, in the *cor*, the heart. The character of sexual desire holds for animals as well as for humans. But in both cases it is linked to the production of offspring. Indeed, the ground of this experience in the organism is the same kind of ground as we find also in vegetative forms—though obviously unexperienced by the plant. In his *Symposium* Plato has Diotima proclaim that sexual desire is the natural drive of the mortal for the immortal. The necessarily mortal organism is linked to the immortality of the species through its reproductive dynamism. Where the living form is such that appearance can come into being, that is, in animals and in humans where awareness happens, the living being need not be aware of the underlying dynamism. The lack of awareness on the part of animals and humans of the unconscious dynamic teleology that generates the level of conscious appearance also occurs at the higher level of human awareness in the native desire of the intellectual soul to seek "the principle of the Whole." It is a desire of which most people are not aware, except as it is already answered in terms of religious belief which fills in the initially empty horizon of our native reference to the Whole with a particular account of the Whole—or, for that matter, in a scientific worldview. In Plato the awakening to that cosmic-metacosmic dynamism requires an *epistrophe*, a complete turnabout—in Augustine's Latin, a *conversio* of the soul to recognize what it is and to what it is by nature directed. The human soul seeks the principle of the Whole of being. It lives out of the answers given to the fundamental question, posed to it by its own nature, of its place in the whole scheme of things.[13] But the desire is not only for an understanding of the place of humans in the Whole; it is a desire of the whole person, the basic desire of the heart.

It being the case that the underpinnings of the field of awareness, both on its sensory and its intellectual levels, involve a search for the immortal, and that the intellectual level is underpinned by the desire of the mind to be aware of its relation to the Whole, human awareness will be restless until it finds the eternal fulfillment of that desire, even though it be for the most part unaware of its native aim. Once again, however, Augustine testifies to the coming to rest of that desire in the communicative presence of a Person

13. Cf. Plato, *Republic*, 508e–509b.

who encompasses and grounds all that intellectual awareness could acquire and who, as Beauty Itself, attracts the restless soul and gives stability to a life flowing toward the divine.

By reason of our bipolar character, our heart of hearts is aimed at the fullness of being. If the human heart desires anything less than that fullness, it cannot be fully satisfied. Hence its essentially restless character. One might say that the task of life is to align the objects of our heart's desires with the fundamental native desire, in our heart of hearts, for full relation to the Fullness of Being.

In working out what the term of that reference might be, pagan thinkers like Plato, Aristotle, and Plotinus located it in an eternal dimension which intersects the temporal: the Alpha and the Omega, the One as Source, the Beginning of everything, and the Good, the End that all things seek to emulate. It displays itself shining through the beauty of things as incomparable Beauty Itself (Plato), as the complete self-presence of Thought that all things imitate and that humans alone can contemplate (Aristotle), as the full plenitude of the Source from which all things emanate and to which humans seek to return (Plotinus). A Christian thinker like Augustine will find this congenial; but he sees, beyond the conclusion to a demonstration or the object of appreciative contemplation, One who personally addresses human beings, both in revelation history and in the intimacy of their hearts. God is not simply a third person object, the Principle of the Whole, but a second person presence whom we address as "You" and in Christian prayer are emboldened to call "Father" (Abba).

As containing the residue of past experiences, the heart is associated with the memory. Augustine considers the memory in a special chapter (Book X) following the narrative of his life (Books I–IX). Memory is the innermost chamber of the mind, that which, in the psychophysical totality of a human being, is closest to the I-*animus*. The I-*animus* is other than the memory because, as Augustine remarks, the I cannot encompass the memory.

Now there are three basic levels of memory: one is the automatic retention of the past through which the Me comes to take on the peculiar thickness it has, filling the empty space between the Now of immediate sensations and the fullness of Being to which our nature refers us. That latter reference is the deeper second phase of memory. Living most fully is learning a type of recollection which returns fully to the self as a whole, remembering what I am: emptiness longing for the plenitude of Being Itself, and on that basis re-collecting the eidetic order of the Whole. In between and third is the deliberate attempt to re-collect the past and, more deeply, to recollect the universal eidetic order.

Crucial to the nature of memory is the reference to the past as past. Though there has to be some trace of past impressions stored in the brain, memory is not the presence of these traces. The traces (as in a computer's "memory") are not the past but the present result of the past. There is a sense, then, in which we are not only living outside our skin in the present, we are also literally *outside the present*. This is linked to the capacity to abstract the universal, that which is recognized to hold all times and all places where the proper conditions are met. Such capacity indicates a being beyond the Now of sensation-desire and, in some way, with the whole of space and time. That in turn, as we have been at pains to point out throughout, is rooted in being referred to the totality of being.

Innermost to the memory is the heart, for not all that is in our memory is close to us. The I-*animus* in Augustine's usage is not broader than memory, for I cannot encompass my memory. Perhaps it is best to say that I as conscious center have as implicit horizon reference to everything, but focally I cannot even encompass that part of the totality that has sedimented in my memory. Aquinas will say that the scope of the intellect exceeds its power to reach and that therefore it is in principle open to having its power raised through grace in "the light of glory."

In the course of describing his life's journey, Augustine addresses God as *"interior intimo meo et superior summo meo"* ("more interior than my most intimate self and superior to my highest self") (VI, 21). What could be more intimate to me than I to myself? But the Me so much escapes the I. One spends a lifetime getting to know Me—my real capacities, my real motivational sources, and, beyond this, the deep structure of human nature that underpins my field of operative awareness. But as created, I presuppose the creative presence of the Divine who, knowing my totality, projects me, throughout my life-span, into being. The act of creating is not simply a "once upon a time" starting up of the universe. In Aquinas, e.g., there is no way to demonstrate a first temporal beginning philosophically, for, from the point of view of philosophic thought without revelation, it might just be, as Aristotle thought, necessary that nature and thus time is eternal. But the very finitude of things within the cosmic Whole requires an explanation, which can only lie in that which transcends finitude and which thus is Infinite Being. This means that, as long as there is finitude, Infinite Being must be creating. That means the Creator is fully present in such a way that every finite being is totally transparent to him and thus he is closer to things than they are to themselves.

In Book X, as a kind of conclusion of his ascent, we find one of the most famous lines of the *Confessions*:

> Late have I loved you, beauty ever ancient, ever new, late have I loved you. Behold you were within me and I without. There outside I sought you; and I, deformed as I was, rushed into those beautiful things which you have made. You were with me and I was not with you. The things that are not if they are not in you held me captive at a great distance from you. (X, 27)

The passage is the real center of the work: it is the divine Beauty which, experienced, can still the restless heart. This clearly recalls the Ladder to the vision of Beauty Itself in Plato's *Symposium*. Looking back to Augustine's vision at Ostia, we note that divine beauty appears suddenly out of the silence into which one enters. The obvious difference is the personal address to "Beauty ever ancient, ever new" as "You." We might on occasion be privileged to gaze upon Beauty Itself, as Diotima and Plotinus testified; but, in Augustine's experience, that Beauty, as the divine You, looks upon us. However, our gazing is not merely the detached look of the intellect. The employment of metaphors drawn from all the senses describes a comprehensive relationship rather than simply the more detached relation of "seeing." This shows something of what, in the immediately following section being "united with God with one's whole being" means (X, 28).

What is one's "whole being"? This hearkens back to the Old Testament command to love God with one's whole heart, mind, soul (Deut 6:5). The heart is the gathering of the Me as tuned, ready to respond in habituated ways to what presents itself; but if it is focused upon anything less than God, it cannot include the I as founded upon desire for God. Belief is not yet union with God with one's whole being. One's wholeness is gathered in the deepest nearness of anything as rooted in the divine plenitude which creatively sustains both the thing and the I entering into nearness. One learns to love everything as created by God. Such love corresponds to one's "heart of hearts," the desire that is one's founding metaphysical reference.

In the divided state Augustine finds that the *animus* cannot operate *ex toto*, from its totality. One can want so to love God, but one might also find no particular relish in the effort. One lives in anguish as having one's heart divided. Its healing and thus its ability to fulfill the command is something only possible through the gift of God's presence inflaming the heart. Strange command, this: one is commanded to do something one cannot do on one's own. Hence the tendency to understand it—and thus misunderstand it—as a matter of willing alone, which is only a precondition.

In Book X, having recapitulated his life, Augustine exclaims in prayer: "*Percussisti cor meum verbo tuo, et amavi te*" (You struck my heart with your word, and I loved you") (X, 6). He goes on to contrast and relate what he loves in God with what he loved in seeking the embrace of a beloved: "Yet I love a kind of light, a kind of voice, a kind of fragrance, a kind of food and a kind of embrace . . . by the interior of my humanity where it flashes forth to my *anima*." When the heart is struck by the word of God, love is awakened, the *anima* receives light, and the equivalent of all the sensory modes of presence is evoked. The light of the *anima*, I would claim, is the sense of divine presence in the heart. The evocation of sensory modes other than seeing is significant—even though light finally takes center stage as that which flashes into the *anima*. It recalls the psalmist's "Taste and see that the Lord is sweet" (Ps 33:9), but it adds embrace and fragrance and sound. Augustine uses metaphors derived from all the senses to hint at what is involved in the experience of the presence of divine beauty. One does not simply "see" this beauty in a "Beatific Vision"; one "hears" it, "smells" it, "touches" it, "tastes" it. The togetherness of these features recalls sexual encounter where all the senses relate to the beloved. It is not an accident that the monastic tradition developed commentaries on the "Song of Songs": the sensuous description, attributed to Solomon, of the physical assets of his beloved were taken as symbol of the soul's nuptial union with God. Not the cognitive distance of *theoria* or "contemplation," but participative union is what is ultimately at stake in bringing the heart's restless desire to its fulfillment.

By that parallel with sexual embrace one at least gets a sense, though in a lower register, of what total presence might mean, and thus what loving God with one's whole heart, soul, mind, and strength might mean. But one must also recall Augustine's apt remarks upon his life of sexual indulgence when he was simultaneously outside himself and locked up inside himself. Sexuality involves a kind of ecstasy, but one which might involve no real entry into the interior life of another but a kind of self-enjoyment, locking one inside of one's own feelings of gratification. But when the word of God strikes the heart, there is an embrace of love that simultaneously brings one outside of oneself and brings one into the presence of the unfathomable interiority of the divine Other. In mature human sexuality the total sensuous experience becomes the expression of personal intimacy and mutual dedication and thus a fuller image of the divine embrace.

But for Augustine, being taken with exterior beauty was a mistake, and he seems to consider the Platonic starting point in the experience of physical beauty a distraction and the result of the fall. After his conversion, the whole realm of the senses, and most especially sexual experience, made him nervous.[14] He required a turn away from the seduction of external beauty and a turn "within." What awaited him within was God addressed at the beginning of Book X as the power of his soul above its highpoint.

<h2 style="text-align:center">3.</h2>

The account of his life that Augustine recollects presupposes being-in-time. But what is time? Here we have the *locus classicus* of the discussion of time and a working out of some of its eidetic features (XI, 26). Augustine remarks that when no one asks him what it is, he thinks he knows. But then when he attempts to answer the question, he is puzzled. The analysis actually goes back to Parmenides who, attempting to purge all nonbeing from the thought of being, eliminated all change (since that involves the no-longer and the not-yet). Being is in a changeless eternity.

What is time? It is the relatedness of past, present, and future—an eidetic structure repeated at every moment of time. How are these features to be described? The past is what was but is no longer; the future is what is not yet but will be; and the present? What is "now"? It is a flowing which disappears into the past as it moves into the future. The beginning of the spoken sentence is gone before the end is reached and the whole sentence is relegated to the past. The Now flows along, an ever-present, nontemporally extended divider moving out of the no-longer into the not-yet. Three interrelated modes of nonbeing! Time is precisely a complex mode of not-being.

Augustine does not stop there. How is it that he can consider all this? Because he is not in time in the mode of the fleeting Now but in a different mode. Augustine goes on to locate the three dimensions of time in the ego-*animus*: the future exists in the expectation of the *animus* now, the present in its current attention, and the past in its remembrance (XI, 28). This accounts for the three temporal dimensions, at least insofar as focal experience is concerned. Awareness retains the past, anticipates the future, and attends to what is present. This is what Husserl will later call "internal

14. Balthasar, "Augustine," in *Studies in Theological Style*, 95–143.

time-consciousness," the flow of consciousness attending in function of retention of the immediate past and protention or anticipation of the immediate future.[15] But we can also refer to and even go in search of the distant
past and deliberately project the future of our own goals.

However, we should not grant that the reduction of the past to recollection is sufficient. We seek the reality of the past beyond our own recol-
lections through the traces left in the present. The past seems to be a reality
beyond the mind by which the mind is measured as it develops devices for
reconstructing the past more faithfully in historical research foreshadowed
in the opening of Plato's *Symposium* which recounts how the then-present
speaker came to know of the past occurrence of the original symposium.
In recent times, Alfred North Whitehead will propose that the past has
"objective immortality" in the memory of God.[16]

Augustine views being-in-time from the perspective of the eternity
that stands beyond and encompasses time. As a Platonist, he sees the eidetic features of any region as eternal, like mathematics, but also like the
features of time itself from which mathematics abstracts. One can grasp
the eidetic because one is, at the deeper levels of one's being, beyond time.
However, the deeper levels are not "the whole soul." They are the anchors
of a life that is spread out in time, indeed, "distended," that is, distracted,
torn asunder by time and tumbling through it. The ego *animus* exists as a
self-presence in the space of self-directive awareness that is a kind of exile
from the divine so deep that it is not usually felt as an exile, except insofar
as a certain restlessness propels it on. That exile is time understood as the
distentio animi, the "distention" of the ego-*animus*, the judging and choosing awareness being dissipated, scattered, subjected to tumult in the heart
as its polar opposite and ground (XI, 26).

His whole life has been a *distentio* that he describes as being dissolved in time, torn (*dilaniatur*) by a tumult of diverse attractions even to
the intimate viscera of his *anima*, the depths of his heart and its desires,
ignorant of their proper order. With this he contrasts the soul's being *exten-
tus*, extended, broadened by following the deliberate intention of eternity
(XI, 29). "Behold, my life is a distention. . . . [However,] not distended, but
extended, not according to distention, but according to intention, I follow
to the palm of the supernal vocation. . . . And I am dissolved in temporal
things, of whose order I am ignorant, and my thoughts, the intimate viscera

15. Husserl, *Phenomenology of Internal Time-Consciousness.*
16. Whitehead, *Science and the Modern World*, 173–79.

of my *anima*, are torn with seething multitudes of things." What brings the soul to rest is the fire of divine love awakened within it that purifies and liquefies the heart flowing toward God.

The notion of *distentio animi* is not simply a neutral analysis of the functions of expectation of the future, attention to the present, and memory of the past. Distention is dis-traction, being torn up, divided, being subjected to constant tumult, never being at rest, never being one. At the same time, being subjected to the turbulence of time is a becoming rigidified, locked into the mode of dispersion. In the most intimate viscera of the *cor/anima* one is deeply restless. What brings the self to unity and peace is the intention of the deep future, the eternity that awaits us at the end. But this intending is not viewed here as a simple act of the iron will that stoically rises above all disturbance and maintains its *apatheia*, its lack of feeling. It is rather rooted in an experience Augustine then describes as one of being both purged and liquefied in the fire of divine love so that one flows into God: "Until I flow into You and am purged and liquefied in the fire of your love" (XI, 29). Paradoxically, being caught within time is being rigidified and being in tumult; coming to intend the final eternal end at the level of the heart burning with divine love both fixes one on the future and renders one liquid. The metaphor of divine fire is significant: not only does it purify and liquefy, it also illuminates so that one may flow, knowingly, into the divine.

The reflection upon time is prolegomenon to an extended interpretation of the early parts of Genesis on creation, recalling Augustine's opening address to God as Maker of heaven and earth. Under Ambrose's guidance, Augustine came to see that the Scriptures he had earlier regarded as only for the naive masses were the repository of truths hidden from the wise of this world. In the beginning of Scripture, God's eternity, encompassing and transcending time, is proclaimed as the ground of the vast totality of creation within which a single human is dwarfed. And yet for Augustine this same God of power and might watches the innermost thoughts and the most fleeting experiences of our lives and gently leads those who seek him to find their rest in that which lies Beyond, here and hereafter. Augustine's prayerful *Confessions* points to what he experienced as that encompassing divine Presence, Maker of heaven and earth, but also Watchman and Guide to our most intimate thoughts, One who speaks to, and who alone can still our restless hearts.

QUESTIONS

1. What were the stages of conversion in Augustine's life? What led him to each stage?

2. How did the Neoplatonists' teaching parallel the Prologue to St. John's Gospel? What was its deficiencies?

3. What do you understand by "the heart" and what is its role in human experience? How is it related to "the intellect"? "The will"?

4. How do you understand the commandment to love God with your whole heart, soul, mind, strength, being?

5. What are the various levels of memory for Augustine?

6. How is God "more intimate to me than I to myself"?

7. What are the essential features of time? What is puzzling about their status? Clarify the two different aspects of time that Augustine considers: time itself and our awareness of it.

FURTHER READINGS

1. Hans Urs von Balthasar, "Augustine," in *Studies in Theological Style: Clerical Styles*, 95–143.

2. Peter Brown, *Augustine of Hippo*.

3. Etienne Gilson, *The Christian Philosophy of Saint Augustine*.

4. Romano Guardini, *The Conversion of St. Augustine*.

5. Robert O'Connell, *Saint Augustine's Confessions: The Odyssey of Soul*.

* * * *

ST. THOMAS AQUINAS,
SUMMA THEOLOGIAE

Grace presupposes and perfects nature.

—*SUMMA THEOLOGIAE*, I, 1

READINGS:

Anton Pegis, *Introduction to St. Thomas Aquinas.*[1]

1. Sacred doctrine (Part I,1, 1 and 8 [pp. 3–5, 13–15]).

2. The existence of God (I, 2, 3 [24–27] and I, 46, 2 [252–57]).

3. The incarnate and incorruptible nature of the soul (I, 75, 6 [28790] and 76, 1 [291–97]), its powers (I, 78, 1–4 [321–35]) and operation (I, 79, 4 and 5 [343–48] and I, 85, 1 and 2 [400–407]).

4. Natural moral law (I–II, 91, 2–4 [617–23], 94, 2, 635–38 and 95, 1 [646–50]).

5. The end of man (from the *Summa contra gentiles* [429–77]—henceforth *SCG*).

---

1. For the course I used the Pegis book. It has a judicious set of extensive excerpts from the *Summa Theologiae*. I refer to the page numbers in Pegis's book in brackets. Except for the last selection (5), the readings refer to the *Summa Theologiae*. The work's division into three parts is indicted by Roman numerals and is arranged in a series of related questions. The Arabic number following the Roman refers to the question treated and the last number refers to an article or sub-question. Thus I, 1,1 means Part One, question 1, article 1.

1.

Thomas Aquinas (1223/4–1273/4) appeared in the wake of the Crusades that had as one of their positive results the first introduction of the total extant corpus of the works of Aristotle into the West. Thinkers in the East like Avicenna (Ibn Sina, fl. ca. AD 1000) and Averroes (Ibn Rushd, d. 1194) worked with the texts of Plato and Aristotle. The West had very few original texts of either thinker. Of Plato there was the first third of the *Timaeus* and (perhaps) the *Meno*, while of Aristotle there were only some of his logical works. The Neoplatonists were present fragmentarily in the so-called *Theology of Aristotle*. The extant corpus of Plato's writings came to the West only after the Fall of Constantinople in 1453. The works of Aristotle came over to the West earlier and in dribbles through contact with Islamic thought. Around 1140 translations began with the logical works and continued until, in the last third of the thirteenth century, the total Aristotelian corpus had been translated.

Confronting Aristotle also entailed confronting Islamic thinkers like Avicenna and Averroes and the leading Jewish theologian, Maimonides, who had themselves commented upon and developed Aristotle's ideas. Aquinas referred to Averroes in particular as "*The* Commentator" and drew positively from Avicenna and Maimonides for the transformation of Aristotle requisite to adapt his thought to the Christian religious tradition. This kind of attention to the non-West has not been a hallmark of most Western thinkers since Aquinas (Nicholas of Cusa, Leibniz, and Schopenhauer are notable exceptions); but it is an imperative in today's world, as John Paul II noted.

The first wave of translations of Aristotle's works was from the Arabic. Only during the time of Aquinas were translations done from the original Greek. The total corpus so translated was finally made available around 1270. William of Moerbeke made several translations to accompany Aquinas's commentaries. And Aquinas wrote commentaries, line by line, on the major works of Aristotle, continuing up to the later years of his life. Just as for him Averroes was "*The* Commentator," so also was Aristotle "*The* Philosopher."

One of the central notions Aquinas took over from Aristotle was his view on the nature of the soul. To recap our earlier treatment, Aristotle's notion of *psyche* was broader than the notion of psyche in contemporary psychology: it was the principle that accounted for the peculiarities of living things generally. Contrasted with the nonliving, organisms "circle back into themselves" and set themselves over against their environment from which they draw the materials for their operations. They are the first examples of "selves": they are *self*-formative, *self*-sustaining, *self*-repairing, and *self*- replicating.

Aristotle sees nonliving things as aggregates rather than selves. The seeds produced by organisms contain the active potentialities that allow them to "become what they are," that is, to develop in actuality what they are in potentiality. In Aristotle's view, the *psyche* is the principle that accounts for the unity of the organism over time and at any given time. He spoke of this principle as the "first act" of the organism insofar as the first thing that grounds all the rest is the determination of the type of the organic process (as formal cause) containing the active powers (efficient causes) that organize the appropriate materials (material cause) drawn from the environment in terms of the goals of the organism (final cause). Explanation of living things requires all four causes, not just the material and mechanical causes studied by modern biology.

The developmental process is the series of "second acts," the activities in which it engages through which the organism progressively takes on its adult features. The thing is called a "substance" and the attributes it takes on, like shape, size, color, acquired dispositions and the like are called "accidents." The latter term is a bit odd in English since for Aristotle it does not mean simply what need not occur. The accidents are the substance's own coming into self-possession as a fully functioning adult member of its species. They might better be called "conjugate forms" as a direct Latinized translation (*con-juncta*) of the Greek *sym-bebekota*, both meaning "co-yoked" or necessarily linked to the substances they qualify. There are three levels to the *psyche* so conceived: plant, animal, and human. Each higher level of soul presupposes the powers of the lower as a condition for its own emergence and functioning. Thus animals and humans presuppose organic, "vegetative" functions. Animal awareness and the sensory level of human experience require the development of the requisite organs (eyes, ears, etc.), and human awareness requires sensory materials as the basis for its operations of abstraction, judgment, reasoning, and choice as well as for the construction of language as transformed sensory material. The higher powers are present from the very beginning in the seed (or fertilized ovum), but require a series of developmental steps before they can come into active function.

Now Aristotle's thought was viewed by churchmen as dangerous territory. After all, he held that the human being is not some separate spirit temporarily embodied and seeking release from the fetters of embodiment—a view still all-too-common in the Christian churches. For Aristotle the human being belongs among the animals as the one who is capable of the individual and collective use of reason: the rational or the linguistic animal. Aristotle also held to the eternity of the world and made no room for a creative and omniscient divinity who would judge the living and the dead: though he argued for the existence of a God as Unmoved Mover of the cosmos, Aristotle viewed God as an exemplar, a final cause, not an efficient cause, not a creator. Furthermore, his God knew nothing outside itself and thus could not be addressed personally in prayer but, at best, praised from afar and emulated. It was Aristotle that was assimilated almost as a whole into Aquinas's theological thought.

2.

Aquinas joined the Order of Preachers, newly founded by Dominic Guzman in the first quarter of the thirteenth century. Along with the contemporary Franciscans, the Dominicans broke with the traditional "vow of stability" that had characterized earlier religious orders. The members of the older orders pledged themselves to remain in a given house for their lifetime. On the contrary, the new orders were "mendicants," originally, like the Buddhists, beggars and preachers who moved from place to place.

The Dominicans were linked to Augustine's early career with the Manichaeans in that they were founded to preach against the Albigensians, the medieval descendants of Manichaeism centered around the town of Albi in southern France. The relation of the early Dominicans to the latter-day Manichaeans also entailed the introduction of the notorious Inquisition whose basic principles Aquinas defended by claiming that political power had the obligation to root out heresy the way a physician is licensed to excise diseased members from the body (*ST* II–II, 11, 3.). Persuasion through discussion is the preferred way; but when that does not work, torture may be a tool; and when that might also fail, the diseased organ must be cut out by execution! As David Hume pointed out, conscience might be sorely tempted in such circumstances to give up and become religiously hypocritical.[2] Noting this, the so-called Catholic Kings, Ferdinand and Isabella, after conquer-

2. Hume, *Dialogues*, Part XII, 122–24.

ing Granada in 1492, the last Muslim stronghold in the Iberian Peninsula, forced the conversion or the emigration of Jews and Muslims and instituted the notorious Inquisition to look into false conversions.

However, Aquinas balanced his support of the Inquisition with a claim that many might find astonishing, namely, the absolutely binding character of individual conscience. He would take this so far as to claim that it would even entail the *obligation*—under pain of mortal sin at that!—to leave the Church, the citadel of truth, if one's conscience so dictated. However, this, in turn, was set in relation to the obligation to seek to form one's conscience in the truth (*ST* I, 19, 5 and 6).[3] So there is a peculiar dialectic or tension between the absolute interiority of conscience and the exteriority of the social order on the one hand, and between both of them and the final truth on the other. (Kant will introduce a version of this in the modern age through his distinction between morality which is interior and legality which is exterior, and in his parallel distinction between the public and private function of the thinker. The private function relates to his professional work, the public function involves obedience to the sovereign.)[4]

Besides the introduction of Aristotle and the operation of the Dominican order, the general theological tenor of the times was expressed in the basic work for training theologians, Peter Lombard's *Sentences*, compiled in 1152. It took its inspiration from *Sic et Non* (*Yes and No*), the work of Peter Abelard (fl. 1140). Abelard developed a heuristic or exploratory scheme of basic questions concerning the Christian faith, to each of which he attached the conflicting opinions of authorities. The upshot was the challenge to side with one line of opinion by developing answers to each of the questions that would be consistent with answers to all the rest. Lombard developed this scheme and gathered especially large selections from Augustine whose authority dominated the West up to the time of Aquinas and beyond.[5] During that period, Lombard's book became the standard work upon which those who sought to become masters of theology were required to comment. The commentaries went to multiple volumes. Aquinas too developed his theological competence through such commentary. However, the introduction of Aristotle substantially modified the standpoint from which one attempted to answer the fundamental theological questions.

3. See also Aquinas *On Truth*, question 17, article 4.

4. Kant, "What Is Enlightenment?," 5.

5. The Council of Trent in the sixteenth century designated Aquinas as the dominant official theologian.

Basically one could say, at least by way of orientation, that Aquinas was Augustinian-Platonic at the highest levels in the doctrine of God and the end of humanness, but that he was Aristotelian at the level of our belonging to the natural world. The dominant Neoplatonic tendency was to think of the human being as basically a soul passing through a period of embodiment, but essentially not belonging to the physical world. In Christian terms, this was, as typical prayers would have it, "a place of exile," "a valley of tears," not our true home. The body with its senses and passions was lowly if not evil. Better to detach oneself completely from sexual experience, from accumulation of possessions, and even from one's own will by the "higher life" established through the vows of perpetual chastity, poverty, and obedience. The way to God was the Neoplatonic way of turning "inward and upward," purging oneself of bodily desires, seeking inner illumination, and opening oneself to final union with the One, "alone with the Alone." This teaching was assimilated into the Christian monastic mystical tradition as the three ways: purgative, illuminative, and unitive.

Recall the implicit question that followed the Pythagorean "discovery of mind" as a peculiar kind of inwardness capable of grasping the underlying mathematical intelligibility of sensorily presented things by a move "inward and upward": What's a nice inwardness like you doing in a place like this—the body with its distracting passions? The Pythagoreans inferred a prior fall of the soul from a situation of "pure spirituality." Plato followed that tendency. In the Judgment of Er at the end of the *Republic* the embodied soul is compared to the sea-god Glaucus who was unrecognizable because he was covered with barnacles and sea-weed that represent embodied experience; only when cleansed of its bodily condition can the human soul be recognized for what it is. On the other hand, as we noted before, in his *Timaeus* Plato also claimed that the body was the *house* of the soul. Though the latter suggests a positive relation, both versions suggest an external relation between soul and body.

For Aristotle the answer to the implicit Pythagorean question was: embodiment is the only condition in which the human mind can be what it naturally is. As we noted, the soul is the underlying principle of the mind as the highest power of the human soul. But in order to exercise that power the soul needs sensory experience as the material for its reflection and for its construction of language; and it cannot get sensory experience without the proper organs. Just as we might have the skill of carpentry but cannot exercise it without saws and hammers and nails, so the soul might have the powers of sensation but cannot exercise them without eyeballs, eardrums, tactual sensors, and the like. So for Aristotle the soul has a hierarchy of powers, the first of which is the power of organic formation and sustenance. The human body is not only the house of the soul; the soul through its "nutritive power" builds, sustains, and repairs its own house as an integral part of its life. If we look at the world around us, we can infer that soul is present in all living things as their underlying principle. At the plant level there is only the power to produce, sustain, repair, and reproduce the organism. At the animal level, the further aim of the nutritive power is to provide the organs for the power to sense that is tied to the awakening of desire and the tendency to move in the direction of the desired object through a variety of flexibly adaptable operations. The process culminates in tactual apprehension: eating, mating, caring for offspring, and fighting enemies.

In the course of human development the animal phase develops up to "the age of reason" when reflection and responsible choice begin to be exercised. We reflect upon sensations, desires, and actions, begin to understand by developing a "conceptual map" of what we can regularly anticipate, and make our choices accordingly. But we do so guided by others through the mediation of a common language. This makes rational or linguistic animals, as Aristotle said, essentially *political animals*, that is, those whose own concrete possibilities are provided by tradition mediated by coming into bodily contact with other human beings. Stimulated by others, we then act out bodily in lending a hand, transforming the environment technologically, forming artistically, speaking and writing intelligently, performing musically. A being so structured belongs essentially "in the world" as intelligent and responsible, essentially embodied, historically situated agent.

In turning to Aristotle, especially for his view of humanness, Aquinas argued that Aristotle's thought in many ways furnished a better basis for understanding the distinctively *incarnate* character of Christianity than traditional Platonism. The foundation of Christianity is the Incarnation of the Word; the end is the Resurrection of the Body; and the way to the Father is through the Sacraments, physical signs that mediate grace.[6] Aristotle made clear the essentially incarnate character of the highest levels of human activity. And Aristotle's basic notion of humans as political animals also linked up with the Pauline notion of the mystical body of Christ of which we are all specialized members.

---

6. See Chesterton, *St. Thomas Aquinas*, 116–19.

3.

Aquinas's major work was the *Summa theologiae,* is a three-part opus developed according to the Neoplatonic scheme of the emanation of all things from God and the return to God through the ascent of the rational creature. Aquinas adds a third part: Christ as the Way. The first two parts are structural analyses; the third part is historical, dealing with how that structure can be fulfilled in time through the mediation of Christ and his church. Aquinas worked on this *Summa* until the last year of his life when a mystical vision occasioned his remark: "I can write no longer. Compared to what I have seen, all that I have written is so much straw." The stop occurred in part 3. Having treated the life of Christ, he went on to treat of the sacraments, and then projected going on to the four last things after death: judgment, heaven, hell, and purgatory. His vision occurred just after he had treated two of the seven sacraments, Baptism and the Eucharist (incidentally, the only sacraments recognized by the Reformation), and had begun work on Penance. The projected work was subsequently completed by others, adding a supplement taken from Aquinas's early commentary on the *Sentences* in the form of an additional ninety-one questions and answers.

OUTLINE OF THE *SUMMA THEOLOGIAE*

(Qq. 611)

FIRST PART

GOD (119 Qs.)

1. The Divine Essence. Qq. 1–26
2. The Trinity of Persons in God. Qq. 27–43
3. The Procession of Creatures from God. [Qq. 44–119]
   A. Creation. Qq. 44–49
   B. Angels. Qq. 50–64
   C. Corporeal Creatures Qq. 65–74
   D. Man. Qq. 75–102
   E. Providence Qq. 103–119

FIRST PART OF THE SECOND PART

MORALS IN GENERAL (114 Qq.)

1. Ultimate End. Qq. 1–5
2. Means to the End. [Qq. 6–114]
   A. Human Acts. Qq. 6–48

The work follows the general heuristic (inquiring) and dialectical (involving the give-and-take of argumentation) structure found in the *Sentences*. It is organized as a set of *questions*—611 in all—each one of which has a series of subdivisions or articles that are themselves questions: over three thousand questions in all! It covers in an orderly fashion all the questions theologians had asked in the history of Christianity, and then some.

Each question and sub-question is organized the same way. After the posing of the question there is a list of objections to the answer Aquinas himself will give, both those objections that have been typically raised and new objections that he himself adds. Then there is the citation of an authority on the side of his own answer, followed, in the body of the *quaestio*, by arguments in favor of the answer. After that come his replies to the objections originally listed. One has to see the answers emerging out of struggle with objections, just as Plato developed his thought through struggle with the sophists and the common opinions they learned to manipulate.

So each question takes this form:

Question

Objections

Citation of authority

Body, presenting Aquinas's own position and reasoning

Replies to objections

This heuristic and dialectical arrangement mirrors the functioning of the arts faculty at the universities, themselves newly emergent in the West. Not only did the doctors provide line-by-line commentaries on Scripture, on theological authorities, and on Aristotle, they also, following the procedures of Abelard and Lombard, held regular sessions of disputation among themselves. So the somewhat dry listing of objections for each question in the *Summa* is a compressed summary based upon the dynamic disputations going on in the university.

4.

In the first question of the *Summa* Aquinas addressed the issue of so-called *sacred doctrine*. Here he introduces one of his most basic principles: that *grace presupposes and perfects nature* (I, 1, 8, ad 2 [15]). Revelation as a manifestation of the grace of God is addressed to a rational nature and calls forth the attempt to understand what has been revealed. Aquinas here follows Anselm's notion of *fides quaerens intellectum*, "faith seeking understanding," and Augustine's witness: *credo ut intelligam*, "I believe in order to understand"—both cited in John Paul II's *Fides et Ratio*. For Aquinas faith is not a blind leap, a sheer act of the will—surely not involving Tertullian's infamous *Credo quia absurdum*, "I believe because it is absurd!" (To which Freud rightly replied: "*Which* absurdities are we expected to believe?")[7] For Aquinas faith is an *intellectual virtue* that extends the light under which the native power of the human intellect operates.

In Aquinas's view, that native operation is best analyzed by Aristotle as reflective alertness to the whole context of human experience and what that entails. If the development of the human being under the impact of grace involves a turn "inward and upward," as Plato and Plotinus indicated, it at the same time remains anchored in attending to what is given from without. The human intellect has a permanent dependency on sensory experience

7. Freud, *Future of an Illusion*, 43.

and therefore on the body as well as on the bodily present human community with which it interacts through the mediation of language. For Aquinas as theologian this points to an intrinsic requirement of the final resurrection of the body, an embarrassment to those who think separation from embodiment is the final thing.

The order of the work is theological, beginning with God and, in the treatment of the human being, with the highest level of the soul. But in both cases, Aquinas launches the inquiry with philosophical considerations, the full evidence for which is not available until the whole view gets worked out. Philosophically one begins with the observation of the operations of sensorily given things, making inferences from that givenness to the set of underlying powers exhibited in the observed operations, and then to the unifying character of the essence that makes all that possible. One also learns to reflect upon one's own operations when making observations and inferences about things and from that to infer one's own powers and the essential ground of those powers. One can proceed from such activities on the object- and subject-side of the field of awareness and infer the character of the ultimate unifying Ground that makes possible the kinds of objects and the kinds of subjects found in experience.

Aquinas practices what I like to call "the Thomistic two-step": a step in philosophy and then a step in theology, or sometimes the reverse, or sometimes several steps in one or the other, alternating throughout the work. Thus in the treatment of God, the first step is philosophical: what can be known of God by human reason without revelation. Then what can only be known through revelation: here he treats of the Trinity.

5.

What can be philosophically known, according to Aquinas, is the existence of God as the one who *is* being rather than *has* being. Technically expressed, God is *Ipsum Esse Subsistens*, his essence is to be and does not limit the degree to which he can be. Aquinas sees this as revealed in the Burning Bush story. When Moses asked Yahweh, "Whom should I say is sending me?" he received the reply, "I am Who am" or "He Who is." Aquinas takes this to mean, "I am the One Who *is* Being Itself" or "I am the one whose essence is to be" (I, 2, 3 [14–27] and I, 3, 4 [30–32]). Aquinas then works in the mode of revelation to examine the Trinity.

As a significant aside we might note that more recent translation has: "I will be there as which I will be there."[8] This does not provide metaphysical information to a not-so-metaphysically inclined Moses. It rather refuses a name by which Yahweh can be conjured. He will be there in whatever way he chooses. Moses's—and our—task is to pay attention. When Jesus came he chided the religious leaders for not attending to "the signs of the times."

At any rate, for Aquinas God is the One whose essence is to be; creatures are those whose essence limits the degree to which they can be. They *are* only by reason of the ongoing causality of God. This follows from the five ways in which creatures show their limitations: motion, efficient causality, contingency, hierarchy, and goal directedness. What alone can explain the limitation of beings in experience is a Being who is not limited: an absolutely Infinite Being we call God. This entails omniscience and omnipotence or the infinity of knowing and doing as well as infinite wisdom.

Some of the ways to prove God's existence depend upon the impossibility of an infinite series of moved movers. By reason of that impossibility, one is too quick to think about motion or causality as necessarily involving a beginning of time. Aquinas resolutely *rejects* such a conclusion (I, 46, 2, ad 7 [256]). A beginning of time is philosophically undecidable—in fact, if you remember, Aristotle rests his proof of the Unmoved Mover upon the premise of the *eternality* of the temporal world.

One might call a temporal series, one which you can trace backward and forward, "horizontal." In geometry there is another kind of causal series we might call, by contrast, "vertical." The theorems follow from and are grounded in the axioms and other more elementary theorems that perpetually intersect the temporal series in which instances of the theorems can be found. For Aquinas, the impossibility of an infinite series of moved movers refers to a like vertical series. Parallel to Aristotle, God as Unmoved Mover is the enduring ground of every finite thing, continually creating it, that is, sustaining it in being. I say "parallel" because Aristotle's God is not a Creator but an eternal exemplar. For Aquinas, all finite being requires an Absolutely Infinite Being as its Cause: One who has no restrictive essence, but whose essence is Being.

However, the notion of in-finity is an essentially negative notion. Its conceivability lies in the scope of reason that is oriented toward *all* being; its limitation lies in the power of reason that can reach into that totality

8. Martin Buber, biblical scholar, twentieth-century co-translator of the Hebrew Bible, in *Moses*, 48–55.

only by way of inference, from what is given in experience, to its ultimate Ground. What God is finally in himself as positive infinity we cannot know by reason alone. But then there is revelation (I, 12, 13 [95]). So Aquinas steps from philosophy to theology in the treatment of the inner life of God as the Trinity. That is entailed by the doctrine of the Incarnation. The inner Other than the Father as the Word, through whom all things were made, entered into the otherness of creation as Jesus Christ. The incarnate Word returned to the Father, resurrected, in order to send the Spirit, the bond of love between the Father and the Word, to establish the inner bond of love in the gathering of those who accept the Word.

6.

In the order of treatment of humanness, Aquinas does not proceed according to the order of knowing—from objects to operations to powers to essence—but the reverse. As a theologian, he moves "from the top down," from that in us which is closest to God—indeed, made in his image—to the lower levels. He begins with the claim to a separate existence for the human soul (I, 75, 2 [283–85]). But the evidences he appeals to in showing the essence of the soul will only be more fully fleshed out when he deals with the soul's operations. From the philosophical point of view, the human being belongs to the animal kingdom, but is differentiated through his rationality. From the theological point of view, the human being is the lowest among the intelligences (the "separate intelligences" being the angels, separated from bodies), requiring a body to furnish the sensory materials upon which it operates intellectually. From the latter point of view the human being is thus *incarnate spirit* who exists on the horizon between time and eternity.[9]

The incarnate character is exhibited in the culminating act of intellectual activity, namely the judgment. Following Aristotle's claims, Aquinas points out that apprehension of the universal and the combination of universals or of particulars and universals in judgments and inferences have a dual root. On the one hand there is that which first occurs within the intellect, name the notion of Being (I, 5, 2 [36]). The mind "shines the light of Being" upon the sensory so that the sensory is not only given but capable of being understood. The light refers us to the Whole that includes *the whole of space and time*. This allows us to see the type in the individual, the repeatability of the type *anytime and anyplace* individuals

9. SCG, ch. 61 [477].

of the type can be met. On the other hand, what judgment begins with are notions abstracted from sensory experience. And what it culminates in is a *recursio ad phantasmata*, a recurrence to unified sense experience (I, 85, 1 [400–405]). We might add that all the way along we think in terms of sensorily produced signs, namely words.

So we begin, as we did with "Phenomenology of the Mailbox," with various presentations of things "outside" through "proper sensibles." Making the same observations as Aristotle, Aquinas noted that each sensory power has its own proper object: for sight it is color, for hearing sound, etc. Actual experience is the spontaneous integration of sensations into an awareness of things as functioning wholes. The integrated object is termed a *phantasma*, etymologically related to the Greek *phainomenon*, an appearance. Intellectual activity abstracts from the sensory experience of individuals such specific notions as "red" and "green" and such generic notions as "color" and "extension." Extension is linked to the so-called common sensibles, that is, features presented to several senses in common. For example, one can *see* an extended object and *feel* its extension. Thus number, length, breadth, depth, and motion as common sensibles apply to the spatial and temporal properties of sensorily given things (I, 78, 1–4 [321–35]). This was all observed before by Aristotle.

Judgment refers the abstracted properties back to the sensorily given things as point of departure for reflective judgments regarding the acts of awareness, sensory and intellectual, involved in the manifestation of sensorily given things and regarding the abstract relations between the abstractions. The latter involve notions such as genus, species, and difference in conceptual relations, the types of judgment and their immediate implications, and the inferential relations between judgments. All of this furnishes the subject matter for the science of formal logic. Logic is the universal instrument not only for the development of the various sciences, but also for the thinking involved in everyday existence. It develops from the principle of noncontradiction: that a property cannot belong and not belong to the same thing at the same time and in the same respect. Such a principle, of unrestricted scope, occurs with the notion of Being as what first awakens in the mind. Because, like the notion of Being that it articulates, it has unrestricted scope, the principle of noncontradiction cannot come from the restricted things given sensorily from without, but comes with the awakening of the intellect itself.

The notion of Being, including all things in its scope, is the ground of both intellect and will. Referred to the Whole, we are able to abstract from the conditions of particular times and places to grasp the universality involved in sensory experience. Reference to the Whole as the fullness of being ultimately implicates a single infinite Fullness of Being of which all things created are finite imitations (I, 85, 1 and 2 [400–407]).

The central idea is the view of the rational soul not only as the inform-ing, *animating* principle of the body, but also as a substance in its own right (I, 75, 2, 4, and 6 [283–90]). This is based upon rationality as transcending the Here-and-Now of the organ-based relation to the sensory environ-ment because one is able to grasp meanings, incarnated in the sound of words which apply *always-and-everywhere* throughout the whole of space and time where the conditions for their instantiation are met. The appre-hended form is found individuated in spatiotemporally located individuals (include one's own individual body). The principle that grounds spatio-temporal existence is *materiality*, originally posited as principle of change under different forms. Spread out in space, a material thing can come apart and come together over time. One can apprehend the formal and material *principles* involved by abstraction from materiality and thus spatiotemporal location. At the level of intellectual operation, this involves our own being abstracted from the Here-and-Now. Aquinas describes this situation as one of *intrinsic* independence of material conditions at the level of intellectual operation and simultaneous *extrinsic* dependence upon sensation and thus embodiment for the presentation of things to be understood.

This follows from the soul's being in a way all things by reason of the notion of Being that is the first notion to arise in the mind. This allows Aqui-nas to describe the human soul as situated on the horizon between time and eternity because, though inserted into space and time in relation to the sensing organism, the notion of Being encompasses time. The notion of Be-ing put us in a space of meaning that is identical for all rational agents. Such an insight is linked to Aristotle's notion of the light of the *nous poietikos* or "making" intellect that was understood by the Islamic commentators Avi-cenna and Averroes to involve a separate Intellect, one for all humankind. This follows Aristotle's claim that such an intellect is "separate, unmixed, coming from without." The Latin translation as *intellectus agens*—translated in turn into English as *agent intellect*—changed the scope of the Greek ex-pression: though agency can also be a making, agency is too wide to cover the explicit meaning of the Greek expression. Aquinas observed that unless we each had our own *intellectus agens*, a separate Intellect's shining upon our sensory experience would make us able to be understood, not able to understand. It would be parallel to a light shining upon a wall that makes the wall visible to those who have the power to see, but would only make the wall *able to be seen*, not *able to see*. But in the end, since all creatures participate in the divine Being, our own individual agent intellects are the way in which the rational creature participates in the divine Light (I, 79, 4 and 5 [343–48]). Things can be understood because they are created by divine Intellect; they can be understood by us because we share in the divine Light and are made in the divine image. Though sensation presents things as separate identities, they are united in the Divine Ground. Being in the Divine Ground for us is being intellectual beings who, as Aquinas said, by nature implicitly know God, but not, to begin with, as God (I, 2, 1, ad 1 [22]). We need to develop proof by beginning with sensory life.

Aquinas also developed Aristotle's notion of *boulesis*, of willing, in the direction of free self-determination. In Aristotle, dynamism follows form. At the level of animals and humans, the apprehension of form involves the evocation of appetite. The appetite that follows intellectual apprehension is the will. For Aquinas, the *primum cognitum*, the notion of Being as first known, refers to everything and thus affords primordial distance from every finite determination. Referred to the Whole, we are free to determine ourselves within the limits of the concrete possibilities afforded by our own prior determinations. Aquinas understands this as involving a natural desire to see God.[10] But were we able to "see God face to face," our will would be related as a falling stone to the ground, unable to resist the natural attraction. However, lacking that in this life, our relation to the divine is indirect, through faith and inference. Consequently, we are free, not only with respect to finite beings, but also with respect to God himself. These observations ground Augustine's claim: "You have made us for Yourself, O Lord. And our hearts are restless and will not rest until they rest in You." Aquinas's observation displays the basic ground for the possibility of free self-disposal of a finite being: through human finitude's being by nature open to, and directed toward the Infinite via the notion of Being.

Such reference entails a *natural* desire for eternity because will as appetite follows intellect as form oriented toward the all-inclusive. Aquinas argues that since natural desires are not in vain, the human soul, by reason of its highest powers, is immortal. By nature it is not "matter-immersed,"

10. *SCG*, 68 [463–67].

though it is necessarily matter-related. It requires a necessary relation to matter because of its starting point in sensation and continual point of reference by recurrence to phantasms. In its native makeup the intellectual power of the soul has "an extrinsic (but necessary) relation to matter" but "an intrinsic freedom from matter" in essence and operation. Aquinas infers from this both personal immortality and the requirement of the resurrection of the body. Even in separation from the body after death, the human soul still retains its native relation to embodiment. This meets with the proclamation of faith that the body will rise again "on the last day

There is another conclusion Aquinas derives from the basic structure of humanness as incarnate reference to the Fullness of Being. He invokes a distinction between the power and the scope of the human intellect.[11] Because it thinks within the horizon of Being, everything—including God—lies within the scope of the intellect. However, we have the power to advance toward that scope only by inference from what we can come to know through bodily based experience, that is, through sensation. The inferential power attributes all positive perfections to God as Infinite Cause of the perfections found in finite beings. But as in-finite, the notion of God requires a negation of the limitation involved in the perfections found in finite things and an affirmation of them as in infinite identity with God. Aquinas concludes that we know best about God when we are aware that we do not know adequately about God. An infinite light in himself, he is hidden in a cloud of ultimate darkness for us. Paralleling Aristotle, our mind is to the Ultimate Intelligible as the eyes of the owl are to the sun.

The distinction between the power of the intellect that depends upon inference from the finite to the In-finite and the scope of the intellect that includes the Infinite in principle though not in fact, opens up the possibility, given through revelation, that God might expand the power to reach the scope. That is how Aquinas understands the biblical "light of glory."[12] Natively our "restless heart" seeks the Face of God, but we cannot encounter that Face without God's free elevation of our nature. A personal relation can only be achieved through free self-donation on the part of each partner.

One might add that human existence as the finite creature open to the infinite Creator, occupying the dividing line between time and eternity, is the creaturely condition for the possibility of the God-Man, just as the internal differentiation between the Word as the Other than the Father is

11. *SCG*, 54 [475].

12. *SCG*, 53 [473].

the divine condition for the possibility both of there being something other than the Father ("through him all things were made") and for God himself entering into the otherness of creation in the God-Man ("and the Word was made flesh"). Again we see the close connection Aquinas sees between what is available philosophically and what is given by way of revelation.

7.

In the journey to eternity and the expectation of the resurrection along the way, reason is able to discern certain necessary conditions for the fulfillment of human nature that constitute the so-called "natural moral law" that is "written on our hearts." The first principle (so-called "*synderesis*") is "Do good and avoid evil" (I, 94, 2 [637–38]). The way to embody that moral law concretely is through the development of virtues.

Virtues are modes of self-possession that allow one to act without inner constraint in relation to the requirements of situations and thus to achieve maximal flourishing as a human being. They serve the intrinsic goals of humanness specified in a general way in natural moral law. The Ten Commandments are applications of the fundamental natural law principles. We will consider, in turn, the virtues, natural moral law, and the Ten Commandments.

The personal conditions for flourishing are what come to be called *the cardinal virtues*, each a hinge (Latin *cardo*) of a full human life. (Here we refer to the line from Plato through Aristotle to Aquinas.) As Nietzsche was fond of noting, any significant human achievement depends upon bringing order into the chaos of natural appetites. Though animals may safely follow their instinctive urges and so fulfill their own wellbeing and that of their offspring, in attempting the same humans only become chaotic. The reason lies in the ontological pole of our being: referred to the Whole via the notion of Being, we are pried loose from anything less that the Whole and are "condemned to choose." We are given over to ourselves to shape what is given in us by nature. It is up to us to shape our appetitive life in the light of our higher commitments. So the premise of all significant human achievement is temperance or *sophrosune*, which Aristotle etymologizes as *sozein phronesin* or preserving your *phronesis*, the capacity for intelligent self-direction.

That capacity is the pivot of the whole of one's life. It is learning to keep one's balance in surfing through the contingencies of life. It is the capacity for sizing up situations and finding the right thing to do. It presupposes temperance learned typically through disciplined upbringing. Parental orders teach the young child that it does not have to follow its appetites but can direct itself according to principle. That is the condition for the rational development of the child, freeing him or her from being governed by appetites so that he or she can be free to govern him/herself.

The exercise of *phronesis*, which is distinct from *cunning*, depends upon the virtue of *justice*, the fixed disposition to give each person one encounters its due. Of course, what that means has to be determined by the practices of a community that can be criticized in terms of consistency of principles and applications and consistency of a community's principles with those that are required for maximum rational flourishing. The notion of justice should be extended intellectually as the fixed disposition to give each interlocutor and each position its fair reading, holding oneself open to being corrected in misunderstanding another or overlooking significant principles, correction that might emerge from dialogical encounter. Acting rightly in situations requires also the fixed disposition to overcome whatever hardships may stand in the way. Thus practical wisdom, temperance, justice, and fortitude constitute the foundations of a rationally free human life.

Virtuous existence occurs in terms of the ends set by the levels of human structure: preservation of one's own life, care for one's offspring, living in community, and seeking truth. The further application of these natural imperatives can, by the exercise of reason, lead to variations on the traditional Ten Commandments. These are imperatives that follow from those built into the levels of human structure. (Here we will align them with natural moral law principles.)

8.

In considering the overall structure of humanness, we found that it is bipolar. One pole is the organism generating the field of sensation guided by the needs of the organism. The other pole is established by the notion of Being, the first notion to arise within the mind; it refers us, albeit initially in an empty way, toward the whole of what-is, for outside being there is nothing. The imperative that follows from this pole is: *Seek the truth.* Actually, this is the first specification in terms of intellectual operation of the most fundamental imperative: Do good and avoid evil. Good and evil are determined by how we relate to the conditions for human flourishing. Truth would be the good and error the evil proper to intellectual flourishing.

In seeking the truth, when we consider the overall framework set up by the notion of Being, the question that emerges is: Is the totality of being the sum of finite beings, hierarchically arranged? Or is there something beyond the finite, an In-finite Being? This question emerges because we can always ask of any putative limit to the cosmos, whether there is something that stands beyond the limit. Stephen Hawking proclaims that asking whether there was time before the Big Bang or space beyond the expanding universe are meaningless questions. But they are not meaningless, and that is because we are oriented toward space and time as indeterminately encompassing forms that we bring to bear upon experience. It is this orientation that allows us to abstract universal meaning, meaning that applies *anytime and anyplace* we find its instances in the Here-and-Now of sensory experience. That orientation toward space and time as empty encompassing wholes, in turn, is rooted in our being projected toward being as a whole, even beyond space and time. Because we are oriented toward the Totality, we can always ask whether what occurs within Hawking's stipulative limits is all there is.

So there are three a priori forms that we bring to bear upon experience: the notion of Being as referred to the Totality, potentially infinite, and space and time as indeterminately encompassing forms. Because of the functioning of the a priori notion of Being in us, we can ask whether there is something beyond any putative limit, indeed whether there might be something beyond the totality of finite being. Is there something which, positively and in its own nature, corresponds to what we grasp negatively as in-finite possibility? The question then emerges as to how finite being can be at all, since being is potentially infinite. And the answer that presents itself: only because absolutely Infinite Being continually gives being to everything finite. Because we are oriented toward the Infinite, finite being presents itself as needing a cause of the limitation of being whose nature is infinite.

When we think of infinite being, we think it as contrasted with finite being; that is why we call it in-finite. However, if we think of *absolutely* infinite Being, it would of necessity have to include finite being, else it would be limited to one side of the finite-infinite distinction. (Here Hegel comes into play.) If there are "gods," they would be "angelic beings," good or evil, great but still finite beings, themselves grounded in the single absolute, infinite fullness of Being. There can only be one such Being, since by its nature it includes everything else, which is necessarily finite. Such inclusion means both that, as absolutely Infinite Being, It completely transcends all finitude and yet is completely immanent in each thing. It is right to call it "God." As Augustine said, he is closer to me than I am to myself. And as St. Paul has it: "In Him we live and move and have our being." As correlate to our reference to Being, he would be "He Who Is" and "He whom my heart seeks."

As absolutely unrestricted, such a Being would have to be omniscient, omnipotent, and all-wise. Nothing escapes him because his knowing and choosing sustains creatures in being and thus he is all powerful. And the interrelatedness of things shows something of his infinite wisdom. As the ground of all finite Being through whose generosity we exist, such a Being deserves our praise and thanks: hence the imperative, *Worship God.*

Seeking the truth is possible for a rational being only through belonging to an antecedent community. We can think at all because we have language through the induction into which we are able to be inducted into all the practices of a given community. Not only is language required for rational development, but also for a developed tradition of inquiry that learns to sort out what is given in experience and to develop modes of explanation. So truth-seeking involves the imperative: *Live in community.* (We will come back to that shortly.)

Following out the imperative to seek the truth, we come to two primary commandments as the first of several imperatives derived from the deepest stem of human existence, namely, human rationality: (1) *There is but one God who gives us being* and thus *He deserves our worship,* that is, our appreciation and service. There is nothing that could be called "God" as the Fullness of Being besides this One. Now, (2) the second commandment, to *Keep holy the Sabbath,* would not be a natural imperative, but a determination of such an imperative, something peculiar to the Hebrew tradition; however, it spells out for a people a way to situate worship of God as a primary response.

Living in community is not simply a prerequisite for rational development; it is the condition for raising one's offspring to be participants in the life of the community—eventually the community of humankind. It follows from the immanent goal of sexual relations: *procreation and care for offspring.* The seven commandments that pertain to interhuman relations spell out the conditions for the possibility of living in community in such a way as to pass on the developments that emerge from past generations. So the first commandment in this regard would be: (4) *Honor your father and mother*, that is, respect them and through them the tradition that they have mediated to you, the tradition that gives you your concrete possibilities of development. Along with acknowledgment and worship of God, this is the only other positive commandment.

Then, if we are to live in community, (5) we certainly cannot kill each other or (7) steal from one another or (6) take our neighbor's spouse for ourselves. Indeed, we should not even (9 and 10) *think* about stealing and committing adultery, for the thought is father to the deed.

There is one more commandment relating to the neighbor: (8) *You shall not bear false witness*, that is, lie in such a way as to harm your neighbor. It is linked to another commandment that pertains to our relation to God: (3) *You shall not take the name of the Lord your God in vain.* I take that to mean: do not swear by God in bearing false witness against your neighbor and compound the evil by directly falsifying your relation to God.

Keeping the totality of these commandments makes one a just man. However, with regard to one's neighbor, the commandments are negative: they establish a fence around the area of human action. We might add that what happens within that area is found in the proclamations of Jesus as the grounding of these commandments in the dual commandment of love: Love the Lord, whom you justly praise and thank, with your whole being; and love your neighbor as yourself. The second is the way to the first: "How can you love God whom you cannot see if you do not love your neighbor whom you do see?" And the second presupposes proper self-love, for one cannot love one's neighbor as oneself if one has contempt for oneself.

These developments constitute principles of human development rooted in permanent features of human existence. They are developments of what comes to be called *natural moral law.* The commandments are secondary principles as applications of the imperatives built into the tri-level structure of humanness.

The command to preserve your own life and to live in community together govern such things as traffic laws. How can automobile traffic be governed in such a way as to maximize not only the efficiency of moving from place to place, but especially the safety of those who travel? One thing that has to be decided is on which side of the road to drive. There are two possibilities: in America the makers of our tradition decided to drive on the right side; in England and parts of Continental Europe, tradition-formers decided to drive on the left: two opposite laws governed by the same imperative.

The deepest level of human activity is seeking the truth that governs all the rest. Such seeking is directed to the ongoing pursuit of understanding the underlying reality of ourselves and the things we encounter in individual sensory actuality. Underlying that actuality are the natural powers of things, and underlying the sensory actuality of other humans are their states of mind and humanly developed skills, both practical and theoretical. Following out the truth imperative launches natural science as an ongoing, expansive, methodically self-corrective process. One might say that the modern specification of the natural law imperative to seek the truth, as formulated by C. S. Peirce, is: *Do not block the path of inquiry.*[13] This is a distinctively modern development that had to fight a long uphill battle against the religious establishments that thought they were in possession of the final truth of all things and consequently limited the things people could say, read, and write—and, with God as the inner spy, even what one could think.

Now the imperative involved in ongoing scientific inquiry has to be understood as itself operating within the principles that specify the dignity and rights of human beings. That is what is involved in the battle over abortion and abortifacients. Even though a fertilized ovum presents itself as a relatively incomplex cell, and detailed scientific investigation uncovers nothing but its relative complexity, nonetheless, it has, unobservable in principle, a set of powers that have been set in motion and that will terminate, unless inhibited, in an adult capable of reproduction and of freely directing itself. Failure to respect this being-underway is what is involved in abortifacients, in destroying fertilized ova for embryonic research, and for infertile couples in artificially producing embryos that are implanted in larger numbers than the desired birth, so that the weakest are destroyed.

This opens a very wide area that is beyond the scope of this presentation. One can see, however, that arguments can be launched for proper procedure in such areas on a natural law basis, not as a religiously sectarian enterprise, even though it is appropriated and even developed by the Roman Catholic Church. Arguing from religious revelation and tradition is not proper to the public forum; arguing from natural moral law as understood above is the only legitimate basis for public policy arguments in a religiously pluralistic society.

13. Pierce, "Scientific Attitude and Falliblism," 54.

Aquinas sees two ways in which natural moral law develops: by way of deduction and by way of application (I, 95, 2 [649]). The deductive leads the way to more concrete specifications of moral requirements as we reach toward the concrete situation. The way of application can take various turns, leading to a legitimate variety of cultures and of individual "lifestyles." To take a trivial example, burping before one's hostess would be understood in the West as extremely impolite, but in parts of the Middle East as an expression of appreciation for a good meal. There are various ways of applying the natural law deduction that living in a community entails showing gratitude for favors received and not giving unnecessary offense, especially to benefactors.

Conscience involves the intelligent assimilation of the tradition's self-understanding and its application to the changing character of individual circumstances. For Aquinas conscience is not a "still, small voice" that prompts us to keep the rules, but involves, as in Aristotle, reflective intelligence in its most alert state, sensitive to all the requirements of circumstances.[14] The community's prior understanding of the development of natural moral law as a set of universal prescriptions has to be applied to differing individual circumstances. And this is rendered possible only insofar as the one applying them has developed the cardinal virtues: fortitude, temperance, and justice pivoting around prudence as practical wisdom.

As we already noted, conscience is so important for Aquinas that he claims its absolutely binding character, even when erroneous. And that might entail following it, even if it dictates leaving the Church! But that also entails making the constant effort to inform one's conscience by being more intelligently alert to all the circumstances of human action. Just as faith must seek understanding, so conscience must seek its formation in the truth.

9.

The insights I have summarized and organized here are woven into the tight fabric of question, objection, answer, and replies structuring each *quaestio* in the systematic heuristic structure of the *Summa theologiae*. Since the Council of Trent (1545–63) that work has superseded Peter Lombard's *Sentences* as the basic text for training Catholic theologians. But the *Summa* also contains a way of developing the central insights, anthropological,

14. *ST* I, 79.

ethical, epistemological, and metaphysical, in the preceding thinkers, both pagan and Christian. Aquinas was on the cutting edge of the Catholic and largely Augustinian tradition. He was able both to assimilate it and to step out of it in order to enter into sympathetic commentary upon a newly available tradition grounded in pagan antiquity, that of Aristotle. This allowed him to bring the tradition forward by assimilating the new insights available from a perspective different than the largely Augustine-based tradition in which he was raised.[15] In doing this he furnishes the strongest example of a Catholic intellectual.

In his encyclical of 1879, *Aeterni Patris*, Pope Leo XIII recommended to Catholic thinkers a retrieval of the Scholastic tradition, with a special emphasis upon the study of the Angelic Doctor. Pope Pius X made mandatory to Catholic philosophers and theologians the defense of twenty-four Thomistic theses and the sealing of that allegiance with an oath—something John Paul II expressly rejected. Fortunately for the objective study of Aquinas, Vatican II removed that mandate, for it entailed, not the development of reason, but the development of rationalization and a closing of the mind to what might lie outside of the Thomistic perspective, rich as it might be. Vatican II opened up the Catholic mind to the modern world to which the actions of previous papal teaching had closed it. Now we can more fully appreciate Aquinas as a philosopher rather than an ideologist.

QUESTIONS

1. Aquinas puts together the Augustinian-Neoplatonic approach with the new Aristotelian approach. How did he do that, and what were the problems with each of the approaches? Why did several bishops condemn Aristotle?

2. What is the relation between faith and reason?

3. What is the status of conscience with regard to the individual and with regard to political authority?

4. What can we know about God from reason alone and what are its limits?

5. Several of his ways to prove God's existence appeal to the impossibility of an infinite series of moved movers. Explain.

15. See MacIntyre, *Three Rival Versions of Moral Inquiry*, 127–48.

6. Explain Aquinas's view of the rational soul being "substance as form of the body." How does that relate to the afterlife?

7. What is the basis for the freedom of the will?

8. How does he develop the distinction between the power of intellect and its scope?

9. Link his assimilation of Aristotle's view of the virtuous life with the Ten Commandments.

FURTHER READING

1. M. D. Chenu, *Toward Understanding St. Thomas.*

2. G. K. Chesterton, *St. Thomas Aquinas: The Dumb Ox.*

3. Etienne Gilson, *The Christian Philosophy of St. Thomas Aquinas.*

4. Josef Pieper, *The Silence of St. Thomas.*

* * * *

DESCARTES'S *DISCOURSE*
ON METHOD

Instead of that speculative Philosophy found in the Schools,
we may find a practical Philosophy . . . and thus render ourselves the masters and possessors of nature.

—*DISCOURSE ON METHOD*, PART VI

READING

René Descartes, *Discourse on Method*, translated by Donald
Cress. This edition is available together with the *Meditations on
First Philosophy* which expands the argument that is compressed
in part 4 of the *Discourse*.

1.

René Descartes (1596–1650) lived in a time of great change characterized
by the Thirty Years' War (1618–1648) and the rise of modern science.
The former was the result of the fracture of Christendom brought about
by Martin Luther's challenge, beginning in 1517, to the corruption of the
Roman Catholic Church. Banners at the celebration of Leo X's coronation
as pope carried the inscription: "First Mars, then Venus, now Apollo." It
referred to the reign of Julius II (Mars, god of war) who lived in his armor
and extended the papal states; of Alexander VI (Venus, goddess of love),
the Borgia Pope whose throne was surrounded by his mistresses and who
elevated his "nephews" to the cardinalate; and to Leo himself (Apollo,

god of the arts, among other things) who was a sponsor of the arts and who, upon his coronation said: "The Lord has given us the papacy and we intend to enjoy it."

Many German princes took up Luther's challenge against such corruption; many did not. This led to bitter religious wars with people slaughtering one another in the name of the Prince of Peace. After the exhaustion of thirty years, the Peace of Westphalia settled the issue according to the maxim, *Cuius regio eius religio*, "Whose realm (it is), his religion (will prevail)." Catholics migrated from Protestant realms and Protestants from Catholic realms; but there was intermingling. Descartes, a Roman Catholic, was involved in the struggle as a mercenary to the Protestant Prince of Nassau.

The second element of overriding significance in Europe at the time was the rise of modern science. Copernicus's *On the Revolutions of the Heavenly Bodies* in 1543 challenged the prevailing view that the earth was the center of the universe. Kepler's careful charting of the movements of the heavenly bodies gave support to the new theory. The theory displaced common sense observations that clearly showed, and still show, the revolution of the sun around the earth. The new theory clarified and unified otherwise anomalous phenomena. In this case, the observed paths of the planets, named "the wanderers" (*planetes*) by the Greeks, which displayed very irregular paths, moving now in one direction, now another, were erratic and thus "irrational" compared to the regular circular motion of the sun and the moon. Taking the sun as the center, the planets ceased appearing to wander and were conceivable now as moving in regular, though elliptical, paths around the sun. So modern science took its rise by the displacement of the common sense evidence that the sun circled about the earth: heliocentrism replaced geocentrism.

Galileo (d. 1632) came on the scene both as a supporter of the new view and as a pioneer in terrestrial mechanics, studying such phenomena as falling bodies, the swing of the pendulum, and the movement of balls down inclined planes. He was forced by the Roman church to recant his astronomical views and was imprisoned (not, one might add, in a dank, rat-infested dungeon chained to the wall, but in a suite at the Vatican with a butler and with access to the Vatican Gardens). The same year Galileo died Newton was born, and it was Newton's *Principia Mathematica* in 1687 that put celestial and terrestrial mechanics together into a single system to produce early modern physics' view of "the clockwork universe."

Descartes played a significant role in relation to both of these cultural elements. The upshot of the fracturing of Christendom was a search for a new foundation for the togetherness of people since the old religious foundation was tearing people apart. The new science cut across religious boundaries and appealed, not to tradition, belief, and authority, but to evidence brought together in a consistent system. Descartes himself contributed to this science, first by the invention of analytical geometry, a method of translating geometric figures into equations through plotting of figures on a grid of squares oriented by what came to be called, after him, "Cartesian coordinates." But he also attempted to lay the foundations for a new mathematical physics. Now there were mathematical physical inquiries in past ages: optics, harmonics, and astronomy. But in the prevailing Aristotelian view, they were "intermediary sciences" between cosmology and mathematics proper. They worked with quantitative form abstracted from the full reality of things made concrete by substantial form and, in the case of living things, made such by their souls organizing matter. As Descartes envisioned it, the new mathematical physics would be an *ontology*, a science of the very *being* (Greek *ontos*) of nature, unveiling, not, as with the Aristotelians, an abstracted aspect, but the full reality of what natural things were. The Aristotelian-Thomistic view of substantial forms working teleologically upon the elements to realize their own immanent goals were eliminated and from then on, the way in which mechanical processes worked were taken to explain wholly the structure and behavior of all bodies.

Faced with the dissolution of the religious sources of legitimation for human togetherness, Descartes observed that cities designed by a single architectural planner showed more coherence than those that simply grew up over time haphazardly and that cities governed by laws promulgated by a single lawgiver, like Lycurgus in Sparta and Solon in Athens, operated in a more orderly fashion than those that did not (Part Two, 12).[1] Descartes proposed to raze the old "scientific" buildings, the haphazard growth of differing opinions over the time of long traditions and, using some of the materials that remained, to reconstruct the field of knowledge as a whole according to a single unified method.

---

1. Internal references are to the *Discourse on Method*, other footnotes to other works. Since there are many translations of Descartes's works, scholarly editions have, in the margins, the page numbers to the critical edition of his works by Adam and Tannery in 1965. We will refer to those page numbers preceded by the part (chapter) number.

This attempt set in motion the Enlightenment's search for a "natural religion" and Lessing's claim that all positive religions were heretics from natural religion, specimens of which were being made available from the Far East.[2] Leibniz even suggested that, though we might send missionaries to the Chinese to teach them about salvation, they also should send missionaries to us to teach us how to live with one another![3]

Descartes noted that, although his own study of the classics brought him into conversation with the greatest minds of the past, one could find no basic agreement among them. He himself chose to write in his native French rather than in Latin, the language of book-learning, so that he could appeal, not to past authority, but to the evidence available to any unbiased observer. Looking back over the history of philosophy, at first sight one sees only the history of warring opinions. Looking back over the history of mathematics, one sees the steady expansion of the house of mathematical thought, adding room after room as time goes on. Descartes himself built one of the new rooms. Mathematics furnishes the paradigm of responsible thought, giving clear and distinct definition to its axioms and postulates and proceeding step by step in its deductions to produce airtight arguments. Descartes proposed to lay the foundations for all the sciences by proceeding in a manner his follower Spinoza termed *more geometrico*, in the geometric mode.

Descartes appealed, not to book-learning, but to "good sense" as the power of judging rightly and distinguishing true from false; and good sense, he claimed, is evenly distributed (Part One, 2). Is this contrary to the obvious differences in intellectual capacity among humans? Or does it mean that everyone has the capacity to restrain his will until sufficient evidence is available? That would make more sense than denying evident differences in intellectual capacity. But this also entails an equality that, functioning with the method of critical doubt, dissolves social hierarchy, undermines monarchy and aristocracy, and sets the stage for democracy.

Descartes gave up on "book-learning" and resolved to read "the great book of the world" and to "search for no more knowledge than I could find within myself" (Part One, 9). He also noted that reasoning about things which are important to oneself and in which false reasoning costs dearly could produce more truth than private reasonings of a man of letters on matters which produced no effect (ibid.). That is why his

2. Lessing, *On the Education of the Human Race*, I §4.
3. See Meyer, *Leibniz and the Seventeenth Century Revolution*.

project was intended to culminate in a moral philosophy; but it did not begin with that. As with the ancients and medievals, Descartes noted that morality is rooted in human structure, and human structure is rooted in the structure of the cosmos.

As with Plato, he noted that the philosophic project begins by considering the human condition as one of dependency represented by prisoners chained from birth in a cave. As children, Descartes notes (Part Two, 13), we are led by appetites and teachers—parents, pastors, school teachers, and peers bound by traditions—what Freud later called the Super-ego that repressed the Id.[4]

Recur to our overall context of the I-Me relation: here again we have the genetic and cultural stamp, the shaping of instinctive urges by significant others. Descartes claimed that "it is more custom and example that persuades us than certain knowledge" (Part Two, 16). His aim was "to try once and for all to get all the beliefs I had accepted from birth out of my mind, so that once I have reconciled them with reason I might again set up either other, better ones or even the same ones" (Part Two, 13). His plan was to reform his thoughts on foundations completely his own, but to measure "his own" by appropriate evidence. Think here of Socrates's "Virtue is knowledge" and the obvious objection provided by situations where I know what to do, feel otherwise, and am consequently suspended in my decision. But what does "know" mean here? Would it not be better to say that "I remember what I have been told to do"? One thinks and acts largely in terms of what one has been taught. "Learning" consists to a great extent in remembering what others—"the greats" or "the authorities"—thought or think.

Recall Plato's analysis of the way *doxa* or common opinion, "the web of belief," functions. Think about science here, especially in terms of the pragmatic criterion of truth to which Descartes appealed. Both science and common sense rest upon the web of belief, and both of them "work." The difference seems to be that common sense is plural, depending upon the plurality of communities. But then, so is science historically plural, though it is sequentially developmental while common sense seems to be just plural. Science is expansive and methodologically self-corrective. Any theory is trumped by sufficient counterevidence. Yet in the wake of Descartes's appeal to humanity, common sense has come to recognize the abolition of slavery, equality of all persons before the law, and "inalienable rights" as

4. Freud, *The Ego and the Id*.

deductions from the transcending character of humanness as such. As both John Paul II and Benedict XVI have noted, these can be rightly regarded as items in the progress of humanity.[5]

Descartes proceeded with great confidence, claiming that there is nothing so far distant that one cannot finally reach nor so hidden that one cannot uncover it with the proper use of method (Part Two, 19). He recounted his early study of logic, geometry, and algebra. Logic, he claimed, serves more to explain to others and to speak without judgment than to discover. He searched for a method that embraces the advantages of those three and came up with several major *"rules for the direction of the mind"* (referred to as RDM in our chart below) (Part Two, 18–19).

The first rule was: "Never to accept anything as true that I did not know evidently to be so" and thus to avoid precipitous judgment and prejudice. This rule introduces what Hans-Georg Gadamer more recently called the Enlightenment "prejudice against prejudice."[6] But Gadamer noted that there are pre-judices, that is, pre-judgments that are enabling— the know-how of a functioning community, especially knowing how to use the ordinary language—and there are prejudices that are matters of blind closure, e.g., those of the Ku Klux Klan, that close one to their possible modification or subversion.

Descartes guided himself by the clarity and distinctness of principles that he found exhibited in an exemplary manner in mathematics. In *Principles of Philosophy* he distinguished *clarity*, as the explicit presence of any object to any attentive mind, from *distinctness*, as the presence of all features of that object.[7] He evoked these criteria especially in regard to the distinction between thought and extension as the principles of mind and things respectively. His second rule embodied the principle of analysis: divide up the difficulties into as many parts as possible so you can see all aspects of what has to be explained. The third rule followed from that: proceed in order from the simplest and move toward the more complex. It is the procedure of geometry: the more complex theorems depend upon the less complex, and ultimately upon the relative simples that are the axiomatic basis of the system. Descartes's final rule was to provide complete enumeration and general review. The aim of the latter was to hold together

---

5. Pope John Paul II, *Fides et Ratio* §18/64.

6. *Truth and Method*, 238–47.

7. *Principles of Philosophy*, vol. 1, part I, xlv. Henceforth, *PP*.

all of the elements and complex derivatives in a single view, to learn to contemplate what we prove.

We should not forget that the aim behind that aim was to secure a view of the universe as a whole in order to be able to direct human life rationally. There was to be a final moral code. But then the question was how to conduct oneself in the interim. For that he developed what he called a *"provisional moral code . . .* where one can be conveniently sheltered while working on the other building" (Part Three, 22–27).

In what consists the "sheltering"? First, protection from censure and sanctions provided by others, both as public opinion and as exercise of official power. Descartes was concerned about what happened to Galileo, but we might also think back to Socrates and to Jesus. (The *Discourse on Method* was written around 1637. Recall that Galileo died in 1632.) Descartes was more generally concerned with what was happening in the Thirty Years' War of 1618–48 where people were killing and being killed for their religious beliefs. The first principle was thus to obey the laws and customs and religion, governing oneself in all other matters by the most moderate opinions. Watch what the most sensible do rather than what they say, because they often do not know how their practices correspond to their explicit beliefs—a significant comment upon the ordinary operation of the mind in daily life. Following the most moderate observers of customary ways not only provides social insurance, it also aids in the conquest of the Id. So, secondly, Descartes also sought sheltering from the appetites, the storms of passion (the Id) which tend to obscure the all-important power of judgment. Hence his third moral principle was to control oneself (to which we will return below).

Descartes notes that "I placed among the excesses all of the promises by which one curtails something of one's freedom" since he observed nothing in life that remains the same and he was working at perfecting his judgments that might undercut what he early promised (Part Three, 24). Freedom here has to be thought in relation to his commitment to working at the perfecting of his judgments in terms of suitable evidence, not in terms of later claims to freedom from anything which might "cramp my lifestyle." What governs here is not free-floating "freedom" but appropriate evidence that frees the mind from ignorance.

His second moral principle was: "Be as firm and resolute in my actions as I could be, and to follow with no less constancy the most doubtful opinions, once I have decided on them, than if they were very certain." Since life requires action, we ought to follow the most probable course. Keeping himself from commitments which would curtail his freedom of inquiry has to do with his relations with others. Holding himself to courses of action, even if doubtful, has to do with learning to establish some kind of extension over time of his own ability to act. One might also consider resoluteness as the basic end, but temper that with the ability to assess the attainability or not of the particular goals to which one commits oneself and the relative worth of the goals proposed in the light of broader reflective experience. One thus retains one's freedom to withdraw from particular goals sought after sufficient reflective experience.

His third principle reads: "Try especially to conquer myself rather than fortune, to change my desires rather than the order of the world." Long meditation is required to become accustomed to looking at things from this point of view. Philosophers have practiced this and viewed themselves happier than others because of it. Students regularly take "fortune" to be "wealth" rather than—as Descartes intended—external circumstance. What Descartes offers is basically a Stoic view. It is rooted in the observation of the contingent character of all external success that depends upon health and favorable circumstances, over both of which one has no ultimate control. But—provided one has lucidity of mind (and this also indicates the contingency of human control)—one can learn to master oneself, to take up one's own inner attitude toward one's circumstances, to fix one's attention upon what lasts, and to work toward significant goals. This retirement from the attempt to control the exterior is provisional. The ultimate goal is "to become lords and masters of nature."

His fourth and final principle was personal: Review occupations so as to choose the best one. "Best" has to be seen in relation to what suited his own peculiar gifts. He concluded his provisional moral code with the note: along with the truths of faith, keep these maxims and rid oneself of all other opinions (Part Three, 28). Believers have seen Descartes's relation to truths of faith as a matter of taking out "social insurance." Some have even argued that Descartes was an atheist! But since Christian believers were doing such naturally abhorrent things—and they had been doing them ever since they got political power back in the days of the Roman Emperor Constantine in the fourth century who converted to Christianity—it is wise to look to discovering and establishing institutions for implementing naturally available truths that allow people to benefit each other mutually. Hence the

Enlightenment's battle to separate the Church and political power, finally recognized in Vatican II after centuries of papal resistance.[8]

2.

Descartes's major interest was in developing the new science for which he attempted to lay the metaphysical foundations, placing science within the largest possible framework. For that he needed a view of nature, of the soul, and of God. In the fourth part of the *Discourse on Method* (31–40) he summarized the arguments he developed in more detail in his *Meditations on First Philosophy*. The path of argumentation follows the direction given by Plato's Cave and Line of Knowledge.

As we have noted, we find ourselves in the Cave of sensation and tradition, having first been determined by our appetites and our teachers. Being freed from our chains and having our heads turned completely around in reflection, we are able to understand both how the opinions and practices were generated and the nature of our sensory involvement in things. Both sensing and opinion present us with *appearance* relative to our sensing equipment and our point of view, but not with full being. The first step out of the Cave is mathematics, an instance of which is provided by the Line of Knowledge, a proportionally drawn *visible* line subdivided by the same proportion and exhibiting the *intelligible theorem* that the central segments would always be equal. This invites a meta-mathematical (beyond mathematics as *meta-physics* is beyond physics) reflection upon the "Forms," the eidetic differences between a visible (the seen line) and an intelligible (the theorem it instantiates). This reflection is located metaphorically at the fourth level of the Line, together with mathematics at the third level after the first great cut dividing visible and intelligible. Plato used the distinction between visible and intelligible to reflect upon the eidetic features of the distinction of and relation between sense and intellect. (Our by now infamous "Phenomenology of the Mailbox" worked at filling in some of the features of this fourth level.)

Descartes followed Plato's lead out of the Cave with mathematics as the paradigm of responsible scientific thought. Both he and Plato were looking for stability in the flux of sensation and opinion. But Descartes sought an

---

8. Compare the "Declaration on Human Freedom" from Vatican II with the "Syllabus of Errors" of Pius IX. "The Church Today," *Documents of Vatican II*, 183–316. *Popes Against Modern Errors*, 27–39.

even greater stability than Plato: he sought *absolute certitude*. For this reason he devised a special method: methodic doubt. Note that it is a *methodic* and not a "real" doubt. It functions as a kind of intellectual sorting device, determining levels of certitude. It functions, first of all, by putting out of play all previous *doxa*, all insufficiently substantiated opinion.

As for Plato, so for Descartes, the sensory world was the first to undergo criticism. Copernicanism cast doubt about the reliability of the immediate deliverance of the senses for theoretical purposes. The readily verifiable movement of the sun around the earth is only apparent. Furthermore, studies in physics and physiology showed that seeing, for example, required a causal series from light sources with light partially absorbed, partially reflected by objects, passing through the lenses in the eyeballs to their retinas and on to the visual center in the back of the brain. It seemed obvious that—again, contrary to immediate experience where color appears to be "on" the things appearing "outside"—color sensation was a psychic effect produced by the causal series inside the head of the observer. So color, sound, smell, and the like are not "in" or "on" things as they appear, but are only "in" the awareness, inside the observer. The world of sensory experience is only apparent. Again, there are perspectival distortions, optical illusions, hallucinations, and dreams. There is the phenomenon of "the phantom limb": patients with a severed leg still feel sensations where their foot used to be. In the dream state in particular, the objects presented are every bit as charged with the index of "reality" as is the wakeful world. Descartes's conclusion was that *for theoretical purposes* the sense world was not *absolutely* reliable. So he began his ascent out of the Cave.

Mathematics was Plato's index of "true being" because it just "is" and is not mixed with the nonbeing of past and future involved in changing things. But Descartes applied the methodic doubt even to mathematics, appealing to a very wild hypothesis: that of the "evil genius" who might be thought of as manipulating my brain to make me *think* that I am carrying out rigorous demonstrations when I am not.[9] The wildness has a quite sober point: mathematics is not *absolutely* indubitable. One might say, so what? *Nothing* is *absolutely* indubitable!

Descartes's ultimate aim is to make it obvious that there *is* something so indubitable: the self-presence of awareness to itself, even when it is deceived about any given object, as well as what is necessarily entailed in that observation. Hence his famous dictum: *Cogito ergo sum*, I think, therefore

9. Descartes, *Meditations of First Philosophy*, First Meditation, 22.

I am. This is the beginning of the modern focus upon subjectivity that John Paul II saw as an essential achievement of modern philosophy, one of modernity's "precious insights."

In this way Descartes goes beyond Plato's focus upon intellect and sense as powers of the soul to the individual as conscious user of these powers. Though each human is such an I and, as such, a unique center of responsibility, it has this "being a unique I" as a feature common to all humans.

Descartes practices *methodical* doubt, not real doubt. As he said, no one in his right mind would really doubt the *reality* of the external world, though the status of its appearance is not its reality.[10] Doubt is a *method*, a sorting device to determine levels of certitude in experience. Before him, Augustine, in his famous *Si fallor sum*, "If I doubt I am," made the same observation that led to Descartes's discovery of the *cogito*.[11] For Augustine it was an isolated insight; for Descartes it was the beginning of a system.

The very task of philosophy is to probe beneath the web of *doxa*, the belief systems that hold everything else in place for a given society, in order to discover the unavoidably given evidences upon which everything else depends, and to make solid inferences from there. The theologian operates in the interplay between that practice and the claims of revelation along with the tradition of its interpretation.

Attend to the *Cogito ergo sum*. There are three increasingly more comprehensive levels to consider here: the individual conscious I, here-and-now aware of itself, the universality of the co-implication of awareness and existence, and the *sum*, the instantiation of being in this instance of that type. The *cogito* displays the uniqueness of the I as the pivot for the appearance of things, the pivot around which every manifest truth arranges itself. But the *cogito* is an eidetic discovery—a truth for any possible consciousness—and not the record of a private episode in the life of René Descartes. The eidetic character is linked to the *sum*, the "I am," the contraction of the meaning of being to *this kind of* being, and, indeed, to *this particular being* pre-reflectively self-present in any state of awareness. The *sum*, invoking the mind's "being in a way all things" by thinking of Being generally or Being absolutely, indicates the encompassing field of intellectual operation. (Remember the question, What's it *all* about? as following from the unrestricted, but initially empty notion of Being.)

10. Sixth Meditation, 90.

11. Augustine, *City of God*, Book XI, section 26.

Descartes appeals here to the traditional notion of the *lumen naturale,* the "natural light," which he claims never to have doubted.[12] Though he does not say this, a reason for it can be advanced: that this alone can ground the eidetic recognition involved in the *cogito* and in every other universal truth. Being, identity, and the principle of noncontradiction provided by the "natural light" are principles of unrestricted scope.[13] But this also provides the notion of perfect, infinite being by which Descartes attempts to ascend beyond his methodological confinement to the initial discovery of the indubitability of the *cogito*. Without the intellectual equipment needed to carry on an intelligent dialogue with oneself and to engage in methodical inquiry, nothing intelligible could be discovered. So what Descartes arrives at is not the bare I but the rational subject with the *lumen naturale.* In his *Lectures on the History of Philosophy*, Hegel exclaimed that with this discovery of the *cogito*, philosophy at last reaches solid land, safe from the sea of opinions that hitherto buffeted it.[14]

In the *Meditations* Descartes expanded on what he meant by the *cogito*. It includes the whole field of consciousness: sensing, feeling, desiring, imagining, remembering, doubting, judging, choosing.[15] It has properties of privacy and inwardness that clearly distinguish it from the character of bodily extension. Descartes concludes that thinking in the wide sense of awareness in general is a distinct substance, hence something that can survive the dissolution of the body.

Methodologically confined within the *cogito* to begin with, Descartes also observed that, whatever our acts of awareness might deliver, I also cannot doubt that they *seem* to deliver a world independent of my awareness.[16] Here is where Edmund Husserl, in his *Cartesian Meditations*, claimed that Descartes discovered a new field for exploration, precisely the field of phenomenology.[17] It was what we began to explore in "Phenomenology of the Mailbox": the field of immediate and indubitable deliverances to consciousness of the multiple essential ways in which things appear and the various acts of awareness in which they appear. Husserl undertook the equivalent of the Cartesian doubt to bracket or suspend any theoretical claims about what

12. Third Meditation, 29.

13. John Paul II, *Fides et Ratio*, section 4, 12.

14. Hegel, *Lectures on the History of Philosophy*, 3:31.

15. Second Meditation, 28.

16. Second Meditation, 29.

17. Edund Husserl, *Cartesian Meditations*, §10, 23–24.

things *ultimately* are in order to pay careful attention to the eidetic features of how they appear to awareness. The inventory Descartes provided when he articulated what he meant by the *cogito* is precisely the field of conscious acts that are the bases for distinctively different modes of appearance. The description of the essential features of these different acts and their correlation with different objects is the task of phenomenology as proto-science. It is a new "first philosophy"—though it had been practiced since Plato's Line of Knowledge. Its task is the delineation of the factual presupposition of any human activity: the structure of the field of awareness.

Descartes—following Galileo and Kepler before him, and followed in turn by Newton, the Empiricists, and Kant after him—made the theoretical claim that the sensory features of the world were effects in the private inwardness of consciousness brought about by wave agitations in the field of bodily extension. The real properties, the so-called *primary qualities*, of bodies were the quantitative, the measurable properties. The sensory features were *secondary qualities* produced inside consciousness by the activity of the primary qualities upon the sense organs.[18] Note that this parallels Aristotle, who distinguished proper and common sensibles and claimed that, as basic quantitative features, the latter were more basic to the bodily thing perceived than the former which depend upon a relation to the perceiver. The radical difference lies in Aristotle's rejection of the notion of private inwardness and the mere subjectivity of the sensory qualities. For Aristotle, sense qualities are distinctive relations, relations of *manifestness* between bodies in the environment of an animal body and animal awareness operating through bodily organs: sensations take the perceiver *out of* its privacy and put it in relation to the things surrounding it.

As the line of development of Empiricism from Locke through Berkeley to Hume showed, the "inwardizing" or "subjectivizing" of sense qualities made insoluble the problem of how we get from our own private inwardness to the reality of the "outward" world so that we can know that objectively knowable wave-agitation produces sensation. Kant later said that the scandal of modern thought was the inability to make that transition.[19] More recently, Heidegger claimed that the scandal was that philosophers thought it to be a problem, for we begin our reflective development of scientific and philosophic thought by reflecting back from our initial Being-in-the-world, finding ourselves in the midst of things with others,

18. *PP*, vol. I, part IV, CXCI–CXCVIII.
19. Kant, *Critique of Pure Reason*, B xl, 34n. Henceforth *CPR*.

living in a sensorily manifest environment and belonging to a linguistic community of shared meanings that makes possible an individual's "talking to himself" in thought.[20] Note that this *is* Descartes's starting point, as it is the starting point of Plato. But in both cases, the immediately given is shown to be factually mediated by the web of belief as a mode of mutual practical adjustment to the environment.

Descartes's cleavage of the field of reality into two sorts of finite substances made problematic the question of how matter can operate upon spirit. Spinoza claimed matter and thought are two sides of a single thing, Malebranche that physical impact was the occasion for God's production of a state of mind in us, Leibniz that the relation was pre-established with creation.[21] What this line of reflection provides us is not necessarily skepticism but an enhanced sense of *the mystery of sensory manifestness* and the correlative *mystery of awareness itself.* But beyond Locke and with Heidegger, the astonishing fact is not only that wave agitation produces sensations "in" us, but that what is shown thereby is shown "outside" us!

Descartes's way of cutting the field of awareness, operating with the notion of clear and distinct ideas, reduced bodies to their measurable properties and thereby eliminated the Aristotelian notion of soul with vegetative and sensient powers operating teleologically upon the elements. For Aristotle, the soul organizes the elements into a set of instruments for the purpose of activating the sensory powers in order to develop and sustain the individual and carry on the species. With the elimination of soul as inner organizing principle, the bodily was considered a distinct realm of measurable extension operating purely mechanically. The coming into being of different types of bodies could in principle be explained mechanically, beginning with extension and motion. In fact, Descartes laid the foundations for evolutionary theory in his claim that, given proto-matter and the laws of combination and separation, he could explain how the current universe was produced—though he grants as probable that God could have made it as it is from the beginning (Part V, 43). Given a mechanical explanation of everything physical, the function of "soul" was shrunk to distinctively human awareness; it became a distinct thought-substance causally interacting with an external mechanism, a position caricatured by Gilbert Ryle as the doctrine of "the ghost in the machine."[22] It is a view that still haunts us.

20. Heidegger, *Being and Time*, 190 (German 205).

21. Leibniz, *Monadology*, §80.

22. Ryle, *Concept of Mind*, 15–16.

Animals turn out to be sheer mechanisms, without awareness. It is considered "anthropomorphic" to read back into them something like humanly conscious states based on their overt behavior. The human body-machine turns out to be useful for providing those filtered appearances—dashboard knowledge—that make possible identification of food, mate, offspring or enemy. But one should not assume the same with regard to animals. Their howling in pain should be thought of as directly parallel to the blowing of a steam whistle under pressure!

All that we observe in animals can be explained in purely mechanical terms. But in humans, the observation of linguistic behavior indicates something more than mechanism (Part Five, 56–57). Human linguistic response is flexible, adapting to all contingencies. Those who want to claim the equivalency of animal use of signals or even more so today of computer programming to human linguistic responses have to face the challenge of the indefinite flexibility of human response. Human language is an instrument that can be used to speak of anything at all and indicates reason rather than mechanism—although it is clear that in speaking one has to employ the mechanisms of the body.

3.

Descartes attempted to move from the *cogito* to what is implicit in and grounds it. He claimed that God's existence is at least as certain as any geometric demonstration (Part Four, 36). In his *Meditations on First Philosophy* Descartes will say that the existence of God is *even more certain* than the existence of the *cogito*![23] One way to see how he might have thought that is to think again in terms of "the natural light," which is excepted from the methodical doubt since one could not even raise questions, pose doubts, think of methodical procedures and arrive at certain conclusions without its operation.[24] Descartes distinguished the natural light from the teaching of nature that provides the sensory field of sensations and appetites required for survival.[25]

The notion of the natural light can be related to Descartes's claim to the certitude of the existence of God via the notion of Being and the

23. Meditation Five, 69.

24. I might add that he also could not do so if he had not a language, French or Latin, in which to think and which indicates those who taught him.

25. Meditation Six, 82.

principles of identity and noncontradiction entailed by that notion. All certitude is grounded in the recognition of any object of attention *as an instance of Being*. But Being is absolutely unrestricted: it includes all that is or can be, even a possibly Infinite Being. Infinite Being, in every way unrestricted, would be Perfect Being.[26] Descartes claimed that the presence of the notion of Infinite Being as the horizon of all awareness cannot be caused by finite processes. Rather, the presence of that notion is "the sign of the creator in the creature," an indication that we are made in his image and likeness.[27] Descartes made a further proposal, along the lines of Anselm's famous argument, dubbed by Kant the "ontological argument" or an argument from the logic of the notion of Being.[28] Descartes claimed that the notion of Infinite or Perfect Being includes the note of actual existence, since it would not be Perfect Being without it.[29] This is in a way parallel to the way the notion of triangle includes the note of having its internal angles equal to 180 degrees, though in this latter case we have an essence that does not include existence.

Anselm claimed that we can think of "that than which none greater can be conceived." "To think" or "to conceive" is not here "to imagine." Think of the various infinite number series or of our own awareness, neither of which can be properly imagined. Anselm's second premise was: that which exists outside of merely being thought about is greater than that which is merely thought of—for example, my nonexistent fifth son. And his conclusion was: that than which none greater can be conceived must exist outside of merely being thought of. Descartes thought along the same lines in terms of absolutely Infinite, Perfect Being whose essence entailed existence.

4.

Once having secured the existence of God as absolutely Perfect, Infinite Being at the heart of the natural light, Descartes saw that God as perfect must be a non-deceiver. He thus would not create a being subjected to

26. Notice here the correlation between unrestrictedness and perfection. The Greeks thought just the opposite: the unrestricted is the indeterminate that required some determination to reach even minimal perfection. Is this shift linked to the rise of choice to a position of absoluteness, for which restriction is diminution?

27. Meditation Four, 57 and 61.

28. Anselm, *Proslogion*; Kant, *CPR*, A 598 (B 626), 504–5.

29. Meditation Five, 66–69.

illusion unless there was a good reason for the illusions and a way to get beyond them. For us, the way is the responsible use of the mind, restraining the will until we have clear and distinct evidence.[30] Again, the path is shown by mathematics as the most responsible use of the mind governed only by the rigor of proper evidence. With regard to the illusions involved in "the teachings of nature," that is, our sensations and appetites, we can explain them by studying the laws of physics and physiology. Optical illusions, phantom limbs, the apparent existence of color "on" things, the apparent motion of the sun around the earth and the like follow from how we are constructed physiologically and situated physically in order to survive. Mind is seated in the midst of the brain, able to think through what is given by nature in order to direct oneself rationally rather than instinctively or merely by way of tradition.

The sense world that was originally subjected to methodical doubt returns again as a mode of appearance for the sake of the adjustment of the human animal organism to its environment. Animals would have the same physical constitution as humans, minus the mode of appearance in the sensory-appetitive circle. Appearance occurs for the sake of providing the materials for human choice that both follows and directs intellectual operations. The environment that appears in this sensory way is reliable for practical adjustment insofar as we can operate on it with principles of coherence and consistency that allow us to distinguish the dream-illusion state from the state of fully functional wakefulness.[31]

In 1633 Descartes had written a work on nature, *Le Monde*, but had not published it for fear of what happened to Galileo (Part Six, 68). Its procedure was to assume God as creator of matter and random motion and to deduce the laws of nature from the perfection of God. But the order of inquiry could not be completely deductive. He instructed us to find in a general way the principles of all from "certain seeds of truth that are in our souls." We are then to examine "the first and most ordinary effects that could be deduced from these causes: heavens, earth, water, air, fire, minerals, etc." But since the actual forms of things are only some among an infinity of possible forms, one then needs to go from effects, i.e., the actually given species, to causes. Since also there are many possible ways to account

---

30. Ibid., 35.

31. Meditation Six, 83. Note the use of the notion of teleology or purpose, which was banished from physics in favor of mechanism but returns here in determining the relation between the body and sensation.

for the effects from the principles, experiments are necessary to rule out possibilities. A purely deductive system needs to be supplemented by recurrence to experiment and thus to sensory experience. Hence Descartes needs the coherence and consistency of the everyday functional dashboard of sensory experience even for theoretical purposes.

Descartes goes on to add that to hide these things he has uncovered would be to sin against the common good of all men since the knowledge of nature can displace speculative with practical philosophy so that we could "use these objects for all the purposes for which they are appropriate, and thus *make ourselves, as it were, masters and possessors of nature*" (Part Six, 62). This promotes both enjoyment of the fruits of the earth and bodily health. And, insofar as "the mind depends so greatly upon the temperament and on the disposition of the organs of the body," the improvement of health could make men generally more wise and competent.

This pragmatically oriented view anticipates the Tree of Knowledge in Descartes's "Letter to Picot."[32] The Tree of Knowledge has as its roots metaphysics; its trunk is physics, its branches mechanics, medicine and morals—all of which allow us to pluck the fruits in the realm of practice. Both the observation on the bad effects of false reasoning upon practice and the establishment of rules for theoretical and practical behavior point to the unity of theory and practice expressed by this tree analogy. Even the most speculative levels of knowledge are linked to the practical fruits which will make us "lords and masters of nature." But the Tree also points to the systematic connectedness of genuine knowledge. As Hegel put it, "The True is the Whole."[33] The insipidity of much academic work is linked to its having been excised from the living whole of human experience, cutting it off from its context. Nonetheless, abstraction from context—as, e.g., in mathematical or formal-logical exploration—is a condition for "making progress" in knowing. Yet for the full truth, the abstractions have to be traced back to their roots in the life-world. This is part of the task of phenomenology.

We might note a transformation of the order from the tradition. For Descartes, the end of knowing is physical practice in the world, not contemplation of the divine. Contemplation takes up one paragraph at the end of the third meditation.[34] He said, "Let us now contemplate the God we have proven." Descartes claimed to deal with metaphysical issues in order

32. "Author's Letter," preface to *PP*, 211.
33. Hegel, *Phenomenology of Spirit*, Preface, §20.
34. Meditation Three, 52.

to get past them to the things that really matter: knowing that culminates in mastery of nature for practical purposes.

Getting past them also involved bowing to the religious tradition through proving the existence of God and an immortal soul so that science can be shielded from the persecution that attended Galileo's publication of his scientific work. If we look back at the third article of Descartes's provisional moral code, "Conquer oneself rather than fortune," we see a focus upon what Aristotle called *praxis* or self-formation, which ultimately for Aristotle was for the sake of *theoria*. In contrast to Aristotle, *praxis* for Descartes is instrumental to *theoria* initially but to *techne* ultimately.

We should note that Descartes never wrote a treatise on morals derived from the roots he cultivated in *Meditations on First Philosophy*. He died of pneumonia contracted by going out in winter time to tutor Queen Christina of Sweden at 5:30 in the morning. Would the treatise on morals have been a treatise on behavioral engineering?

In a concluding section he adds: "If I write in French, the language of my country, rather than in Latin, the language of my teachers, it is because I hope that those who use only their natural reason will judge my opinions, rather than those who believe only in old books" (Part Six, 77). He had earlier noted that in books one can encounter the minds of the greats; but one soon finds that they are not in agreement. He turned to "the book of the world" to learn his lessons, appealing to "good sense" (Part One, 9–10). He thus cut off contact with the past and set the world resolutely toward the future of scientific technology.

5.

In his essay "The Way Back into the Ground of Metaphysics," Martin Heidegger recalls Descartes's Tree of Knowledge and inquires as to the character of the soil in which that tree is planted.[35] What is the "ground" of metaphysics? That ground is the life-world of a given people. The *cogito* as the I is rooted in *Da-sein*, the fuller human reality as *Being-in-the-World* into which any I is "thrown" and which gives the individual field of awareness a peculiar tuning. Descartes, in spite of himself, could not escape the world that shaped him. The great historian of medieval philosophy Etienne Gilson worked at showing the medieval roots of Descartes's thought.[36]

---

35. "The Way Back into the Ground of Metaphysics," 277–90.

36. See *Études sur le rôle de la pensée médiévale*.

Nonetheless, Descartes stands at the border between two worlds and neatly divides the enlightened modern world of natural science, technological application, and isolated individualism from the medieval world of theology, contemplation, and communal belief and practice.

QUESTIONS

1. What is a society to do when its religious foundations are no longer accepted by large numbers? What have been the historical responses?

2. How do you understand each of the four rules for the direction of the mind in intellectual inquiry?

3. How do you understand each of the four principles of the provisional moral code? Why is it provisional?

4. What are the implications of Descartes's recognition of the indubitability of the "*cogito*"?

5. Link Descartes's discussion to the "Phenomenology of the Mailbox."

6. What are the two ways Descartes attempted to prove the existence of God?

7. How does Descartes's path of inquiry parallel Plato's Cave and Line of Knowledge?

8. What is the nature of mind and of body for Descartes? How are they related? How does his notion of body differ from the "common sense" view? What is the nature of the sensory features we common-sensically attribute to bodies? What about animal awareness? How does Descartes view of the mind-body relation differ from that of Thomas Aquinas? How does it parallel Plato's views?

9. How does Descartes's overall view of our relation to nature relate to the views of contemporary science and the reasons our society supports scientific research?

10. How does Descartes view the relation of faith and reason?

FURTHER READING

1. John Cottingham, ed., *The Cambridge Companion to Descartes*.
2. René Descartes, *Meditations on First Philosophy*.
3. Marjorie Grene, *Descartes among the Scholastics*.
4. S. V. Keeling, *Descartes*.

* * * *

HEGEL AND RELIGION

The True is the Whole.

—*PHENOMENOLOGY OF SPIRIT*, §20

READING

Section on Religion in G. W. F. Hegel,
On Art, Religion, and Philosophy.

1.

The thought of G. W. F. Hegel is important to our study of philosophy for theology in that he maintained, with Aquinas, the autonomy of philosophy and also an overlap between what is revealed and what can be found by independent human thought. However, unlike Aquinas, Hegel maintained that philosophy can advance considerably further than Aquinas had into the territory of revealed thought. For Hegel all the basic categories hitherto taken solely on the basis of faith could be shown to be approachable philosophically through a reformation of philosophical logic.

A first approach to Hegel may be taken in terms of a comparison between two ideal-typical positions: what I will call the Enlightenment Heritage and Orthodox Christian Theology respectively.[1] The approach is ideal-typical, i.e., it develops in terms of a projection of certain tendencies in different thinkers that are viewed as heading toward an ideal term which may be held completely by none of them, but which illuminates tendencies in them all. And I want to approach the three positions—En-

1. This essay draws heavily upon the chapter on Hegel in my *Placing Aesthetics*.

lightenment, Orthodox Christian, and Hegelian—in three areas: theology, anthropology, and Christology. We take this approach partly because it allows us to fill in something of the thought-movements to which we have paid insufficient attention, but which are required by an overview of the salient points in the whole of Western thought; but mainly because it is particularly illuminating with regard to Hegel. Some of the typical contemporary rejections of Hegel have the same Enlightenment basis as some of the typical rejections of orthodox Christianity (which is not to say that Hegel was entirely orthodox).

In the Enlightenment theological heritage, there is the tendency to consider God as a separate entity, absolutely one and apart from things in a manner like one might envision the separation of one atom from another in Greek atomic theory. Creation is the fashioning of preexistent material by this God as a Divine Architect or Watchmaker.[2] (The position is called "Deism.") What he creates, according to Newton, is a set of atoms, externally related to one another according to invariant mechanical laws to establish the Clockwork Universe. In the area of anthropology, there is a tendency to view the human Spirit as spatially locatable, inside the head. Locke's view comes to mind: awareness as a dark, empty chamber into which light enters through the slits of the senses.[3] Spirit is considered as either separated from the brain, e.g., in Locke's inner chamber, identical with it in Hobbes's or La Mettrie's materialism or ephiphenomenal to it (that is, produced and controlled by it) or in Hume's phenomenalism.[4] In either case, experience is something subjective that occurs inside the head as an effect of exterior causal processes, which tend to be viewed as so all-encompassing that even so-called free acts are explained in terms of antecedent causal processes. On the social level, there is social atomism. Paralleling methodical procedure in classical physics, society is considered in terms of its ultimate constituents, isolated individuals, starting from which thinkers constructed a comprehensive view of society through the positing of a founding contract between such individuals.[5] Original innocence belongs to human nature

2. Cf. Hegel, *Encyclopaedia Logic*, §128, Addendum, 198 (henceforth *EL*). For a general account, see Smith, *History of Modern Culture*, 2:410ff.

3. *Essay Concerning Human Understanding*, bk. II, ch. XI, 17.

4. See, e.g., Hume, *Dialogues Concerning Natural Religion*, II, 148.

5. Locke, *Second Treatise on Government*, bk. II, ch. II, 4; Hobbes, *Leviathan*, I, ch. XIII.

which is corrupted through social structures.[6] The Good Life is viewed as satisfaction of appetite and thus as freedom from pain. Medical research aims especially at the latter, technological advancement in general at the former.[7] Following the Cartesian project, mankind progresses in enlightenment as we learn the mechanisms of nature and use them for our benefit, i.e., health, the procurement of pleasure, and the avoidance of pain.[8] If we wish to retain Christianity in such a view, Christ is viewed as the good man, the moral exemplar.[9] Grace, though incongruous, if considered at all, is conceived of as an outside aid in reaching the Good Life.[10]

If we compare this set of related views with an ideal-typical analysis of orthodox Christian theology (at least pre-sixteenth-century orthodoxy), we find a significant contrast on all scores. Many of the things for which people blame Hegel are actually closely related to the claims of traditional Christian theology. Among other things, Hegel is trying to give a conceptual transcription of that theology. He claims that Christianity has revealed the basic truth; but he also claims, following Lessing, that revelation was not rational when it occurred (it was received from without and not at all understood in its basic grounds), yet it is directed toward our rational comprehension.[11] Thomas Aquinas says something similar in his *Summa theologiae* where he talks about things that are available through philosophic inference as well as through revelation. Aquinas includes in the latter such things as the existence of God, those of his attributes inferable as the causal grounds of the objects of experience, and the natural moral order, specifically the Ten Commandments as secondary precepts of natural law. They were revealed, according to Aquinas, because they are necessary for proper human behavior, but can only be discovered through reason by thinkers of significant capacity, with great effort, over long stretches of time, and with significant admixture of error. But once given, such truths can be underpinned and fully integrated into our lives by reaching them through the extensions of our experience by means of the work of reason. However, there is a limit: for Aquinas some

6. Cf. the treatment of the issue in the Enlightenment by Cassirer, *Philosophy of the Enlightenment*, 137–60.

7. Smith, *Enlightenment*, 202–11.

8. Ibid.

9. Cf. Hegel, *Lectures on the Philosophy of Religion* (henceforth *LPR*).

10. *LPR*, 422.

11 *LPR*, 144ff.; cf. Lessing, *Education of the Human Race*, §72.

truths—those that are not inferable as causally implicated in what we can experience—can only be known through revelation.[12] That includes the central Christian dogmas of the Trinity, the Incarnation, and the nature of the Sacraments. Hegel, on the contrary, acknowledges no limits: we can give a conceptual transcription of revelation that makes sense out of it, i.e. integrates it into our experience as a whole—and that likewise makes sense out of the entire history of Western philosophy as well.[13]

In the orthodox Christian theology we are considering, the first truth is that God is Trinity.[14] This is one of the things that Aquinas places beyond the scope of reason's power of inference. Not so for Hegel: God as sheer identity, the One as First Principle, is dead; God as Trinity, as identity-in-difference, is alive, a moving Ground, the very paradigm of Reason.[15] In the traditional teaching, common to both Plotinus and Augustine, God as Father/One others himself in the Logos/Son which is the basis for the outpouring of the otherness of creation.[16] The Logos pre-contains all the ways the One can be mirrored outside the Godhead in creation. The Holy Spirit is the union of the otherness of the Father and the Logos: Being is trinitarian in its ground. This is among the basic truths, essential to Christianity, that Augustine claimed to find in the Platonists.[17] In traditional orthodox Christology, the Logos was made flesh in Christ who was not only the good man, the holy rabbi, the great teacher, but God in his otherness.[18] Only the Logos, as the internal otherness of the Father, through whom there could be something other than God, could enter into the otherness of creation.[19]

In creating, God does not simply remain separate; but, by reason of the fact of perpetually giving complete being to creation, he is, in the words of Augustine, nearer to creatures than they are to themselves.[20] God, being absolutely infinite as the ground of the total being of the finite, is

---

12. 102 *ST* I, 1, 1.

13. 103 Cf. *LPR*, 418.

14. Cf. Aquinas, *ST*, I, 27ff.

15. Cf. *Hegel's Philosophy of Mind*, §566–70, 299–301 (henceforth *HPM*); also *LPR*, 418.

16. Plotinus, *Enneads*, VI, 1; Augustine, *On the Trinity*, bk. XV, 23ff.

17. *Confessions*, VII, 9.

18. *ST*, III, 2.

19. Cf. Rahner, *Foundations of Christian Faith*, 223ff. See also *Encyclopedia of Theology*, 1755ff. (henceforth *ET*).

20. *Confessions*, III, 6.

more transcendent than the Watchmaker God of the Enlightenment or the "Demiurge" in Plato's *Timaeus*, a divinity who fashions matter separate from him, or, for that matter, than the finite, non-creating, exemplar divinity of Aristotle. At the same time, he is more immanent than in either view as the Ground of Being of all that is, having to sustain freely and knowingly all that is. God is not simply Fashioner but Creator, not simply giving form and furnishing exemplarity as in Plato and Aristotle respectively, but also giving full being to all outside himself.[21] For Aquinas, unlike the case of the Trinity, this is something both revealed and accessible to human reason. Hegel, of course, maintains the same.

For orthodoxy, only humanness, as sole locus of openness to the Infinite in material creation, constitutes the external condition for the possibility of being assumed by the Logos in the God-Man.[22] Humanness is understood as the image of God and is thus not wholly locked up in the finite, but is finite-infinite, finite having designs on the infinite. The human being as the image of God consequently involves a view of the Spirit that is not simply identical with the body, nor simply contained within the head or even totally within finite conditions. The human being as aware and responsible, having intellect and will, is openness to the totality of Being.[23] Again, for both Aquinas and Hegel, this is available to unaided reason.

However, historically human beings are in a darkened condition brought about by an Original Fall that is passed on to the whole race.[24] This is linked to the fact that a human being is not an atomic individual, but is intrinsically social, and, indeed, as believer, a member of the Mystical Body of Christ, the Incarnate Logos. That is not intended merely as a metaphor but as an ontological reality.[25] There is an internal connection between all believers, who share in a common life, the life of grace which is not only an outside aid but, more deeply, a participation in the divine life, the indwelling of the Trinity in our own togetherness as a community of love. Love as the bond of the Spirit in the community is an identity-in-difference: not simply an external connection or an interior merging, but the fostering of difference by identifying with it and discovering one's own identity in the process.

21. Cf. my *Path into Metaphysics*, 187ff. for fuller exposition and references (henceforth *PIM*.)

22. Cf. Rahner, *ET*, 690ff.

23. Cf. *PIM*, chs. 2 and 3.

24. Cf. Rahner, *ET*, 1148ff.

25. Pius XII, *Mystical Body of Christ*.

For Hegel, this becomes the formula for Being itself. God is an identity-in-difference as divine Love; so also with God and creation, Spirit and body, individual and community—they are intelligible as identities-in-difference, each dyad in its own way. God is love. Trinity expresses that: the Spirit is the bond of love between the Father and the Son who are other than one another and yet are united in the deepest and most complete manner possible.[26] Divine love is what pervades the believing community.

That has implications for thinking about interpersonal relationships that Hegel does not miss. For Hegel the trinitarian structure of identity-in-difference is the logical genetic code for *all* reality. Creation is God's own othering for Hegel—though this is far from being orthodox. In orthodoxy the Trinity is complete before creation, needing nothing outside Itself. God creates out of love and out of choice to share divine goodness.[27] In Hegel, by contrast, God apart from creation contains empty possibility developing out of the empty notion of Being and requiring, needing instantiation in the concrete realms of Nature and History.[28] For Hegel, God *needs* creation and *must* create. The logical grounds for this lie in the relation between the infinite and the finite. Abstractly considered, they are simply opposed; but if we consider infinity as *absolute* infinity (not, for example, the infinity of differing number series, unlimited in the number of individuals belonging to the respective series, but with each individual and the whole series with it limited to its type), then we see that the absolutely Infinite *must* include the finite, otherwise it is limited to one side of the infinite-finite relation. The logical consequence for Hegel is that God as the *absolutely* Infinite *must* create in order to be himself as the absolutely Infinite. Creation for orthodoxy is *other than*, not the *othering of* God. The latter is, in orthodoxy, the Incarnation. Further, the point of creation is that God be manifest in knowledge and love, and in orthodoxy

---

26. *ST*, I, 37, 1 and 2.

27. *ST*, I, 46, 1, ad 6.

28. *EL*, §212, addendum. There is the enigmatic and undeveloped declaration in the *EL* that God is eternally complete and eternally completing himself, which seems to give the lie to understanding the Trinity containing in itself the realm of possibility and thus empty and requiring creation of nature as its own fulfillment. In *SL* (50) logic is said to consider God in his eternal essence before creation. There is also the declaration in the *Philosophy of History* that "Spirit is immortal; with it there is no past, no future, but an essential *now*. . . . What Spirit is it has always been essentially." *Philosophy of History*, 79 (henceforth *PH*). Of course this could be true of an eternal universe.

the Incarnation is the in-principle final manifestation of God that is completed in fact through the completion of history.

Finally, in Christianity one does not flee from pain but, when it is inevitable, embraces it, not masochistically but by identifying with Christ on the cross Who asked precisely not to have to undergo it—though one finds it difficult to resist seeing masochism in much of the spiritual tradition that relishes suffering. It is through his suffering and death that his resurrection and consequently our redemption occurs.

There is clearly a vast difference between the Enlightenment heritage, that we all share rather spontaneously and are inclined to defend rationally, and the Christian tradition, which Hegel attempted to interpret rationally in the modern era. He claimed to be an orthodox Lutheran to the end of his life. The claim has been challenged in different ways, based upon differing interpretations of what he actually did. But that depends upon how one understands the relation between reason and dogmatic proclamation. For Hegel orthodoxy is right in principle, but lacks the proper conceptual framework that he thinks his system provides.

The identity of the divine and the human, the infinite and the finite, with each retaining their differences, was revealed in Christ; and that implied the Trinity as the primordial Identity-in-difference. Hegel sees *that* as the philosophic key to the Whole. Experience is global, everything appearing together within an overarching view of the Whole. The human mind isolates the distinguishable aspects within that Whole—like color and sound with their differing eidetic features. This is the work of what Hegel calls *Verstand*, translated as "Understanding," the key function of what the Enlightenment called "Reason." It is the power of the negative, the ability to separate in the mind what is linked in experience, and the I that uses it is absolute negativity, standing back from everything and able to choose its own way. The basic principle of the Understanding is the principle of identity: each thing is what it is. It led to a view that considered all relations as external: God and the world in Deism, atoms linked to atoms in cosmology, mind and body in psychology, and external contractual relations in politics. One Enlightenment wit described love as "the contact between two epidermises."

But Christianity revealed the basic principle as identity-in-difference. The work of showing that principle through internal relations in experience itself is the work of what Hegel called *Vernunft*, translated as "Reason." Note that this is poles apart from what the Enlightenment called "Reason" that is actually Hegel's abstractive "Understanding." So there are quite different forms of so-called Rationalism. In Hegel's Rationalism the principle of identity-in-difference breaks Aquinas's "glass ceiling" for philosophy and allows the entrance of Trinity and Incarnation into philosophy itself. Christianity intuits the basic principles of the Whole; revealed theology works at their integration with philosophy by taking them as starting points; Hegelian philosophy develops them within philosophy itself.

2.

Hegel is the great synthesizer who sought to contain the entire philosophic tradition, with its Greco-Roman and Hebrew-Christian sources, in a single system of astonishing power and insight. There is a very real sense in which he establishes a persuasive synthesis of Parmenides, Plato, and Aristotle, mediated by the dominant symbols of Christianity and grounded in the turn to the subject focused in a special way in Descartes.

Parmenides opened Western metaphysics with the proclamation of the identity of Thought and Being and presented a claim to knowledge of the essential features of being. He described a goddess revealing to him that "It is" and "It is not" is not. He proceeded to a conceptual analysis that removes all elements of nonbeing (It is not) from the notion of Being (It is). If we perform that analysis, being shows itself as changeless and absolutely one: changeless because change involves the nonbeing of the no-longer and the not-yet in the never-finally-there of the moving Now; absolutely one, and not a one of many that is itself composed of a multiplicity, because any one among many is *not* the others, and any one composed of multiplicity is such that one aspect is likewise *not* the others.[29] However, for Hegel, as for Nietzsche, such being is not the fullness of reality but the last trailing cloud of evaporating reality.[30]

If we think how we might arrive at such a notion starting from the things of experience, we might set in motion a sorting process that, by leaving aside concrete differences, arrives at progressively higher logical order, i.e., more universal, more encompassing logical classes. Beginning with the multiplicity of actual people, we leave aside the many interesting things that distinguish each of them to arrive at the notion of "humanness" that is

29. Cf. *PIM*, ch. 6, 125–32.

30. Hegel, *Hegel's Science of Logic*, 82ff. (henceforth *SL*); Nietzsche, *Twilight of the Idols*, 37.

their common identity. Thinking in terms of the next wider class, we arrive at the identical notion of "*animal*" that leaves aside the concrete differences between the various species of *animals*, humans included. Moving further upward and leaving progressively more aside, we arrive at the identical notion of "organism," and further still at the notion of "body." Finally, in the Aristotelian line, we reach the category of so-called "substance" (*ousia* or beingness) which includes the bodily on the one hand and the mental on the other.[31] Going back to the concrete things from which analysis began, we are able to sort out common features in all substances: quantitative features such as weight or extension, qualities such as sensory features or powers or habits, relations of various sorts, including the spatial and temporal, actions and passivities and the like. The features fall into the general notion of "attributes" (Greek *symbebekota* or things that are yoked together with the basic beingness of things). Substance and attributes are described as "Being-in-itself" and "Being-in-another" respectively: a substance, such as a person or a tree, exists as self-grounded (in itself), as distinct from the features of things, such as their color or height, which exist only in and on the basis of the things that ground them. Hegel takes us one step further: leaving aside the in itself and the in another, we arrive at the pure notion of "being." Since (as we followed in the line of substance) every logically higher order, i.e., more inclusive category, can be inclusive of broader ranges of things only insofar as it leaves aside more and more differentiating aspects of those things in order to concentrate upon commonalities, the last move, isolating the notion of Being from the two modes of Being-in-itself and Being-in-another, leaves us with a notion that is completely empty. Hence it turns out to be identical with its opposite, Nothingness or Nonbeing. But then, far from being changeless, as Parmenides claimed, such a notion is identical with Becoming or process, for, as Plato indicated, process is the mixture or synthesis of Being and Nonbeing: being no longer what it was and not yet being what it is to be.[32]

Here we find Aristotle's notion of nature as *phusis*, a straining to emerge. The notion of Being is not only the empty notion of process; it is also all-encompassing, for outside Being there is nothing. Hence the empty notion of Being strains toward its own unfolding in the totality of the concrete universe. Being has an erotic structure in the Platonic sense of the term "erotic": it is emptiness that has designs upon plenitude. But

31. Cf. Aristotle, *Categories*, 5, 2a 11.
32. *SL*, 105ff.

in contrast to Plato, it is the Eternal having designs on the Temporal for Its fulfillment. At the same time, Parmenides's claim that Thought and Being are one gives the *telos* to the process: Being in its inner nature is directed to manifestness, is intrinsically related to Spirit and is completed in being understood.[33] So, it would make no final sense to have a world in which Spirit did not appear. Hence the embarrassment that surfaces today in the all-too-common epiphenomenalist notion of spirit that is left over once we turn over all explanation in the sciences to observation and mechanism. In such a view, Spirit as awareness is a residual by-product of the nervous system that is able to do absolutely nothing, not even practice science.[34] Its functional place is taken by brain mechanisms; its appearance is undeniable, but also inexplicable because by hypothesis, totally inactive. It is the locus of a wholly passive display of part of the workings of the nervous system. But if Nature can be understood, so, contrary to the epiphenomenalist, can the locus of its manifestness, namely human understanding. And Nature comes to fuller manifestness when we understand that it strains to produce, in increasingly more complex and centralized animal organisms, the conditions for its own progressive manifestation. It is this link between Being and manifestness that sets the immediate context for Hegel's view of art that heals the rift between the abstractions of science and the immediacy of sensory experience. Far from being irrational, such a view leaves no dangling irrationals such as appear in that scientific view which leaves out conscious spirit, except as functionless epiphenomenon.

Being-Nonbeing-Becoming constitutes the first triad of Hegel's System and exhibits the kind of formulaic structure that Fichte had described as thesis-antithesis-synthesis.[35] The synthesis is called *Aufhebung*, an ordinary German term that can mean three apparently quite different and even opposing things: cancellation, preservation, and elevation. The notion of Becoming cancels out the one-sidedness contained in the notions of Being and Nonbeing, preserves what is seen in each of them in isolated fashion, and elevates the insights contained in them to a new and higher level of mutual compatibility.[36]

In a sense this is the strategy for approaching any great thinker in the history of thought. What we have to realize and what I have been at pains

33. *SL*, 479ff.

34. Cf. Wooldridge, *Mechanical Man*.

35. Cf. Kaufmann, "Hegel Myth and Its Overcoming," 95ff.

36. *EL*, §96, addendum.

to show is that each classic has a hold on something of crucial signifi-cance, else it would not have continually drawn the attention of those who think seriously in these matters. But thinkers hold opposite views. What is seen by a given thinker? Preserve that. What is one-sided about the un-derstanding of what is seen? Cancel that. How can we put the insights of two thinkers together and do justice to what is seen in them singly? The Spirit drives in this way over time through all partialities to a more comprehensive understanding of things: generating positions, evoking counter-positions, and finding higher syntheses.

When we arrive at the empty notion of Being, we find something that is there for Spirit as something manifest to us. So going back to Par-menides, the first great metaphysician, there is a sense in which Thought and Being are one. The question is, in what sense are they one? At least in this sense, that Being is there for manifestation to Spirit and that mani-festness is an identity-in-difference. We stand over against what is being revealed to us; it is being manifest precisely as it is and where it is, other than us; but it is also in us as our knowledge. Thus there is also a kind of identity: what is called in the Scholastic tradition an *intentional* or *cognitive* identity. Knowing is, in Scholastic terminology, being the other *as other*.[37] Being other is involved in all change; knowing is being *the* other, precisely as it is *other than the consciousness* to which it is manifest. Thought is not just present to itself in blank self-identity; it is there as the center for the manifestation of the cosmos. The whole of Being is there for manifesta-tion; the *point* of Being is to show itself.

So what we get in the Parmenidean formula on the identity of Thought and Being is a statement of the fundamental teleology, the goal-directedness of the process of reality. The reality-process is not simply that of empty Being trying to become fully what it can be—though that is the case; it is, more fundamentally, Being as aimed at creating the conditions for its being fully manifest by producing the conditions for the locus of manifestation: human existence.

The manifestness of the Whole is the Notion of notion or the Idea fully returned to itself in comprehensive thought.[38] Hegel uses the image of a tree to give a graphic conception of the main lines of his System. The first triad of the Logos gives what we might today call the basic "genetic code" and the Logos-system constitutes the seed. Nature is the tree ramifying

---

37. Maritain, *Degrees of Knowledge*, 112.

38. *SL*, 576ff.

into its various branches according to the logical code. The Logos-system is Being-in-itself or potentiality; Nature is Being-outside-itself or spatio-temporal existence; and Spirit in its history is Being-in-and-for-itself or actualization, Being returned in manifestness to the Logos-system.

Spirit divides into three forms: Subjective, Objective, and Absolute Spirit. *Subjective Spirit*, the structure of the individual human, is the bud on the tree of life; Objective Spirit the flower; Absolute Spirit the fruit, the *telos* of the tree. Subjective spirit divides again into three: *Anthropology*, as the realm of the states of mind following the physical articulation of the organism, grounds *Phenomenology* or the realm of the appearance of things and persons to awareness and thus of an inwardness that makes manifest-ness possible; both are surmounted by *Psychology* which comprehends the conditions in the human subject for intelligent fashioning and intelligible manifestness.[39] The ultimate distance from the Now (which Hegel calls negative or formal freedom) afforded by our reference to the Whole makes possible both freedom of choice in the practical order and intelligible man-ifestness in the theoretical order.[40] Freedom of choice introduces a vast level of contingency, in and beyond the contingencies of Nature, of arbitrariness, irrationality and also of creativity characteristic of humanness. The struc-tures displayed at this level are the conditions for the possibility of the next two levels: Objective and Absolute Spirit.

The essentially embodied Spirit is, to begin with, merely Subjective Spirit, merely the basic set of human potentialities in concrete individuals. It requires *Objective Spirit*, i.e., the development of the objectifications of thought in institutions, habits, customs, ways of life, traditions, in order that, through time, Spirit might come more fully to itself through the growing manifestness of the Whole. Subjective Spirit does not develop its potenti-alities without a social matrix which is the objectification brought about by past and present human subjects. One does not arrive at even a rudimentary self-consciousness without the presence of the human other, threatening or confirming.[41] But that does not occur without a developed institutional matrix, beginning with the institution of language. Objective Spirit is the other in relation to the Subjective Spirit, the instantiations of which—hu-man individuals—stand in dialectical relation to one another.

---

39. This is the basic outline of the level of subjective spirit in *HPM*, §387–482, 25–240.

40. *HPM*, §465, 224, §469, 228, §481–82, 238–40.

41. *Phenomenology of Spirit*, §175 on Self-consciousness (henceforth *PS*).

Following Aristotle and anticipating Heidegger, Hegel observed that human beings conduct their lives by being rooted in a community that is the residue of centuries-long practices. Hegel calls this *Sittlichkeit*, which might be translated as "customariness." German *Sitte*, Greek *ethos*, and Latin *mores* all refer to the practices of a people. We live in that way of life as our element, the way fish live in water and birds live in the air. Aristotle focused especially upon two institutions: the family as basic unit and the *polis* or small city-state as the place of human flourishing. The individual is typically submerged in those elements. In the development of the modern world, the individual appears on the scene with its newly discovered or asserted rights against the community. Freedom of religious choice and practice, freedom of enterprise, inquiry, publicity, and choice of marriage partner, along with equality before the law: such rights create an unprecedented situation. So Hegel sees the new arena of *Civil Society* as a social region of free activity, limned by law, inserted between the family and the overarching polis, now grown into a modern State. Hegel develops a view of the State as hierarchically arranged, culminating in a constitutional monarch, but arranged in such a way that sets of institutions protect the rights of individuals and communities from lawless intrusion of the higher levels of organization upon the lower and upon the individuals whose rights and dignity is the whole point of the modern State. It is in such a State that the ongoing study of the order of things and the ongoing development of art and enterprise can carry humankind to more and more sophisticated levels of operation.

Not all people are on the same level historically except as Subjective Spirit which, from the point of view of the *telos* of history, can participate in it more deeply as it unfolds. Social, political, and economic institutions become, in a sense, more rational over time, not only in the sense of becoming more subjectable to calculation, but also in the sense of becoming more articulated and more understood, providing more amplitude for the exercise of individual choice, and, above all, coordinate with and supportive of the growing manifestness of the intelligibility of the whole of Being. Intelligibility and freedom develop because intelligence objectifies itself more and more through history.[42]

Now we should underscore, contrary to an army of critics, beginning with Kierkegaard, that Hegel's view does not involve the swallowing up of the individuals but rather their location within a vision of the whole.

42. See *PH*, 54ff., 69ff.

Furthermore, the development Hegel envisions is rational precisely insofar as it advances in maximizing opportunities for individual choice—of occupation, marriage partner, religious affiliation, speech, assembly, and the like—though within the structures that make possible "substantial freedom," i.e. identification with family, state and God, ultimately making possible "absolute knowledge" as the comprehensive view of the Whole.[43] We should note that absolute knowledge is not omniscience: it is awareness of the systematic togetherness of those features that make intelligent existence possible. Within the System, thought and action go forth, forever finding and establishing new relations.

What speculative knowing comprehends is the moral necessity of a community, rooted in the inwardness of the presence of the divine Spirit of love revealed historically through Christ. Such community is characterized by its awareness of the necessity of each—whether at the level of taking responsibility for oneself or at various hierarchical levels for the community—to choose a course of action existent within contingent contexts and generative of consequences that cannot be fully envisioned; hence the necessity of the fallibility of choice. But by reason of being bound to the community, there is also the necessity of offering grounds for the course chosen and being open to correction by others. By reason also of the bond of the community, there is the correlative need of forgiveness for mistaken choices. Absolute knowing is the manifestation of the necessary interrelatedness of categories that culminates in the coming into being of such a fallible, dialogical community bound together by the spirit of sharing in the divine.[44]

For Hegel the coming into being of such a community and its development through time according to the lines of the System follows Christ's pronouncement that "it is expedient for you that I go [from your presence to My absence into heaven]. If I do not go, the Spirit of the Father will not come. When he comes he will teach you to worship in spirit and truth."[45] Spirit reaches its deepest inwardness by appearing in bodily presence in Christ and withdrawing from there into inwardness and encompassment of all bodily presence.

43. See Hegel's *Elements of the Philosophy of Right* on freedom of property acquisition, cf. §62, 51; on freedom of the press, of speech and of thought, §319, 205–6; on freedom of conscience, §124, 84, on freedom to choose a marriage partner, §162, 111.

44. *PS*, §641–71.

45. John 16:6; *PH*, 325; Hegel's *Aesthetics*, 1:80 (henceforth *ALFA*).

Objective Spirit is not the goal but merely the flower that precedes the goal. The final fruit of the tree of Nature is the realm of Absolute Spirit or Spirit absolved from the mere abstract possibility characterizing the Logos-system considered by itself, the concrete but non-self-present realm of Nature, and the conscious but finitely bounded realm of human awareness constituting history prior to the emergence of the Hegelian System. Through history Spirit returns to itself. This occurs first in the realm of Art where, in its highest function, the Absolute is displayed in sensory form; then in the realm of Religion where the turn within, to the heart, is accomplished. The process is completed by the comprehension of the main lines of the Whole made possible over time through the development of Philosophy.[46]

The mode of interiority that rises above art is *Religion* which gives expression to the human heart's rising up from the everyday to the Encompassing and Eternal.[47] But Religion tends to think about the Absolute in pictorial terms: God is a father, the Logos a son, the Spirit a dove.[48] In the development of theology, it thinks conceptually, but only with the static, regional abstractions (*Vorstellungen*) of the Understanding (*Verstand*), not in the developmental and comprehensively related categories (*Begriffen*) of all-encompassing Reason (*Vernunft*). One has to give conceptual cash value to the pictures and life to the abstractions through philosophic comprehension which thus rises above Religion, moving even more inward because it reaches the deepest inwardness of Spirit.[49] But in rising above Religion, Philosophy preserves and clarifies the inner movement of the heart in its rising to the Eternal and Encompassing and finding reconciliation with the community of confession and forgiveness.

Philosophy begins in Parmenides with the notion of Being and the proclamation that Thought and Being are one.[50] But this occurs at the beginning only abstractly and apart from the world of our everyday experience. It has to descend into the world to comprehend it totally. Its in-principle comprehension is displayed in the System we have sketched. Such a sys-

46. EPM, §§553–77, 292–315.

47. *Lectures on the Philosophy of Religion*, vol. I, 4. This is a version of Hegel's lectures other than the Hodgson version which was based on the 1827 series.

48. LPR, 146.

49. LPR, 144ff.; cf. Hegel, ALFA, vol. I, 108 (I, 149): *Vorstellung* includes images but also abstract concepts like "man" and "the quality of blueness," while *Begriff* contains opposite factors in unity.

50. LHP, vol. I, 249ff.

tem not only comprehends the main lines of Nature; it also, and especially, includes the main lines of History. For Hegel, the divine Spirit operates even more in History than it does in Nature.[51] Providence governs what occurs, driving toward the full disclosure of the meaning of the Whole. But History, like Nature, is no serene unfolding of a harmonious Whole: it involves the pain of struggle and destruction, even at the level of the history of philosophy. However, in and through the cross of contradiction, suffering and destruction, the meaning of the Whole is progressively displayed and worked into institutional form.[52]

As we said, "absolute awareness," which stands at the end of the process is not the same as divine omniscience. There is an indeterminate amount of material to discover and create. What Hegel claims to have shown are the interlocking set of categories required for rational existence, that is, for ongoing exploration of the nature of things and ongoing interaction between human beings in constructing institutions and inventing new means for fashioning and uncovering Nature. Revelation has acted as an external beacon that has led Reason to this shore upon which it can be most fully itself.

3.

For Hegel Religion is rooted in the elevation of the heart out of the everyday to the Eternal and Encompassing. He who has not experienced that has not the basis from which Philosophy of Religion follows as the height of Philosophy (131, 178).[53] Such elevation is rich in proportion as it is mediated by religious doctrine (190). But in modern times development has led to the side-lining of doctrine as now an object of historical study, that is, as someone else's thought—directly parallel to the way in which the history of philosophy is all-too-often treated (165). (That is why we have continued to recur to our phenomenological analysis to show how one might appropriate the thoughts of the great thinkers.) Some theologians have gone out of their way to de-emphasize dogma and have shown contempt for philosophy (162). And the modern examination of the biblical sources has

51. *PH*, 15; *ALFA*, I, 30 (I, 40).

52. *LPR*. Cf. *ALFA*, I, 97 (I, 133).

53. References in parentheses within the body of the text are to Hegel's introduction to his *Philosophy of Religion*, the introduction to which appears in *On Art, Religion, and Philosophy*, edited by J. Glenn Gray.

all-too-often failed to attend to the categories the interpreter unreflectively brings to bear upon the sources (153).

The history of doctrine is the history of the employment Reason upon the Bible and previous tradition. The early Church Fathers and later the Scholastics recognized the role of examining presuppositions by studying those who were best at doing that: first Plato and Plotinus, then later Aristotle, as we have seen (146). Those three pagan thinkers performed an essential service to Religion by giving content to the elevation of the heart. Absent doctrine, Religion shrivels up into empty elevation, a kind of wallowing in subjectivity (141).

The development of Religion as such is the work of Reason. Just as the history of doctrine and the history of philosophy should be a study of the development of one's own Reason, so also the study of the history of Religions should put us in the position to assimilate whatever belongs to Reason as such. The study of that history, as for Hegel the study of any history, is a developmental process. It culminates in what he calls *Revealed Religion*, that is, Christianity, for at the ripe time it reveals the final character of the Divine in the God-Man and his presupposition as the Logos in the Trinity (204–6, 155).

Christ is born, "grows in wisdom and knowledge before God and man," preaches, suffers, dies, and is risen. In his post-resurrection appearances he announces, "It is expedient for you that I go. If I go, I will send the Spirit Who will teach you how to worship in Spirit and truth."[54] And, as Martin Luther held, it is the inner witness of the Spirit that stands at the center of religious experience (167). For Hegel that does mean individual inspiration, but for him, the deepest witness of the Spirit lies in coming to understand, since Reason is deeper than feeling. Indeed, Reason is the Divine in us and feeling is subjective peculiarity (157). Even Aquinas noted that the human intellect is a kind of participation in the divine light. The one who learns to follow Reason gives up his peculiar individuality in order to stand at the level of the universal. However, standing at the level of the universal creates a rift between the abstractness of the universal and the concreteness of individual life. For Hegel, one without the other produces inauthentic existence. Let us not have hearts without heads or heads without hearts.[55] Remember, the center of Religion lies in the elevation of the heart to the Eternal and Encompassing and thus involves radical subjectivity.

54. John 4:20–24.
55. *HPM*, §445.

When philosophy takes Revealed Religion as its beacon, it is able to extend beyond where unaided Reason tends to take us and bring together the whole of history: of Religion, of thought, of human practice as such. Religion develops its self-conception in terms of mental images, feeling, and art-works. The work of Reason is to translate those into adequate conceptions and into a way of life consonant with the character of free spirit (199). History culminates in the establishment of proper human freedom: freedom from enslavement to passions, from narrowness of outlook, and freedom for the development of substantial community and the development of institutions, of the arts, and the sciences within that community (199).

> Going out into the actual world is essential to religion, and in this transition religion appears as morality in relation to the state and to the entire life of the state. According as the religion of nations is constituted so also is their morality and their government. The shape taken by these latter depends entirely on whether the conception of the freedom of spirit which a people has reached is a limited one, or on whether the nation has the true consciousness of freedom. (192)

4.

Hegel's thought is profound and challenging for any reader. But for one who takes the time to get inside it, it is full of significant insights. I find particularly attractive his claim, in effect, to remove the "glass ceiling" Aquinas posed between natural knowledge that can reach God only as the One but cannot move into a knowledge of him as Trinity. Hegel's principle of Identity-in-Difference, announced in the Incarnation, is a revealed beacon for philosophic thought. Aquinas seems based upon the principle of Identity alone. Employing Hegel's principle, all the philosophic dualisms can be reduced to dualities within a single whole. In the case of God, one might argue for a principle of otherness within God as the basis for the possibility of there being something other than God. That suggests the possibility of that principle of otherness being able itself to enter into the otherness of creation at the point where the created is founded on openness to the Infinite, that is, in the case of the human being. The identity within the difference of God suggests a third principle. . . . But these are only tantalizing suggestions. . . .

However, there are significant problems with Hegel's thought for Christian theology. The dialectical relation between the Infinite and the finite requires that the absolutely Infinite cannot remain one side of that relation, but must encompass the finite under penalty of being limited to being one side of the relation and thus being finite. That means that God *must* create. But central to Christian orthodoxy is the freedom of God to create or not.

Hegel further claims that God himself is completed through the development of the rationality of humankind through history. God not only *must* create, he must await the development of history (which he guides) to reach the point of his own completion, the basic moment of which is the Incarnation. This stands quite opposed to the notion of God, central to the Christian tradition, as having the fullness of perfection and thus being omniscient. But then Hegel also claims, paradoxically, that "God is eternally complete and eternally completing Himself"—which seems to cancel out the claim of God's dependence upon creation for his completion.

After Hegel's death, followers split into two camps, the Right which emphasized the religious and political in a positive way and the Left which moved to atheism and revolution. Hegel's texts are a Rohrschach test: one configurates them in terms of one's own leanings. Nonetheless, Hegel is a gold mine of insights for philosophical development, but also the source of divergent schools and a challenge to Christians to enter sympathetically into his thought.

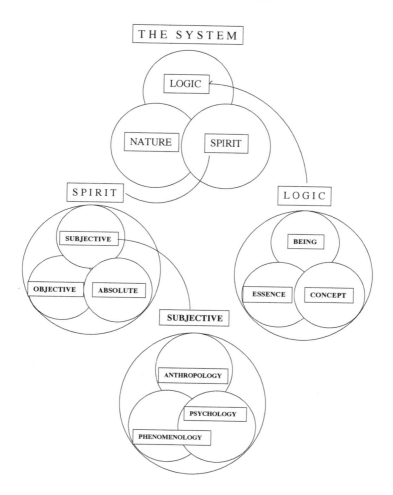

QUESTIONS

1. Compare Hegel's notion of the relation between reason and revelation with Aquinas's. Link that to #2.

2. In what ways does Hegel's view differ from orthodoxy, Catholic or Lutheran?

3. How is the structure of humanness the external condition for the possibility of the Incarnation as the structure of the Trinity is the internal condition?

4. How is the Vatican II Declaration on Religious Freedom an application of Hegel's thought?

5. Compare the function of the notion of Being in Hegel with our "bipolar view" of human existence.

6. Compare the role of tradition and community in Hegel with our view of the I-Me relation.

7. Discuss Hegel's notion that there can be no existence apart from mind and that the point of being is to be for manifestation. Link that to Christian orthodoxy.

* * * *

FURTHER READING

1. G. W. F. Hegel, *The Philosophy of History.*

2. G. W. F. Hegel, *Hegel's Introduction to the System: Phenomenology and Psychology.*

3. Emil Fackenheim, *The Religious Dimension of Hegel's Thought.* A quite readable and sympathetic (though not uncritical) approach to Hegel.

4. Stephen Houlgate, *An Introduction to Hegel: Freedom, Truth, and History.* A clear introduction at a high but readable level.

5. Terry Pinkard, *Hegel.* One of the best approaches to Hegel's thought through his biography.

* * * *

HEIDEGGER'S THOUGHT

Man is a thinking, that is, a meditative being. . . . Man today
is in *flight from thinking.*

—"Memorial Address," 47

READING

"Memorial Address," *Discourse on Thinking.*

1.

Descartes had invoked the image of the Tree of Knowledge with roots in
metaphysics, trunk in physics, branches in mechanics, medicine, and morals, with practical application as the fruit, learning to become "lords and
masters of nature." His vision lies at the background of the contemporary
view of science grounding technology and impacting society through indus-
try. It aims at relieving the human condition through labor-saving devices,
medicine, and the provision of enjoyment. Heidegger terms such a view the
Gestell, the "enframing": a view that puts everything through the methodical
grids of science and subjects it to our practical projects.[1] He sees it as having
its deep historical roots in Plato's view of the Ideas or Forms as the models
the Demiurge follows in producing the universe.[2] It operates in the mode of
thought Heidegger calls "representative-calculative" (46).

---

1. *Question Concerning Technology,* 19. Henceforth *QCT.*
2. *An Introduction to Metaphysics,* 66. Henceforth *IM.*

Heidegger's question with regard to the Tree of Knowledge is: What is the ground in which the tree is planted?[3] He is led to that by the conjunction of two peculiar experiences: on the one hand, an experience, rooted in his Bavarian Catholic peasant environment and in Benedictine monastic life, of the living presence of the divine Mystery and, on the other hand, an experience of "startled dismay" at the absence of such presence in the contemporary *Gestell*.[4] The tradition of metaphysics is rooted in a sense of overarching meaning experienced in "the heart," but does not think that rootage. The distinctively modern tradition rooted in Descartes leads to the progressive atrophy of that sense.

Heidegger is working out of a distinction given in experience and made central by the nineteenth-century Danish philosopher-theologian Søren Kierkegaard (together with Friedrich Nietzsche, one of the fathers of twentieth-century Existentialism) between *subjective* and *objective* thinking—though Heidegger would not approve of the terms. In the latter, the operative mode of the philosophical tradition, the accent falls upon the content, the *What* of our thought. In the former, the accent falls upon the individual's mode of relation to the content, the *How* of one's mode of existence.[5] This is what is at stake during the rise of Scholasticism in the distinction between its mode of understanding and that of the monastic tradition. In the former, the aim is to get our concepts straight, to achieve truth as correctness of assertion. In the monastic tradition, the aim is to bring the content to presence. Religiously, one might believe in the existence of God as omnipresent; philosophically, one might attempt to exhibit some proof of the claim by inference from what is given in experience, as did Thomas Aquinas and Hegel; meditatively, one would aim to appropriate the belief and/or inference or rather be appropriated by it in becoming more deeply aware of, and indeed, by being gripped by the presence of God. This is what is at stake in Jewish Existentialist Martin Buber's distinction between I-It and I-Thou relations with everything: the distinction between object and presence; or Catholic Existentialist Gabriel Marcel's distinction between abstractive and participative thinking.[6] Along these lines, Heidegger contrasts representative-calculative thinking with meditative thinking (46). The former belongs in a special way to those with peculiar intellectual

---

3. "The Way Back into the Ground of Metaphysics," 277–90.

4. *Contributions to Philosophy.*

5. *Kierkegaard's Concluding Unscientific*, 181ff.

6. *Mystery of Being*, vol. II, 95–126 and 260.

gifts—mathematicians, scientists, philosophers, and academic theologians; the former belongs to humankind as such. Meditative thinking cultivates what Heidegger calls "the element" in which humans live, like fish live in the element of water.[7]

2.

In his first and most famous work, *Being and Time*, Heidegger indicates the distinctive character of humanness by the term *Dasein*, sometimes set off from its ordinary usage, which means "being there" or "being here," by a dash and a capitalization: thus *Da-Sein*.[8] Human being is the *Da* or the "there" or "here" of *Sein*, of "Being," a notion that, as we have been at pains to show, includes the Whole. *Dasein* is the place where a relation to the Whole is set up. Because everything is encompassed by the notion of Being, the notion functions to pry us loose from animal involvement in the environment given in sensation and to refer us to the Whole. Sensation carves out a field of limited manifestation tied to organic structure and need; the notion of Being poses the question of the "meaning" of what goes on in that field. Meaning, in turn, involves the positioning of environmentally given things in relation to the Whole, but positioning in such a way as to involve "the whole man," "heart" as well as "intellect" and "will." The notion of Being basically involves the question: What is the Whole? and, simultaneously, How are we related to the Whole? This "How" spells itself out in terms of establishing ways of thought, action, and feeling that coalesce into a "world" of meaning developed in the deep past and passed on over generations to give a certain directed tonality to the human heart. Human being as *Da-Sein* is thus essentially Being-in-the-World. And any given world, though intending the Whole, is in its details only one way of manifest relation to the Whole.

Heidegger attempts to show how the theoretical approach that has guided the metaphysical tradition has emerged out of a more basic relation to Being found in inhabiting a world as the true ground of metaphysics. Whatever we encounter we always encounter "as" something—even in so rudimentary a context as seeing this page "as" black on white, but even more immediately "as" writing which we examined in "Phenomenology of the Mailbox." This is correlated with the distinction between two modes of

7. "Letter on Humanism," 239–76. Henceforth LH.

8. *Being and Time*. 10. Henceforth *BT*.

truth expressed in two Greek terms, *orthotes* and *aletheia*, literally translated: correctness (as in "ortho-doxy," "ortho-dontia," and "ortho-pedics") and unconcealment, each corresponding to a different "as."[9] Things are manifest as fitting in the functional context of living prior to expressed articulation in judgment. Judgment interprets explicitly and correctly what has been already interpreted implicitly-functionally, what has stepped out of concealment to enter into the functional context of human life. "Unconcealment" is how Heidegger proposes we consider the etymology of the Greek term *aletheia*, from the privative *a-* and *lethe* or the concealed. What he sees as crucial here is the sense of the *Lethe*, the hidden or "the Mystery of Being" that surrounds our everyday adjustment to our world.[10]

Things are essentially hidden: hiddenness is their default mode. Heidegger cites Heraclitus's dictum "Nature loves to hide."[11] Things rise up to initial manifestness in sensation correlated with our desires. Although Heidegger does not say so, but as Aristotle pointed out, nature in us "interprets" the sensorily present as beneficial, harmful or neutral with respect to our own organic needs. But distinctively human existence has always already taken up things so given into a world of distinctively human meaning. Consider, again for example, your taking up these black on white patterns at which you are now looking, not only as writing, but as exhibiting the working of my mind in attempting to communicate with you. The natural organic resonances fade away in favor of our inhabiting together the space of philosophic inquiry for which the sensory patterning is strictly subsidiary and non-focal—until we direct our attention to it, as we are now doing, deliberately looking away from its function in the communication of philosophic meaning.

3.

One term the Greeks used for things was *pragmata*, objects not of "theory" but of *praxis*; another term was *chremata*, what one uses. In *praxis* things perform a function within a larger context. Unless one understands that context, one cannot understand what a thing is. In contemporary museums of fine art we find artifacts from the deep past, for example, stirrup vessels from pre-Columbian Peru, of whose function we have scarcely a

9. "On the Essence of Truth," 136–54.

10. Ibid., 148–50.

11. *IM*, 181.

clue. But they are now descriptively there with certain colors, textures, and shapes that we might find particularly attractive; we can contemplate them aesthetically. They probably were some kind of religious ceremonial vessels, but the world of meaning in which they originally functioned has disappeared. They are works that were, but are now objects shorn of the world in which they functioned.[12]

Heidegger uses a more pedestrian example: a hammer.[13] Describing scientifically its empirically given structure—its color, shape, size, weight, smoothness, hardness—does not tell us what it is. One has to understand it in its relation to nails and wood and to whatever it is used to build. To understand the hammer one has to understand the ultimate purpose—for example, housing as shelter for our domestic activities—and its relation to a complex of other tools. Though sensorily descriptive properties are present in our ordinary relation to the hammer, they are usually only implicit. They come to the fore when there is some dysfunction: it is too heavy or broken. Otherwise we immediately recognize it in terms of its function, that is, in terms of its fitting into the world within which it operates. We do not find that *in* sensation but bring it to bear *upon* sensation. Heidegger speaks here of the *Zuhanden* and the *Vorhanden*, the present-to-hand and the present-at-hand. The former is the functional presence of a thing related to its functional world, the latter its immediately descriptive presence abstracted from that world.

Plato made a similar observation when, in his *Theaetetus*, he has Socrates ask whether one understands a wagon when one inventories its parts: wheels, spokes, axel, bed, sides, tongue, fasteners.[14] The inference is that one understands the wagon only when one understands its function, that is, how it relates to a context defined by certain ends and correlated with certain needs. Then one even knows why the parts are formed the way they are and can see that some parts in the list are parts of parts. A few decades ago, Robert Pirsig, in his *Zen and the Art of Motorcycle Maintenance*, claimed that a complete descriptive inventory of all the parts of a motorcycle laid out on a table will not aid in understanding what a motorcycle is; but once we understand its function, we can understand why the parts are shaped the way they are.[15]

---

12. "Origin of the Work of Art" (1971), 41. Henceforth OWA.

13. *BT*, 64–67.

14. *Theaetetus*, 207A.

15. Epigraph to Persig, *Zen and the Art of Motorcycle Maintenance*.

The point here is to understand Being-in-the-world by distinguishing belonging to a world from being abstracted out of a world, like the ancient Peruvian ceremonial vessels. The focus is not immediately upon *Dasein* but upon the things in which *Dasein* is interested; but Heidegger's aim is to understand the peculiarities of *Dasein*. That is because *Dasein* exists only in relation to what is given "outside" as things and persons and projects; it exists only as Being-in-the-world with others.

In the notion of Being-in-the-world, Heidegger repudiates the tradition stemming from Descartes for which a central problem is how one gets out of a supposedly self-contained *cogito*. The latter arises by means of a methodically guided abstraction. As we noted in a previous chapter, Kant had said that it was a scandal that philosophy had as yet found no way out of the Cartesian *cogito*.[16] Heidegger said the real scandal was that this was taken to be a real problem. We begin "outside" with others in relation to what is in the environment and artificially construct a self-contained *cogito*.[17]

In a Cartesian framework, the methodical abstraction also raises the problem of "other minds." Being-in-the-world involves not only our always being with things "outside"; it also involves our having been assimilated to a tradition mediated by significant others. As in Hegel, language is the primary exhibition of this being-with-others. We formulate our notions of our "inner space" in terms derived from a common tradition, that is, in a public space of meaning.

Being-in-the-world distinguishes *Da-Sein* from everything else. World is not given in sensory experience but comes to it. It is a historical a priori, a set of structures operating prior to any particular experience and mediated by others who anteceded us. For this reason it would seem to be better to distinguish *Dasein* by Being-in-*a*-world rather than in *the* world. However, Heidegger's choice reflects his view that *a* world of historically constructed meaning reveals something of *the* world, that is, the cosmos. A world is human living space carved out of the Whole within the overarching awareness of *the* Whole; it is a perspective on the Whole that is basically practical, rooted in human concerns.

16. *Critique of Pure Reason*, B xi, 34.
17. *BT*, 190.

4.

In approaching humanness, the theoretical properties we can describe as attributes of individual substances, the Aristotelian categories, have to be supplemented by what Heidegger calls *existentials*, of which Being-in-the-world is fundamental. Existentials are the peculiar properties of human beings.[18] They are named from the feature most basic to Being-in-the-world: the human orientation toward the future that Heidegger calls, somewhat idiosyncratically but following Kierkegaard, "existence," the background of twentieth-century Existentialism.

Notice the technical narrowing of the field of application of the term to the human being, and specifically to the human being's "being ahead of itself." "Existence" does not simply apply to individuals as distinct from "essences" that apply universally. *Dasein* as human reality ex-sists, "stands out" (Latin *ex*, "out of" and *sistere*, "to stand") from actuality by being projected into its own possibilities. (We might suggest that the disclosure of possibilities is linked to the distinctive human ability to grasp the universal as universal.) Everything is determined from how we project our future, what we ultimately seek to accomplish in whatever we do.[19]

The possibilities are afforded by the pre-given world within which *Dasein* is born. Heidegger calls this second feature "thrownness" or "facticity" which plays in relationship to "existence" so that *Dasein* is described as "thrown project" or "factical existence." We are "thrown" into a world not of our own choosing and projected ahead of ourselves so as to be given over to ourselves to choose as we will. Thrownness is manifest in the basic moods in which we find ourselves.

A third feature arises from the fact that we occupy the present with others through the interplay between the past and the future, between what is given and how we take it up in communication. Existence, thrownness, and communication in their interrelatedness spell out how we inhabit our world in relation to future, past, and present respectively. "Existence" toward one's possibilities involves a mode of understanding as disclosure of possibilities for choice. Being thrown into our situation is manifest in our prevailing mood or how we each find ourselves.

18. *BT*, 50ff.

19. The three relations to time are called the "care-structure" of the human being and are treated in *Being and Time*, 178–83.

Existence and understanding, facticity and mood are what we might call "neutral" features of our being in time. While Heidegger speaks of existential understanding and mood neutrally as modes of futurity and pastness respectively, the mode of being in the present he often terms "fallenness" (*Verfallen*)—not so neutral a term.[20] This entails deflection from a certain "ought," a deflection within which we for the most part find ourselves. He calls this state "inauthenticity" or, better, though a bit clumsy, "unappropriatedness." The German word is *Uneigentlichkeit*. The *eigen* is cognate to Greek *autos* (coming into English in "authenticity") and Latin *proprius* (coming into English in "proper" and in "appropriation"), all three referring to what is "one's own." The term "unappropriatedness" describes the situation in which we are mostly social reflexes, "owned" by *das Man*, the anonymous One or They, who determine what "one does" or what "they say." This situation that prevails "proximately and for the most part" is also called "average everydayness." We are what we are, do what we do, think how we think, even feel how we feel because that is the way One is, does, thinks, feels in our culture or subculture. We are functions in a larger, all-encompassing social world formed by tradition that is essential to our own existence.

In this situation our relation to the future tends to be one of mere *curiosity*, pursuing now this, now that object of interest. The search for novelty plays a significant role and our culture especially caters to that. Our relation to the past is one of *ambiguity*. There is no distinction between what is grounded and what is not, what is manifest or what is only passed on. The present is governed by *Gerede*, usually translated as "chatter," the passing around of what is currently "in." The situation corresponds to Plato's Cave ruled by *doxa*, the collection of judgments handed-on, the shadows on the wall to which we are chained, some of which include "ortho-doxy."

The opposite situation is one of "authenticity," *Eigentlichkeit* or "appropriatedness." Here the emphasis lies on the ultimate future of one's Being-in-the-World, one's Being-toward-death. Death is *Dasein*'s essential possibility, necessary regarding the fact, unknown regarding the time. As Heidegger describes it, it is the necessary possibility of the impossibility of all our other possibilities as Being-in-the-world. The co-implication of curiosity, ambiguity, and chatter belonging to average everydayness is linked to a flight from facing up to this ultimate term. It grounds our "fallenness" into unappropriated existence. Its presence is nonetheless manifest in the

---

20. *BT*, 156–68.

encompassing mood Heidegger calls *anxiety* and which he distinguishes from *fear*. Fear always has some object about which one is afraid. Anxiety is objectless: it is the manifestation of the essential unsettledness of human existence as a whole, a kind of verification of Augustine's "restless heart." No matter how "confident" we are, there is always, as a kind of enduring background, an inescapable anxiety.

Facing up to my own mortality, running ahead to my end, allows my life as a whole to come into focus. It was what initiated the discussion in the *Republic*, old Cephalus asking what really counts when death is on the proximate horizon. In the light of having to die, what is the significance of what I do "proximately and for the most part"? In that light I am in a position to take over my own thrownness, retrieve what is genuine from the past, sort out what fits and what doesn't fit into my life, attend fully to all the parameters of the situation in which I am called upon to act, and act resolutely as "my own person," "authentically," appropriating my most meaningful possibilities. Here we see a heightening of what Heidegger calls the *Jemeinigkeit*, the "ever-mine-ness" of *Dasein*. It is the sort of state of mind ideally arising in the situation of religious retreat or in adult preparation for Confirmation, only Heidegger is here retrieving it for human existence as such, regardless of religious affiliation or lack thereof.

This "mine-ness" necessarily plays in tandem with Being-in-the-world with others formed by the tradition. "Appropriated" existence is always linked to "unappropriated" existence, since the latter contains the thrown possibilities for the former. Average everydayness also contains the routinized thinking and acting necessary for the coordination of larger groups of people upon whose face-to-face relations as well as more indirect, anonymous functioning we all depend. (Recall the discussion in "Phenomenology of the Mailbox.") But even in average everydayness, "ever-mineness" belongs to each *Dasein*. Each *Dasein* is a responsible center within a tradition, living in a common world but always responsible for its own choices. As Hegel noted, each of us is an I, abstracted at one level from everything, so as to be able to choose among my options within the *Sittlichkeit* I inhabit.

The driving force of human existence lies in *care*. *Dasein* is always concerned with the meaning of its existence as a whole. Anxiety is the background sense of that concern. Being ahead of oneself (existence), being already in (facticity), being with others (communication): the togetherness of these features is what Heidegger calls the basic care-structure of *Dasein* polarized by the future.

5.

Heidegger indicates that the analysis of *Dasein* thus far presented is only preliminary. It is intended as a mode of access to renewing the question of the meaning of Being, not *my* being or just *human* being, but Being as related to each and every being. It is the first step on the way back into the ground of metaphysics.

The title *Being and Time* indicates the ultimate aim of this work: rethinking the question of Being through the question of time. Heidegger sees the traditional Aristotelian notion of time as a series of Nows arising from average everydayness. Large numbers of people are coordinated through the clock which is linked to the movement of the sun around the earth and broken up into a series of discrete numbers. The analytic of *Dasein* involves a different notion of time, what Husserl termed "internal time consciousness." It involves the "equi-primordiality" of the three temporal dimensions—past, present, and future—where the character of the present is determined by how the past and the future enter into it. How we choose our possibilities implicates what we take over from the past and how we are present to things and persons in the Now. The reciprocal is also the case. Heidegger refers to these three dimensions as "temporal ecstacies," modes of "standing out of" (Greek *ek-stasis*) our putative "inwardness." We come to the present by being linked to or spread out over the past and the future through our commitment to various projects. And we stand out from our "inside" by allowing what is over against us right now to draw near, to concern us, to matter.

As we saw, Augustine carried out a similar analysis in his *Confessions*. When he approached time in terms of a kind of "objective" notion, it all but disappeared as a non-temporally-extended, flowing divider between a no-longer-existent past and a not-yet-existent future. Attending to a more "subjective" approach, Augustine viewed time as a *distentio animi*, as a distention or dis-traction of the soul, its being stretched and torn, tumbling through time. The past is present in memory, the future in expectation, and the present in attention. Augustine's notions of dis-traction and the restless heart are parallel to Heidegger's anxiety, a state of perpetual unsettledness.

Heidegger focuses upon the interplay of these three "internal" dimensions of time. The future dominates in terms of the projects we choose, which determines what we take over from the past, how we are attentive and active in the present, and consequently how things and persons are allowed to draw near or are set at a distance. A change in how we project our future transforms the way we tell the story of our past.

As we have noted in the beginning, Heidegger's analytic of Dasein has a metaphysical purpose: to retrieve the grounding understanding of Being from its forgottenness in the metaphysical tradition. That tradition has been dominated by one of these dimensions: the present viewed apart from its co-implicated determining dimensions of past and future. The Greeks understood being as standing presence, ever-now. So Plato considered as true being the Forms that are not subjected to coming into being, changing, and passing out of being, while the things that are so subjected are "mixtures of being and non-being" happening according to their respective Forms.

Heidegger's idea is to reconnect such presence with a coming into presence out of the interplay of past and future. He considers presence consequently in terms of nearness and distance to *Dasein*. This leads him to the notion of the "historicity" of Being. So conceived, Being is not eternal; it is historical. What Being means is historically determined and historically variable. Governed by the notion of Being as standing presence, the metaphysical tradition has produced certain variations on that theme: Platonic Form, Aristotelian isolated self-absorbed Thought, Hebrew-Christian-Islamic creator God, Schopenhauerian-Nietzschean cosmic Will.

6.

But there is a further dimension, for there are two sides to the forgottenness of Being. One is conceptual: the assumption of the notion of standing presence. The other side involves the notion of inhabitance. The metaphysical tradition assumed that conceptual clarification through judgments that correspond to the facts is primordial. In so doing it failed to attend to what we might call the "lived sense of things" that guides conceptuality. Heidegger's expression for such a lived sense is linked to the notion of "world space." It is the space of inhabitance which Plato called the realm of *doxa*. According to Heidegger, through the work of the poet or philosopher, "so much world space is created that even the ordinary appears extraordinary."[21] But when such activity becomes peripheral to a culture, there is a universal flattening out of the sense of Being.

21. *IM*, 28.

In Heidegger's reading, the metaphysical tradition, from its early determination by Plato, was conceived of in terms of production (Forms as models for the production of things by the divine) and thus, in principle, in terms of mastery. Modern life develops out of that view, minus the sense of awe that informed Plato's search.

In the period during which *Being and Time* was written, Heidegger spoke of the metaphysical tradition originating in Plato as "production metaphysics." In the tenth book of the *Republic* Socrates chose the example of the bed with its three epiphanies: the bed, made by the carpenter and copied in one of its surface perspectives by the painter, depends upon the initial idea of the bed, the Form of bedhood "made by God." Plato's *Timaeus* carried that forward: the world itself is made by the divine artisan according to the Forms as blueprints or patterns. In his later reading of the history of metaphysics, Heidegger sees that view carried forward and joining the Hebrew-Christian view of the world as created by God. Creation occurs according to the archetypes contained within the eternal *Logos*.

Descartes's focus on certitude achieved through methodological mastery underscored the disposition of mastery. This comes to fruition in the dominant contemporary mode of approach to Being that views everything as "standing reserve" for human projects. When that became omnipresent through the technological development and application of modern science, the sense of being as dwelling tended to dry up. Contemporary people are like fish out of water, falling out of the element in which alone we can live, and floundering in a morass of nihilism.

However, Heidegger differentiates the contemporary epoch of the *Gestell*, placing everything within the framework of our projects, from the view of things as *pragmata* among the Greeks. The contemporary trend includes humanness in its project. The human being is a complex material mechanism capable of being manipulated and, indeed, manufactured (such is the dream) by modern technology. This is in a way like the metaphysical tradition's view of humanness in terms of the categories drawn from things *shorn* of their practical involvement in *Dasein*. But the Greeks had a nonreductive view of human functioning. Heidegger opposes modern reductionism by attempting to show the origin of the categories taken as all-comprehensive and the lack in the tradition of a full appreciation of the essential differentiation between things with their categories and *Dasein* with its existentials.

The initial approach to Heidegger's project in terms of a distinction between what is present-to-hand (tools functioning in a world) and what is present-at-hand (exhibiting sensorily describable properties) gives priority to the former, whereas the metaphysical tradition reverses that. Underscoring the care-structure as the basic structure of *Dasein* strengthens that priority of *praxis*. It would seem then that the practical would be more important than the theoretical. And yet in his *Letter on Humanism* Heidegger claims that what he is after, Being as the "element" in which humans live, undercuts the distinction between theoretical and practical, as it does the distinctions between subjective and objective, active and passive.[22]

Heidegger contrasts the disposition of mastery with his notion of *Gelassenheit* which the translators render as "releasement toward things," the German title for the essay translated as "Memorial Address" that is being read for this section of the course (54). Things are not to be approached primarily in terms of their suitability to our practical ends but in terms of how they can come to make their claim on us. The latter is especially exhibited in poetry. But poetry operates within the space occupied by the arts in general. Finally for Heidegger art becomes "the saving power" in our epoch of nihilism.[23] Art opens the Whole for human dwelling, appealing as it does to the human heart.

7.

In his later work Heidegger deepens his hold on what it means to inhabit a world. He follows out further his initial analysis in *Being and Time* of the distinction between the present-to-hand and the present-at-hand. Recall that focus upon things present to *Dasein* is the starting point for the analysis of *Dasein*. Here Heidegger is at one with Aristotle and his follower, Thomas Aquinas. We come to apprehend our own awareness on a rebound off of our awareness of things. For these thinkers, this is the necessary condition of an embodied intellect.

In his 1934 essay, "The Origin of the Work of Art," Heidegger distinguishes three traditional views of the nature of a *thing*, two Aristotelian, one Berkeleyan: substance with attributes, formed matter, and the unity of the sense manifold.[24] The first is inadequate because it projects the subject-

22. LH, 272.
23. QCT, 35.
24. BT, 153–60.

predicate structure of language upon things; the second, because it applies primarily to artefacts; and the third because, with its focus upon sensation, it puts the thing too close to humanness. Heidegger proposes that art presents the authentic view of the thing: the thing is a form arising in the tension between World and Earth that gives the thing a charged presence and opens world-space for human dwelling.[25]

The peculiar notion of Earth brings the sense-manifold to the fore. Whereas in our ordinary relation to things sensory properties are subsidiary to our practical involvements (the sensory properties of the hammer are only implicit and non-focal in our attending to the nail going into the board), in the work of art the sensory features become focal, though not as in Berkeley's reduction of things to sensory unities. But Earth is not the sum total of sensory features that are themselves relative to our own embodiment. Earth is the opaque "sheltering" of everything in this world, an ultimate impenetrable darkness that, nonetheless, rises up to partial manifestation in sensation. Our being made out of the earth plays in relation to the same factor with regard to whatever we might encounter sensorily. Because we are made of matter, there is an element of opaqueness in our own self-presence. Though Heidegger does not expressly treat embodiment, it is indirectly present through his central focus upon mortality which is linked to the *humanum*, our being made of humus and our having to return to the soil in death. It is indirectly present in that full dwelling in a world entails the component of earth as it rises up in sensuousness both as perception and as bodily based desire.

The notion of World is the space of meaning "carved out" from the Whole by a tradition as an interrelated set of paths for thinking, acting, and feeling. It creates a Way for humans to inhabit the earth and coexist with each other. World is the "open," the "clearing/lighting" (*Lichtung*) that displays possibilities for human action. The work of art creates a form that gathers a World of meaning as it brings sensory materials into focus, setting it upon the Earth. It creates "World space" and everything is bathed in its light. Though focused on the individual object or set of objects presented, in its light everything else, even the most ordinary, steps out of indifference or routinization and appears extraordinary. But though World is open, it is carved out of the Whole as but *one* way and is thus related to an encompassing darkness. A kind of inverse of Earth that is essentially dark but rises to partial manifestness in sensation, World is essentially light but is also

25. OWA, 137–39.

essentially related to the encompassing darkness which Heidegger calls the *Lethe*, "the mystery of Being" out of which everything arises and into which everything ultimately sinks. The term for mystery in German is *Geheimnis*, or *Ge-heimnis*, where *Heim* means home and the *Ge-* connotes a kind of gathering—as *Ge-birge* is mountain (*Berg*) chain and *Ge-stell* is a bookcase or a skeleton that allow places (*Stellen*) for other things—books or organs respectively. The quality of the World as "dwelling place" for humans is linked to how a place is made for relation to encompassing Mystery.

In his later work Heidegger, following the poet Hölderlin, articulates the notion of World differently: World is not other than Earth, but Earth is included in World. World is "the play of the fourfold," Earth and Sky, Mortals and Immortals. Each feature interplays with the others. Earth retains the meanings it has in the earlier exposition; but humans, as the Mortals, are expressly integrated into the Earth. The *humanum* derives from *humus* or soil as in the biblical notion that we are fashioned from clay. This notion surfaces especially in relation to our Being-toward-death. It is interesting that the Greek expression, "the Mortals," singles out humans, since death is endemic to all the living, not just humans. But we are the distinctive Mortals because we live out of a background awareness of our own Being-toward-death by reason of our living out of the encompassing sense of the Whole that encompasses our short time on the earth.

Earth is related to Sky as the unreachable encompassing openness that provides the basic measures of human existence as embodied: the days and nights, the seasons of the year. It plays in metaphoric relation to the Immortals whom Heidegger designates as "messengers of the Most High." They appear in the tradition as Angels or Muses, sources of inspiration regarding the spiritual measures of human existence: high or low, victory or defeat, honor or disgrace. "The Most High" is shrouded in the darkness of the encompassing Mystery of Being. Our relation to The Most High is revealed in the poets and prophets.

World that corresponds to these features is a dwelling place. When these features in their togetherness disappear, when essential measure is lost, when we flee our mortality, when the sense of encompassing Mystery disappears, when we fall away from the natural bodily measures of our existence and treat the earth as reducible to material for our projects, we are indeed like fish out of water. We have lost the element in which we naturally exist.

Prior to the rise of modern science, i.e., prior to the deliberate pass-ing of all manifestation through controlled methodological grids, there was a place established, through poetic-religious proclamation, for the mysterious background into which receded everything jutting into the world of everyday manifestness. Poetic-religious proclamation is the typi-cal modality in which the sense of Mystery, of the hiddenness behind all manifestation is preserved; and it is preserved in a way that establishes its significant presence.

Metaphysics may have established a conceptual place for this, but does not as such access it. Consider, for example, the metaphysical attempts to prove the existence of God, such as the famous Five Ways of Aquinas. If they prove, they prove within the same kind of space of distance involved in a mathematical proof. An intellectually proven God is no closer to us than a Euclidean right-angled triangle. Hence Pascal, the thinker of the heart, con-trasted the God of the philosophers with the God of Abraham, Isaac, and Jacob and proclaimed that "the heart has its reasons of which reason knows nothing."[26] It is just this sense of the overwhelming presence that speaks to the heart and that we examined in Augustine, which has been occluded through metaphysics and then in principle lost through the rise of the modern sci-entific technological world. Poetry as the vehicle of expression for the truths of the heart is pushed to the periphery as a kind of superfluous icing on the cake, as mere subjective response to objective truth, not as the preservation of the Mystery in the concreteness of the life-world.

8.

In attempting to get back to the ground of metaphysics Heidegger consid-ers its inception in Parmenides. He sees a peculiar relation here between *noein* and *legein* usually translated as "thinking" and "speaking" in relation to the Parmenidean notion of Being.[27] *Noein*, thinking, is taking-to-heart which is letting-be. *Nous*, which becomes in Plato the term for intellect, is here understood differently as related to the *thanc*. According to Heidegger, *thanc* is related to an old Anglo-Saxon term for thought that survives in English in the term "thanks."[28] It is intimately linked with the heart via its association with memory considered as the seat of devotion. Memory is

26. Pascal, *Pensées*, IV, §277.

27. *IM*, 145ff.

28 *What Is Called Thinking?*, 139–48. Henceforth *WCT*.

"the gathering of the constant intention of everything that the heart holds in present being." And intention is understood here as "the inclination with which the inmost meditation of the heart turns toward all that is in being," something not necessarily within one's own control. Taking to heart allows us to exercise memory in the celebration of memorials, such as that which occasioned Heidegger's reflections in the "Memorial Address." Delivered to the villagers in his familial home at Messkirch, this address rests upon a distinction between meditative and calculative thinking. The former belongs, as we have said, to humans as such, the latter especially to peculiarly gifted types—mathematicians, scientists, philosophers, and theologians.

In Heidegger's reading of Parmenides, taking-to-heart meditatively allows the presence of what is present to make its claim. Taking to heart presupposes the gathering (*legein*) performed by language that lets things be present in the way they are present. Linguistically mediated manifestness precedes taking to heart as "letting-lie-before." But it also follows as safeguarding in the gathering of what is taken to heart. The two together, *legein* and *noiein*, rooted in language and the heart, show what meditative thinking most fundamentally is. Letting-lie-before corresponds to the theoretical moment, but taking-to-heart fulfills our belonging to Being.[29] Philosophy as fulfilled attunement to Being sets the conceptually elaborated within the framework of fundamental awe attuned to the encompassing Mystery out of which all that comes to presence comes to presence. As in his "Memorial Address," Heidegger expressly appeals to two modes of thinking: thinking in terms of *logos* that becomes dialectic and logistics, and thinking as memory, devotion, and thanks. Thinking as Heidegger here promotes it is the conjunction of these two modes. Thinking stands in a deeper relation to art than it does to science, for the former grounds the latter in a world of dwelling.

Art, in revealing the fundamental character of the thing as an assembling of the Whole for meditative dwelling, leads us back from the abstract one-sidedness of science, the all-sided abstractness of philosophy, and the partiality of all our particular interests, even our aesthetic interests, to the wholeness of meaning. Art brings us from our various modes of absence and imposition to the presencing of the Whole in the sensuously present. It teaches us to "let things be"; it speaks directly to "the heart," the center of thought, action and feeling; it teaches us meditative rather than simply calculative and representative thinking. It brings us back to the ground of

29. *WCT*, 196–295.

metaphysics: it articulates our sense of Being as the Whole within which we come to find our own wholeness.

We should not fail to note that all is not completely rosy in Heidegger's relation to faith. Early in his life he was for a rather short time a Jesuit seminarian. At the time of his classic *Being and Time* (1927) he had turned to Lutheranism and was an inspiration for Rudolf Bultmann's scriptural interpretation. The tragic side concerned his embracing of National Socialism, and even a form of anti-Semitism. (We should add that the latter was in conflict with his long love affair with Hannah Arendt, the Jewish political theorist.) His disillusionment with Nazism led to his embracing the Catholic mystic Meister Eckhart's notion of *Gelassenheit*. He was finally buried in the Catholic Church.

QUESTIONS

1. Distinguish meditative thinking from representative-calculative thinking.

2. How do the notions of the experience of encompassing mystery and the experience of "startled dismay" function as "the ground of metaphysics"?

3. Distinguish categories from "existentials." What are the existentials? (List and discuss them.)

4. Distinguish truth as correctness from truth as "unconcealment."

5. Contrast the tradition's notion of Being as "standing presence" with Heidegger's notion of the relation of being and time.

6. How is Heidegger's thought related to Plato?

7. How is Heidegger's thought related to Augustine's notion of the heart and his discussion of time?

8. How is Heidegger's thought related to Aquinas?

9. How is Heidegger's thought related to Descartes?

10. How is Heidegger's thought related to Hegel?

11. What is the role of the arts in Heidegger's thought? How does "the play of the fourfold" function in the arts?

FURTHER READING

1. Martin Heidegger, *Pathmarks.*

2. Rüdiger Safranski, *Martin Heidegger.*

3. Charles Guigon, ed., *The Cambridge Companion to Heidegger.*

* * * *

CONCLUDING OVERVIEW

In our exposition, we have covered a good deal of historical ground, though our aim was not simply to recount *how they used to think* in the past; our aim is rather to learn *how to think for ourselves* by attending to the things to which past thinkers refer and to the ways in which they throw light upon those matters. To that end, we have anchored our reflections in phenomenological exercises which teach us how to see, in relatively trivial things in our own experience, the universal features found in all things. Most particularly, we have zeroed in on the overall structure of the field of experience within which everything occurs in our lives. In our exposition of each thinker, we have constantly referred back to the field of experience. We have also tried to show how each thinker treats three basic themes: the Soul, Morality, and God.

THE SOUL

Regarding the soul, we have shown in *Plato* the basis for a dualism that sees a certain tension between rational activity and embodiment. The embodied soul is imprisoned, buried, embarnacled, distracted. Plato follows the Pythagoreans who discovered rational geometry. Such geometry requires prolonged concentration, so the practitioners formed the first monastic brotherhood based upon a functional asceticism aimed at refocusing the field of experience "inward and upward" instead of "outward and downward" in sensory extroversion. Silence, abstinence from sex, and reduction of food intake were the conditions for a concentrated existence that moved from sensory surface to the underlying mathematical order of the universe.

Socrates speaks of the practice of dying, separating the rational soul from the body, gathering the soul from all sides out of the flowing distractions of the body, as requisite for intellectual concentration. But he has other images for the soul, especially that of the spinning top: if upright, the spinning of the outer surface (bodily based desires) supports the up-right position; deviating from uprightness, the top wobbles; if it wobbles so much that it hits the ground, it is carried erratically by those surface movements. In this image we see a possible harmony of body and soul. And in Plato's later work *Timaeus*, the body is spoken of as the *house* of the soul, the place made for it to dwell. One can reconcile these tensions by viewing the first negative set of remarks as *psychological* remarks concerning the experienced difficulty of concentrated intellectual work. The positive set of remarks refers rather to an *ontology* of the soul-body relation, the mode of being, the essential nature of the relation.

Remember that *Aristotle* followed the ontological remarks and added that the soul *builds and sustains* its body in order, through the sense organs, to have the sensory materials it needs for intellectual opera-tions and self-direction in life. So there is a tri-leveled soul: the nutritive sustaining the organism, the sensient, and the rational, where the lower two levels exist as conditions for the fulfillment of the highest, the level of intellectual responsibility.

Augustine picked up on the Platonic view through Plotinus whose work culminated in the achievement of "being alone with the Alone," separate from things and at one with the One as the Alpha and the Omega of all things. In Augustine, there are hints of the soul's fall from heaven to which it strives to return. But Augustine adds the crucial dimension of *the heart*. He picks up on Plato's notion of *eros* as the passion of the soul for the Good and translates into it the personalist language of the heart: "You have made us for Yourself, O Lord, and our hearts are restless and will not rest until they rest in You."

In *Aquinas* we have a wedding between the Aristotelian and the Pla-tonic views in a somewhat strange amalgam: the rational soul is *substance as form of the body*. The rational power abstracts from the Here-and-Now to grasp the universal concepts that transcend the Here-and-Now because rational power itself exists in relation to Being as a whole and thus also in relation to space and time as encompassing but empty wholes. Intellectual operation, reason, though dependent upon embodiment and the sensory presence of material things as starting points, nonetheless transcends them by employing concepts that apply *always and everywhere* their instances are met. The rational power, having an operation *intrinsically independent* of matter—that is, of what locates us in the Here-and-Now—is a thing-in-itself, a substance; nonetheless, such activity is *extrinsically dependent* upon matter for the materials it needs to operate, so that the human soul is substance *as form of the body.* The soul's rational power has a kind of extrinsic relation to the body, but it is the highest power of a soul that is intrinsic to bodily being as its *anima*ting form.

The relation of the rational soul to Being as a whole grounds an implicit longing, Augustine's longing of the heart for God as the eternal Beauty of Being Itself; and since natural desires cannot be in vain, the human soul is naturally immortal. But as immortal, it retains its orientation toward embodiment—and thus the fittingness of the final Resurrection of the Body.

Lastly, the notion of Being gives the unrestricted orientation of the mind, which can only move into that space of meaning opened up insofar as it can infer from what is given in sensorily based experience. By reason of revelation, Aquinas sees the "light of glory" as a grace that brings the *power* of the intellect up to its unrestricted *scope* in seeing God face-to-face. For Aquinas, God as the Infinite Fullness of Being is implicitly known in whatever is known since the mind thinks in terms of its orientation toward Being as a whole.

Descartes returns us to a dualism of a sort completely different than in Platonism. From what is given in experience he focuses upon the interiority of consciousness and the complete exteriority of bodies. Body turns out to be mathematically measurable *extension,* colorless, odorless, soundless, with elements combining and separating according to invariant laws. This is the world of modern physics which became, with Newton, the Clockwork Universe. Sensations are inner, psychic events produced by wave agitation affecting the nervous system. Soul is identical with consciousness, and soul in the Aristotelian sense disappears. What seem to be ensouled entities or organisms, ultimately explainable in terms of the ends they seek, turn out to be simply a peculiar way in which mechanical laws operate and are thus explainable wholly in terms of mechanisms. If matter is thus utterly different than soul as human awareness, when the body-machine falls apart, the inner consciousness continues to exist.

Hegel returns us to an Aristotelian view of the soul with teleology or goal-seeking activity restored to the cosmos as a whole. The cosmos is there as the arena within which human beings arise who can come to know and transform what is given. The operations that transcend the Here-and-Now are related here-and-now to the Eternal. In that sense, the soul is immortal: in its rational activity it belongs to the Eternal. But for

Hegel; when the body dissolves, the relation to the Immortal dissolves too. There is no personal immortality beyond the grave. In this he is the line of Plato for whom the argument for the just life abstracts from the afterlife and its rewards and punishment. With Plato, they are tacked on at the end, but in a mythical mode.

Heidegger retains the notion of the human being as essentially belonging to the earth. The earth-bound character of one's sensory organs corresponds to the rising up of earthly things to manifestation in sensation. But the human being transcends the sensory as *Da-Sein*, the place where, by reason of the notion of Being (*Sein*), relation to the Whole of what-is opens up among sensorily perceivable things. This grounds an essential relation to the Immortal that comes to us through "messengers of the Most High," Angels or Muses as the sources of inspiration who give essential direction to human life. Relation to the earth shows itself most fundamentally in the human being's *Being-toward-Death*, toward the end of all our possibilities as Being-in-a-World. The human is rooted in the *humus*, the soil that makes humans *the mortals*, those who live out of an awareness of having to die because we live out of a background awareness of the Whole that encompasses all.

MORALITY

In *Plato's Republic* we have the first presentation of the grounds for what come to be called *the cardinal virtues*, i.e. the hinges (from the Latin *cardo*) of moral life: practical wisdom or prudence (*phronesis*) as the capacity to realize justice, courage, and temperance in determinate situations. Plato links them to the three levels of the soul: the desirous, the spirited or aggressive level, and the rational. Justice consists in each part doing its own thing, courage as acting under conviction, temperance as the two lower appetites being ruled by reason exercising practical wisdom. But reason in this operation is "looking down" to rule what is lower. Its ultimate end is "looking up" to the Cosmos and its principle in the Good as the One, Source and End of all.

Aristotle sees the moral virtues as dispositions to act, governed by *phronesis* as the ability to size up situations and find the mean between extremes: courage between cowardice and mere boldness, generosity between stinginess and prodigality, justice between giving or getting too much or too little. In fact, for Aristotle the virtue (*arête*) or excellence of each thing lies in just such a mean. In the case of drama, its excellence lies in its having every part together with every other part, like an organism: everything is there that needs to be there for the work to hang together, and nothing that is there is superfluous to that end. And just as in Plato, so for Aristotle, the higher work is "looking up" through the development of the sciences and speculative wisdom as the study of first principle and first things, namely the divine: as the highest end, contemplation is higher than action.

Aquinas presupposes Aristotle's analysis of the virtues but digs further to find the roots of what comes to be called *natural moral law*. There are imperatives built into the natural structure of every thing. In us there are three levels of imperative. At the organic level, striving for its complete actuality, works under the imperative: *Preserve the conditions of your life*. At the sensient level, there is in addition the imperative: *Procreate and care for your offspring*. At the distinctive human level there are two imperatives: *Live in community* and *Seek the truth*. Aristotle underscored the first imperative at the rational level by showing that the human being is essentially a *political animal*, one who can only flourish on the basis of institutions passed on by predecessors. This is the only way in which the highest imperative, *Seek the truth*, can be realized, for the discovery of truth is an ongoing activity spanning the millennia. Also in Aristotle we are called *zoion logon echon*, the living being that has the *logos*, which can be translated as *rational animal* or as *linguistic animal*, the first being the internal ground of the second, but the second being the external ground upon which alone the first can develop itself. We can only think conceptually on the basis of language, and language is the basic institution through which the achievements of tradition can be passed on.

The Ten Commandments are further specifications of the conditions for living in community and seeking truth. The first three presuppose that the ultimate truth is found located in a single all-powerful, all-knowing, and all-wise Being we call God who is the first and enduring ground of everything other than God. All other conceptions of the gods are reduced to illusions or creatures grounded in such a God. As perpetual Ground of all that is, such a God deserves our worship, which, for the Hebrew tradition, is found by the practices involved in keeping holy the Sabbath.

The second set of seven commandments spells out conditions for living in community. Honoring one's parents is keeping alive the tradition that they transmit as the condition for the ongoing unity and development of the human community. Further, one who fosters community does not kill or steal from his neighbor or commit adultery with one's neighbor's spouse; in fact, he does not even entertain the thought of such things. One who fosters community does not bear false witness, that is, lie to get another in trouble, nor compound the offense by bringing in the name of God (third commandment) in order to witness to the (dis)honesty of the testimony.

With the rise of philosophy and, following from that, the rise of modern science, the commandment to seek the truth takes center stage and sets humankind on the way to its ongoing development in knowing and transforming the world through science and technology.

Descartes's project was to bracket out all the claims of tradition in order either to replace them or to place them in an evidential context provided through methodic doubt. But to hold himself to the project, he had to develop what he called "a provisional moral code" to shelter him from dominance by his own passions but also from coercion from without by the community. Regarding the latter, he proposed to follow the religious tradition in his conduct and pay attention to the most moderate people. Regarding the former, he resolved to conquer himself so that he could hold himself to the long-range project of wholesale intellectual reconstruction. His early death did not permit his getting beyond the formulation of the provisional code.

In *Hegel* the philosophical and theological tradition gains its first systematic grounding in so-called *Absolute Knowing*. Though it sounds like omniscience, it is actually something much more "modest": it is knowing the interlocking sets of conditions—ontological, logical, psychological, historical, institutional, and cosmic—for the possibility of rational existence and development. What kind of universe does this have to be in order that a rational being can emerge and flourish within it? Following Aristotle and anticipating Heidegger, Hegel observed that human beings conduct their lives by being rooted in a community that is the residue of centuries-long practices. We live in the way of life of our community as our element, the way fish live in water and birds live in the air. In premodern times, the individual is typically submerged in family and in the overarching community. In the development of the modern world, the individual appears on the scene with its newly discovered or asserted rights against the community. Freedom of religious choice and practice, freedom of enterprise, inquiry, publicity, and choice of marriage partner, along with equality before the law: such rights create an unprecedented situation. So Hegel sees the new arena of *Civil Society* as a social region of free activity, situated by law, inserted between the family and the overarching polis, now grown into a modern State.

Hegel develops a view of the State as hierarchically arranged, culminating in a constitutionally limited monarch, but arranged in such a way that determinate levels of institutions protect the rights of individuals and communities from lawless intrusion of the higher levels of organization upon the lower and upon the individuals, the protection of whose rights and dignity is central to the modern State. It is in such a State that the ongoing study of the order of things and the ongoing development of art and enterprise can carry humankind to more and more sophisticated levels of operation. But that requires in each individual self-mastery, bringing the potential chaos of desires, natural and cultural, to some kind of coherence requisite for commitment to long-range projects, individual and communal.

In *Heidegger*, there is a powerful emphasis upon individual integrity and responsibility in relation to the everyday world in which we are all immersed. But he also underscores that, by reason of our being *Da-Sein*, the place where relation to the Whole appears in the midst of beings, our home lies in relation to the Divine conceived of as encompassing Mystery. Following out the direction indicated by Hegel, we are led by talented individuals to make continual progress in knowing and transforming; but we tend to lose sight of the Mystery of Being that is our home, home for every human being, talented or not. The Mystery makes its appearance in silence and speaks to our hearts, the center of the self that has set up around it various centers of attraction and repulsion. It is the arts that are the locus of the cultivation of meditative awareness which, as we continue to carry on our progress in knowing and transforming, can conduct us back to the Mystery.

GOD

In *Plato* the place where the question of the divine arises is where the Forms have their origin and end: in the Good as the One. As such, the divine is an impersonal principle of cosmic order.

Aristotle comes at the question from a consideration of the hierarchy of things. Everything we experience is formed matter. In living things the form as soul is not simply passive shape but an active principle, using nonliving matter to form and sustain the organism. In animals there arises the immaterial level of *manifestation* whereby they receive the cognitive specification of sensory things, detached from embodiment in physical things, but serving organic need. In humans, the form is rendered universal, implying a level abstracted from the individuating characteristics of sensorily given things found Here-and-Now and a distancing from being governed by appetite. In human knowing we have two factors: the universality of the Form known and what makes it possible for a given universal Form to be multiplied in an indeterminate number of individuals of the kind involved. The principle of such multiplicity is what Aristotle calls *matter* that is, at the same time, the principle that explains the mutability of the Forms in things. Matter in this sense is the basis for the spatial and temporal location of Forms in individuals. But when the Forms are known intellectually, that is, in abstraction from their instances, they are displayed as universals. We can consider Form as universal because, at the level of intellect, *we ourselves* are abstracted from the Here-and-Now involved in organic and sensory life by being referred to the Whole. Both sentient and rational life involve a form of life that transcends simple location in a Here-and-Now and that is the basis for the *appearance* of things. Distance from matter involves self-presence. Animals live in relation to what spatially surrounds them and out of learning from the past and anticipation of the future in the light of organic need. Human intellection involves a mode of self-presence that goes beyond the spatiotemporal location within which animals conduct their lives, driven by appetite.

The upshot of this all is the notion of an Intellect that is absolutely separate from spatiotemporality and that is absolute Self-presence. That is Aristotle's notion of God as Pure Form, as Awareness of Awareness or Self-Thinking Thought. Aristotle backs into that notion by considering the nature of time as involving past-present-future in such a way that any present is inconceivable without past and future. So the changing world is *eternal*, requiring a Before and After for every Now. But since everything in this world is able not to be, there must be something that keeps it in being and that must not then be involved in time. Things keep their species going forever because they seek to be as like that eternal Being as possible: each thing seeking its proper place, moving from potency to actuality and from growth to reproduction, enjoying fulfillment, knowing intellectually. However, such an eternal Being can neither know nor act upon anything outside it, else it would be changed by the encounter and thus subjected to time. It can only be the *exemplar* of perfection which natures seek to emulate, each in their own way. It involves no immediate ethical consequences, judging, rewarding, punishing. Ethics in no direct way involves Aristotle's God.

In *Plotinus* we have a development of Plato in such a way that *Augustine* could find much of Christianity in the Platonists. For Plotinus the One as final Good is the Source of all the kinds or Forms of unity that are possible. The One flows outward like light that generates the illumined region of the Forms as the place of the World-Intellect or Logos through which all things came to be. The procession flows further into the World-Soul which produces and sustains everything under it where the Forms are multiplied through matter as the principle of darkness that terminates the outward emanation of light. Together, the One, the Logos, and the World-Soul are the eternal Trinity which is the ground of all things. For Augustine, such a structure shows how the human heart is restless until it returns to the Three-in-One God.

The human soul has its origin in this eternal realm, but for some unaccountable reason turned away from the One and was plunged into the body as the principle of darkness. So deep is the immersion that the soul is inclined to see itself, like most neuro-scientists and their popularizers today, as wholly material. The chains have to be taken off, the soul turned completely around and dragged upward toward the intelligible light. This return of the rational creature to God is a three-step process: first, *purgation* or the practice of bodily self-denial in order to concentrate the soul; then *illumination* as the concentrated soul begins to grasp more and more of its cosmic situation; and finally *union* with the One as the mystical end of the process. Through the Logos all things were made and the same Logos is the light of men. Of course, what Plotinus did not see is what makes Christianity Christianity: Christ as the God-Man is the Logos-become-flesh.

Aquinas also assimilates and transforms Aristotle in his philosophical theology. Aristotle's God as Self-Thinking Thought is finite, since for the Greek the in-finite is the indeterminate and thus the imperfect. Perfection consists in the full actuality of a given Form. In Aquinas, the unrestricted character given to the mind by the notion of Being allows it to question beyond any putative limit, so that Being presents itself as absolutely unrestricted. This grounds the question implicit in Aquinas: since Being itself is unrestricted, how can finite beings be? The answer he gives through Five Ways is that only an absolutely unrestricted Being whose Essence is To Be, who is *Ipsum Esse Subsistens* or To-Be as a Nature, can be such a Cause, and a Cause not "once upon a time" but always. Creatures are permanently rooted in God, even if the world were eternal. Omniscience, omnipotence, and absolute wisdom and goodness follow. For Aquinas, it is only through

Revelation that we can come to see that the inner life of such a Being is Trinitarian, even though Plotinus, anticipating Hegel, seemed to show otherwise through reason.

In *Descartes*, the idea of the Infinitely Perfect lies in the mind—I would say, as the basis for the mind itself under the note of unrestricted Being—as something we could not have derived from the finite. For Descartes this is an indication that the Infinitely Perfect Being or God is the cause of the mind in which such a notion is the sign of the Creator in the creature.

Descartes also revived the so-called *ontological argument* of Anselm: the thought of that than which no greater can be achieved or the thought of absolutely Infinite Being must have within it the notion of existing outside of merely being thought about, so that its essence, as containing the perfection of Being, entails its existence. As such, God is the guarantor that he would not willingly deceive us, provided we use our faculties properly, moving from clear and distinct ideas and only giving our intellectual assent to what follows from that.

Hegel in effect goes back to Plotinus in his claim to be able to show the Trinity and even beyond that, the Incarnation as implied in the overall character of Being, breaking through the glass ceiling Aquinas claimed with respect to those ideas as accessible by unaided human reason. In effect, Aquinas's restriction followed from too close an adherence to *the principle of identity*. Hegel claimed that insoluble problems arise from this adherence. In the Enlightenment, whose "Reason" is really abstract Understanding, God is thought of as separate, things as composed of externally combining and separating atoms, soul as separate from body, knowledge as inward impression from externally acting things, and individuals as external to the community, entering it only through the external relation of contract.

What the Incarnation displayed is *the principle of the identity-in-difference* of the divine and the human. The relation of creation itself is a matter of identity-in-difference, God being both wholly immanent in things and at the same time completely transcendent of all finitude. The relation of knowing, as in Aristotle, is cognitive identity in ontological difference. The same is true of the relation of soul and body and of individual and community, each an example of identity-in-difference. Actually, both Aristotle and Aquinas hold such a view. But Hegel thinks it applies likewise to God himself.

In order that there be something other than God there has to be a principle of otherness within God, the Logos, locus of the eternal Forms, through which all things came to be; and the differences are bridged by the

Spirit of Love. For Hegel God remains empty unless the world proceeds from him, which it does eternally. The principle of identity separates finite and Infinite; but thinking through the notion of the absolutely Infinite leads to the conclusion that it *must* include the finite, under penalty of being *limited* to one side of the finite-Infinite divide. Hence God *must* create. And the identity-in-difference of God and Man in Christ lets out the secret that this is true of human beings as such. One can see both why he makes such claims and also claims to remain a faithful Lutheran: he is giving rational form to the truths announced with what for him are inadequate concepts for truths revealed in the prior faith-tradition.

Finally, *Heidegger* has no direct doctrine of God, though he says that thinking of God has to be preceded by the philosopher's thought of Being echoing against the poet's proclamation of the Holy, after which we might consider the nature of the divine, and only after that the nature of God. His fixation on the notion of Being as the ground for our relation to the surrounding Mystery and the openness to being apprehended by Mystery are necessary prolegomena to thinking of God as other than an intellectual object.

* * * *

We have presented the key concepts of the thinkers covered as the skeletal framework of each thinker's thought, anchored in the ever-present structure of the field of experience. Today where the reduction is widespread of the human being to a complex of biological, and especially neurological mechanisms, it is of the utmost importance to learn to *pay attention to paying attention*, to note the essential differences between distinctive human awareness and sensorily available things, and most especially, the grounding of distinctively human awareness in the notion of Being. For it is that notion which gives us primordial distance from the Here-and-Now and thereby grounds our ability to form concepts which apply always and everywhere their instances are met and which thereby also condemns us to choose, to freely take responsibility for our lives.

We have approached the texts with those structures in mind. And as I noted several times, our primary aim was not to report on what they *used to think*, but to learn *how to think* about ultimate things. Having a hold of the skeletal framework of each thinker and its origin in, and commentary upon what is involved in the field of experience, the reader should be in the position to revisit the classic texts.

One summer a student of mine was working as assistant to a Texas Utility lineman who discovered that he was majoring in philosophy. "Philosophy!" he said. "I *love* Plato's *Republic!*" When asked what else he read in philosophy or even in Plato, he said, "Nothing, just the *Republic*. Whenever I finish it, I start all over again, rereading and rereading." The man had discovered a classic, a work that has been reread innumerable times by reflective readers throughout the centuries. As I tell my students, Aristotle gets smarter every time I reread his work. My hope is that readers will have been led to recognize what makes classic several key philosophic classics and to revisit them often to deepen their own thought about the matters presented in the texts.

But our ultimate aim has been to prepare the way for a deepened approach to the study of theology. We have seen the ways in which Platonism and Aristotelianism, in Augustine and in Aquinas, furnished the deep reflective basis for the interpretation of Scripture and the tradition of reflecting upon it. One cannot get around bringing one's own self-understanding to bear upon any interpretation, for it is the basis for such. Though there is truth in complaints about philosophy's possible distortion of the Hebrew and early Christian mentality, nonetheless, those who interpret inevitably do so on the basis of their own self-understanding; and philosophy involves an enhanced self-understanding, making explicit what is only implicit in ordinary human experience, as well as exercising critique upon it. As sophisticated as neurophysiological research is, it does not, as such, make explicit the features of awareness brought to bear upon the discipline by the neurophysiologist. As sophisticated as biblical studies may be, they do not, as such, make explicit the features of awareness brought to bear upon the Bible by the interpreter.

The development of philosophic insight in the tradition is in some ways parallel to the development of quantum physics or neurophysiology, about which the Bible says absolutely nothing. Of course the difference is that, unlike quantum physics, both the Bible and philosophy are concerned with God, the soul, moral action, and the community. And there is the philosophic question of the relation of the developed scientific regions to the persons who engage in their expansion. The mentality displayed in the Scriptures is still undeveloped in comparison with all that has been achieved in terms of human understanding of the self and of the cosmos and in terms of institutional development as well. One can see something of the difference by comparing Christian, Hebrew, and Muslim fundamentalism with those modes of faith that have given free reign to the development of reason. It is important to remember the words of John Paul II: faith and reason are the two wings upon which the human spirit soars. I fondly hope that those who have passed through this study will go on to read and reread the classics as the basis for reading more carefully, not only the Bible, but also the Church Fathers, the Doctors of the Church, council documents, and papal encyclicals. In bringing your developing philosophic awareness to the study of the faith, I hope that your spirits can learn to soar.

FURTHER READINGS

One who has worked through this book and has become accustomed to my style of presentation will find further background and extensions of the notions explored in this text in three of my other works:

1. Robert E. Wood, *A Path into Metaphysics*. A phenomenological framework is used to interpret and carry on dialogue with the metaphysical positions or first philosophy of Parmenides, Plato, Aristotle, and Aquinas as a single developing position, followed by a treatment of the line of modern thinkers from Descartes, Spinoza, and Leibniz, to Kant, Hegel, Whitehead, and Heidegger as related to that prior tradition.

2. Robert E. Wood, *Placing Aesthetics: Reflections on the Philosophic Tradition*. The book contends that aesthetics is central to a long tradition of speculative thinkers from Plato and Aristotle, through the Latin Middle Ages, and on through Kant and Hume, Hegel, Schopenhauer, to Nietzsche, Dewey, and Heidegger. There is a threefold placing of aesthetics: phenomenologically placing aesthetic experience in the heart; placing discussion of aesthetics in the historical line examined; and placing aesthetics within the overall conceptual framework of each thinker.

3. Robert E. Wood, *The Beautiful, the True, and the Good*. Studies from Heraclitus to Paul Weiss, Buber on Oriental Thought, and Marcel and Heidegger on relation to Mystery.

4. Robert E. Wood, *Being and Cosmos: From Seeing to Indwelling*.

* * * *

BIBLIOGRAPHY

Abbott, Walter M., ed. "The Church Today." In *Documents of Vatican II*, 183–316. New York: Guild, 1966.

Adler, Mortimer. *Aristotle for Everybody*. New York: Macmillan, 1978.

Anselm. *Proslogion: With the Replies of Gaunilo and Anselm*. Translated, with introduction and notes, by Thomas Williams. Indianapolis: Hackett, 2001.

Apostle, Hippocrates G. *Aristotle: Selected Writings*. Des Moines, Iowa: Peripatetic, 1991.

Aquinas, Thomas. *The Disputed Questions on Truth*. Translated by Robert W. Mulligan. Chicago: Regnery, 1952.

———. *Summa contra Gentiles*. Book 1, *God*. Translated by Anton Pegis. South Bend, IN: University of Notre Dame Press, 1991.

———. *Summa contra Gentiles*. Book 2, *Creation*. Translated by John Anderson. 1976.

———. *Summa contra Gentiles*. Book 3, *Providence*. Translated by Vernon Bourke. 1975.

———. *Summa contra Gentiles*. Book 4, *Salvation*. Translated by Charles O'Neil. 1975.

———. *Summa theologiae*. St. Louis: Aquinas Institute, 2012.

Aristotle. *Categories*. Translated by J. Ackrill. In *The Complete Works of Aristotle*, edited by Jonathan Barnes. Princeton, NJ: Bollinger, 1984.

———. *Metaphysics*. Translated by W. D. Ross. In *The Complete Works of Aristotle*.

———. *Nicomachean Ethics*. Translated by W. D. Ross and J. Urmson. In *The Complete Works of Aristotle*, edited by Jonathan Barnes. Princeton, NJ: Bollinger, 1984.

———. *On the Soul*. Translated by J. A. Smith. In *The Complete Works of Aristotle*.

———. *Poetics*. Translated by I. Bywater. In *The Complete Works of Aristotle*.

———. *Politics*. Translated by B. Jowett. In *The Complete Works of Aristotle*.

Augustine, Aurelius. *The City of God*. Translated by Marcus Dods. Peabody: Hendrickson, 2009.

———. *Confessions*. Translated by Wiliam Watts. 2 vols. Cambridge: Harvard University Press, 1977.

———. *On True Religion*. Translated by J. H. S. Burleigh. Chicago: Regnery, 1959.

———. *Soliloquies*. Translated by Rose Cleveland. Boston: Little, Brown, 1910.

Balthasar, Hans Urs von. *Studies in Theological Style: Clerical Styles*. Translated by Andrew Louth et al. Vol. 2 of *The Glory of the Lord*. San Francisco: Ignatius, 1984.

Brown, Peter. *Augustine of Hippo*. Berkeley: University of California Press, 1967.

Buber, Martin. *Moses*. New York: Harper, 1946.

Cassirer, Ernst. *The Philosophy of the Enlightenment*. Translated by Fritz Koelln and James Pettegrove. Boston: Beacon, 1951.

Chenu, M. D. *Toward Understanding St. Thomas*. Translated by Albert Landry and Dominic. Hughes. Westminster, MD: Regnery, 1964.

BIBLIOGRAPHY

Chesterton, G. K. *St. Thomas Aquinas: The Dumb Ox*. Garden City: Doubleday, 1956.

Cottingham, John, ed. *The Cambridge Companion to Descartes*. Cambridge: Cambridge University Press, 1992.

Descartes, René. *Discourse on Method*. Translated by Donald Cress. Indianapolis: Hackett, 1990.

———. *Meditations of First Philosophy*. In *The Philosophic Works of Descartes*, translated by Elizabeth Haldane and G. R. T. Ross, vol. 1. New York: Dover, 1955.

Dostoevsky, Fyodor. *The Brothers Karamazov*. Translated by Constance Garnett. Revised by Ralph Matlaw. New York: Norton, 1976.

Emerson, Ralph Waldo. *Representative Men*. Cambridge: Belknap of Harvard University Press, 1996.

Foster, David Ruel, and Joseph Koterski, eds. *Two Wings of Catholic Thought: Essays on Fides et Ratio*. Washington, DC: Catholic University of America Press, 2003.

Freud, Sigmund. *The Ego and the Id*. Translated by Joan Riviere and James Strachey. New York: Norton, 1960.

———. *The Future of an Illusion*. Translated by W. D. Robson-Scott. Garden City: Doubleday, 1964.

Friedländer, Paul. *Plato: An Introduction*. 3 vols. Translated by Hans Meyerhoff. New York: Harper and Row, 1958.

Gadamer, Hans Georg. *Truth and Method*. New York: Crossroads, 1982.

Gilson, Etienne. *The Christian Philosophy of Saint Augustine*. Translated by L. E. M. Lynch. New York: Vintage, 1960.

———. *The Christian Philosophy of St. Thomas Aquinas*. Translated by Lawrence Shook. South Bend, IN: University of Notre Dame Press, 1994.

———. *Études sur le rôle de la pensée médiévale dans la formation du système cartésien*. Paris: Vrin, 1930.

Grene, Marjorie. *Descartes among the Scholastics*. Milwaukee: Marquette University Press, 1991.

———. *A Portrait of Aristotle*. Chicago: University of Chicago Press, 1963.

Guardini, Romano. *The Conversion of St. Augustine*. Chicago: Regnery, n.d.

Guignon, Charles, ed. *The Cambridge Companion to Heidegger*. Cambridge: Cambridge University Press, 1993.

Hegel, G. W. F. *Elements of the Philosophy of Right*. Translated by Robert Nisbet. Cambridge: Cambridge University Press, 1991.

———. *The Encyclopaedia Logic*. Translated by T. Geraets et al. Indianapolis: Hackett, 1991.

———. *Hegel's Aesthetics: Lectures on Fine Art*. Translated by T. M. Knox. Oxford: Clarendon, 1975.

———. *Hegel's Introduction to the System: Phenomenology and Psychology*. Introduction, translation, and commentary by Robert E. Wood. Toronto: University of Toronto Press, 2014.

———. *Hegel's Philosophy of Mind*. Translated by Michael Inwood. Oxford: Clarendon, 2007.

———. *Hegel's Science of Logic*. Translated by A. V. Miller. London: Allen and Unwin, 1969.

———. *Lectures on the History of Philosophy*. Translated by Robert Brown et al. Berkeley: University of California Press, 1990.

———. *Lectures on the Philosophy of Religion.* Translated by E. B. Speirs and J. B. Sanderson. London: Paul, Trench, Trübner, 1895.

———. *On Art, Religion, and Philosophy: Introductory Lectures to the Realm of Absolute Spirit.* Edited by J. Glenn Gray. New York: Harper, 1970.

———. *Phenomenology of Spirit.* Translated by A.V. Miller. Oxford: Oxford University Press, 1977.

———. *The Philosophy of History.* Translated by J. Sibree. New York: Dover, 1956.

Heidegger, Martin. *Being and Time.* Translated by Joan Stambaugh. Albany: State University of New York Press, 1996.

———. *Contributions to Philosophy (Of the Event).* Translated by Richard Rojcewicz and Daniella Valega-Neu. Bloomington: Indiana University Press, 2012.

———. *An Introduction to Metaphysics.* Translated by Gregory Fried and Richard Polt. New Haven: Yale University Press, 2000.

———. "Letter on Humanism." In *Pathmarks,* edited by William McNeill, 239–76. Cambridge: Cambridge University Press, 1990.

———. On the Essence of Truth." In *Pathmarks,* 136–54. Cambridge: Cambridge University Press, 1990.

———. "Origin of the Work of Art." In *Poetry, Language, and Thought,* translated by Albert Hofstadter, 15–88. New York: Harper and Row, 1971.

———. *The Question Concerning Technology.* Translated by William Lovitt. New York: Harper, 1977.

———. "The Way Back into the Ground of Metaphysics." Introduction to "What Is Metaphysics?," in *Pathmarks,* 277–90. Cambridge: Cambridge University Press, 1990.

———. *What Is Called Thinking?* Translated by Fred Wieck and J. Glenn Gray. New York: Harper and Row, 1968.

Hemming, Laurence Paul, and Susan Frank Parson, eds. *Restoring Faith in Reason.* Notre Dame: University of Notre Dame Press, 2003.

Hobbes, Thomas. *Leviathan.* London: Penguin Classics, 1985.

Hume, David. *Dialogues.* In *Dialogues and Natural History of Religion,* edited by J. D. Gaskin. Oxford: Oxford University Press, 1993.

Husserl, Edmund. *Cartesian Meditations.* Translated by Dorion Carins. Dordrecht: Kluwer, 1999.

———. *The Crisis of European Sciences and Transcendental Phenomenology.* Translated by David Carr. Evanston, IL: Northwestern University Press, 1970.

———. *The Phenomenology of Internal Time-Consciousness.* Translated by James Churchill. Bloomington: Indiana University Press, 1966.

John Paul II. *Fides et Ratio: On the Relationship of Faith and Reason.* Boston: Pauline, 1998.

Kant, Immanuel. "What Is Enlightenment?" In *On History,* translated by Lewis White Beck et al. Indianapolis: Liberal Arts, 1963.

Kaufmann, Walter. "The Hegel Myth and Its Overcoming." In *From Shakespeare to Existentialism,* 88–119. Boston: Beacon, 1959.

Keeling, S. V. *Descartes.* London: Oxford University Press, 1968.

Kierkegaard, Søren. *Kierkegaard's Concluding Unscientific Postscript to Philosophical Fragments.* Translated by David Swenson and Walter Lowrie. Princeton: Princeton University Press, 1941.

Leibniz, Gottfried Wilhelm. *Monadology.* Edited and translated by Robert Latta. Oxford: Oxford University Press, 1951.

BIBLIOGRAPHY

Lessing, Gotthold Ephraim. *On the Education of the Human Race*. Whitefish, MT: Kessinger, 2005.

Locke, John. *Second Treatise on Government*. New York: Dover, 2002.

MacIntyre, Alasdair. *Three Rival Versions of Moral Inquiry*. Notre Dame: University of Notre Dame Press, 1990.

Marcel, Gabriel. *The Mystery of Being*. Translated by G. S. Fraser. Chicago: Regnery, 1960.

Maritain, Jacques. *The Degrees of Knowledge*. Translated by Gerard Phelan. New York: Scribner, 1959.

Meyer, Rudolph W. *Leibniz and the Seventeenth Century Revolution*. Translated by J. S. Stern. Chicago: Regnery 1952.

Moran, Dermot. *Introduction to Phenomenology*. London: Routledge, 2000.

———. *The Phenomenology Reader*. London: Routledge, 2002.

Newman, John Henry. *The Idea of a University*. Notre Dame: University of Notre Dame Press, 1960.

Nietzsche, Friedrich. *Twilight of the Idols*. Translated by R. J. Hollingdale. Baltimore: Penguin, 1968.

O'Connell, Robert. *Saint Augustine's Confessions: The Odyssey of Soul*. New York: Fordham University Press, 1989.

Pascal, Blaise. *Pensées*. Translated by A. J. Krailsheimer. Baltimore: Penguin, 1966.

Pegis, Anton. *Introduction to St. Thomas Aquinas*. Chicago: University of Chicago Press, 1948.

Persig, Robert. *Zen and the Art of Motorcycle Maintenance*. New York: Bantham, 1974.

Pieper, Josef. *The Silence of St. Thomas*. Translated by John Murray and Daniel O'Connor. New York: Pantheon, 1957.

Pierce, C. S. "The Scientific Attitude and Falliblism." In *Philosophical Writings of Pierce*, edited by Justus Buchler, 42–59. New York: Dover, 1955.

Pinkard, Terry. *Hegel: A Biography*. New York: Cambridge, 2000.

Pius IX. "Syllabus of Errors (Pope Pius IX)." In *The Popes Against Modern Errors*, edited by Anthony Mioni, 27–39. Charlotte, NC: TAN, 1999.

Pius XII. *The Mystical Body of Christ*. Translated by J. Bluett. New York: America Press, 1943.

Plato. *Apology*. Translated by G. M. A. Grube. In *Plato: Complete Works*, edited by John Cooper. Indianapolis: Hackett, 1997.

———. *Crito*. Translated by G. M. A. Grube. In *Plato: Complete Works*.

———. *Phaedo*. Translated by G. M. A. Grube. In *Plato: Complete Works*.

———. *The Republic of Plato*. Translated by Alan Bloom. New York: Basic, 1968.

———. *Symposium*. Translated by Alexander Nehamas and Paul Woodfuff. In *Plato: Complete Works*. Indianapolis: Hackett, 1997.

———. *Theaetetus*. Translated by M. J. Levitt and Myles. Bernyeat. In *Plato: Complete Works*. Indianapolis: Hackett, 1997.

Plotinus. *Enneads*. Translated by Stephen MacKenna. London: Penguin, 1991.

Rahner, Karl, ed. *Encyclopedia of Theology*. New York: Seabury, 1975.

———. *The Foundations of Christian Faith*. Translated by William Dych. New York: Seabury, 1978.

Ross, W. D. *Aristotle: A Complete Exposition of His Works and Thought*. Cleveland: World, 1995.

Ryle, Gilbert. *The Concept of Mind*. Chicago: University of Chicago Press, 1949.

BIBLIOGRAPHY

Safranski, Rüdiger. *Martin Heidegger: Between Good and Evil.* Translated by Ewald Osers. Cambridge: Harvard University Press, 1998.

Schmitz, Kenneth. *At the Center of the Human Drama: The Philosophical Anthropology of Karol Wojtyla / Pope John Paul II.* Washington: Catholic University of America Press, 1993.

Schopenhauer, Arthur. *The World as Will and Representation.* 2 vols. Translated by E. T. J. Payne. New York: Dover, 1969.

Smith, Preserved. *A History of Modern Culture.* Vol. 2, *The Enlightenment, 1687–1776.* New York: Collier, 1962.

Sokolowski, Robert. *An Introduction to Phenomenology.* New York: Cambridge University Press, 2000.

Veatch, Henry. *Aristotle: A Contemporary Appreciation.* Bloomington: Indiana University Press, 1974.

Voegelin, Eric. *Plato and Aristotle.* Vol. 3 of *Order and History.* Baton Rouge: Louisiana State University Press, 1957.

Weigel, George. *Witness to Hope: The Biography of John Paul II.* New York: HarperCollins, 1999.

Whitehead, Alfred North. *Process and Reality.* New York: Harper, 1957.

———. *Science and the Modern World.* New York: Free Press, 1967.

Wood, Robert E. *The Beautiful, the True, and the Good: Readings in the History of Thought.* Washington, DC: Catholic University of America Press, 2015.

———. *Being and Cosmos: From Seeing to Indwelling.* Washington, DC: Catholic University of America Press, 2018.

———. *A Path into Metaphysics: Phenomenological, Hermeneutical, and Dialogical Studies.* Albany: State University of New York Press, 1991.

———. "Phenomenology of the Mailbox: Much Ado about Nothing." *Philosophy Today* 47 (2003) 147–59.

———. *Placing Aesthetics: Studies in the Philosophic Tradition.* Athens: Ohio University Press, 1999.

Wooldridge, Dean. *Mechanical Man: The Physical Basis of Intelligent Life.* New York: McGraw-Hill, 1968.

Zuckert, Catherine. *Postmodern Platos: Nietzsche, Heidegger, Gadamer, Strauss, Derrida.* Chicago: University of Chicago Press, 1996.

INDEX OF SUBJECTS

INDEX OF SUBJECTS

INDEX OF SUBJECTS

INDEX OF SUBJECTS

INDEX OF SUBJECTS

Vernunft (Hegelian Reason), 135, 144

Verstand, *See* understanding

virtue, 3, 61–63, 72, 100–1, 113, 173–74; cardinal virtues, 42, 61, 100, 106, 173; *intellectual* virtue, 62, 92. *See also phronesis*

Whole (totality), 3, 5, 9, 10, 17, 27, 31, 32, 33, 34, 35, 42, 45, 46, 47, 56, 60, 64, 69, 71, 73, 74–76, 95, 97, 98, 100, 101, 126, 136, 137, 140–45, 153, 156, 163, 164, 165, 167, 168, 173, 176, 177

will, 34, 62, 78, 92, 97, 98, 112, 125, 134, 153, 161

word, 19, 30–31, 40, 60, 64, 72, 78, 96, 97; Word, the, 78, 89, 94, 95, 99, 100

world, 11, 16, 27, 32, 40, 42, 44, 45, 46, 52, 57, 61, 63, 64, 69, 70, 71, 72, 73, 74, 81, 84, 86, 88, 89, 94, 107, 112, 116, 118, 119, 120, 121, 125, 126, 127, 128, 136, 139, 142, 144, 147, 153, 154 155, 156–59, 161, 162, 163, 164, 165, 166, 167, 172, 173, 175, 176, 177, 178, 180. *See also* life-world

writing, 3, 18, 19, 29–31, 89, 153, 154

INDEX OF NAMES

INDEX OF NAMES